The
Best
Teen
Writing
of
2019

**Scholastic
Art & Writing
Awards**

Table of Contents

Flash Fiction

Short Story

Humor

Dedication

The Best Teen Writing of 2019 is dedicated to Dr. Ernest B. Fleishman, a longtime member of the Board of Directors of the Alliance for Young Artists & Writers, former senior executive at Scholastic Inc., and a beacon of light to the education world.

Dr. Fleishman's remarkable career in education has been shaped by the many roles he has played—as a leader of Scholastic Inc.'s National Advisory Council and holder of executive positions at the organization; as Superintendent of Greenwich Public Schools; and as a builder of partnerships among school districts, superintendents, teachers, administrators, and the U.S. Department of Education. He has been on the Board of the Alliance since its inception in 1994.

Improving student and staff writing has always been Ernie's priority and passion, and to that end, he established one of the best writing-focused professional learning programs in the country. For his accomplishments, Williams College conferred an Honorary Doctorate of Humane Letters in 1984. Dr. Fleishman also received his B.A. from Williams College, and his M.A. in the Teaching of English and Ed.D. in Administration from the Harvard Graduate School of Education.

In honor of his contributions to the Alliance and writing education, the Alliance is proud to launch the Dr. Ernest B. Fleishman Educators' Fund, which helps the Alliance provide recognition and professional-development opportunities to educators working with under-resourced communities, and whose students excel in the Scholastic Art & Writing Awards.

About *The Best Teen Writing of 2019*

The pieces featured in *The Best Teen Writing of 2019* were selected from works that earned National Medals in the 2019 Scholastic Art & Writing Awards. The Scholastic Awards, a national program presented by the Alliance for Young Artists & Writers, identifies and showcases teenagers with exceptional artistic and literary talent. Founded in 1923, the program celebrates the accomplishments of creative students and extends opportunities for recognition, exhibition, publication, and scholarships.

This year, nearly 1,200 students earned National Medals in writing categories. The works selected for this publication represent the diversity of the National Medalists, including grade, gender, geography, genre, and subject matter. They also present a spectrum of the insight and creative intellect that inform many of the pieces.

A complete listing of National Medalists and online galleries of awarded works of art and writing can be found on our website, **artandwriting.org**. Visit our site to see how to enter the 2020 Scholastic Art & Writing Awards, as well as a list of our scholarship partners and ways you can partner with the Alliance to support young artists and writers in your community.

Some of the writing selections have been excerpted.

Go to **artandwriting.org/galleries** to read all of the work as it was submitted.

About the Scholastic Art & Writing Awards

Since 1923, the Scholastic Art & Writing Awards have recognized the vision, ingenuity, and talent of our nation's youth, and provided opportunities for creative teens to be celebrated. Each year, increasing numbers of teens participate in the program and become a part of our community—young artists and writers, filmmakers and photographers, poets and sculptors, video game designers and science fiction writers—along with countless educators who support and encourage the creative process. Notable Scholastic Awards alumni include Andy Warhol, Sylvia Plath, Cy Twombly, John Baldessari, Ken Burns, Kay WalkingStick, Richard Avedon, Stephen King, Luis Jiménez, Paul Chan, Marc Brown, Truman Capote, and Joyce Carol Oates—to name just a few.

Our Mission

The Scholastic Art & Writing Awards are presented by the Alliance for Young Artists & Writers. The Alliance is a 501(c)(3) nonprofit organization whose mission is to identify students with exceptional artistic and literary talent and present their remarkable work to the world through the Scholastic Art & Writing Awards. Through the Awards, students receive opportunities for recognition, exhibition, publication, and scholarships. Students across America submitted nearly 340,000 original works during our 2019 program year across 29 different categories of art and writing.

Our Programs

Through the Scholastic Awards, teens in grades 7–12 from public, private, or home schools can apply in 29 categories of art and writing for a chance to earn scholarships and have their works exhibited and published. Beyond the Awards, the Alliance produces a number of programs to support creative students and their educators, including the Art.Write.Now.Tour, the National Student Poets Program, the Scholastic Awards Summer Workshops and Scholastic Awards Summer Scholarships programs, the GOLDEN Educators Residency, and many more. The Alliance features art works by National Medalists that received our top awards in *The Best Teen Art*. Additionally, we publish a collection of exemplary written works in this anthology, *The Best Teen Writing*, and a chapbook that features works from the National Student Poets. These publications are distributed free of charge to schools, students, educators, museums, libraries, and arts organizations across the country.

2019 National Writing Jurors

Rasha Abdulhadi
Olga Abella
Elizabeth Acevedo
Dilruba Ahmed
Antonio R. Aiello
Neil Aitken
Hanna Ali
Ignatius Valentine Aloysius
Hasan Altaf
Stephanie Jonell Alvarado
Corina L. Apostol
Joseph Tyler Arnold
MK Asante
Laura Ascenzi-Moreno
Louisa Anne Aviles
Lucas Baisch
Quenton Baker
Dan Barden
Cinelle Barnes
David Basena
Robert Beatty
Danielle Bennett
Sherwin Bitsui
Sarah Blake
Amy Brewer
Lois Bridges
Ryan D. Brinkhurst
Kathryn Brohawn
Nicole Brown
Joseph Bruchac
Tobias S. Buckell
Sarah Shun-lien Bynum
Francisco Cantu
Orson Scott Card
Christopher Carmona
Ellen Carpenter
Rafael Casal
Cecil Castellucci
Angela Cervantes

Pearl Chan
Sophie Charles
Cortney Lamar Charleston
Ching-In Chen
Karissa Chen
Farai Chideya
Brandon Ray Christophe
Darin Ciccotelli
Allicia Clark
Ian Clarke
David Clawson
Ian M. Cockfield
Andrei Codrescu
Gerald L. Coleman
Paige Cornwell
Teri Ellen Cross Davis
Matt Crowley
Jackie Cuevas
Alexander Danner
Peter Ho Davies
Geffrey Davis
Lorna Dawes
Philip De Guzman
Michael J. Deluca
Anna deVries
Natalie Diaz
Mitchell L. H. Douglas
Timothy DuWhite
Cornelius Eady
Summer Edward
Philip Elliott
Kali Fajardo-Anstine
Claire Farley
Aimee Felone
Tim Floreen
Enrique Flores-Galbis
Gwen Florio
Kim Fu
Ifeona Harrison Fulani

Eric Gansworth
Jonathan F. Garcia
Rohan Gavin
Rigoberto Gonzalez
Jillian Goodman
Alison Granucci
Harold Green
Camille Griep
Cassie Guinan
Ben Guterson
Marissa A. Gutierrez-Vicario
Leslie C. Halpern
Betty J. Harris
Lynn K. Harris
Levi Higgs
Brandon Hobson
Luke N. Hodges
John Holman
Yahdon Israel
Lucy Ives
Naomi Jackson
Victor Babatunde Jatula
Miah Jeffra
Kij Johnson
Lonnell Edward Johnson
Fabienne Josaphat
Zeyn Joukhadar
Rachel Graham Kagan
Ilya Kaminsky
Mwende K. Katwiwa
David James Keaton
Jack Kelly
Oonya Kempadoo
Christine Kendall
Angel A. Kimble
Cheston Brian Knapp
Chelene Knight
Mary Knight
Geeta Kothari

Michelle Koufopoulos
Meghan Lamb
Rich Larson
Brett Fletcher Lauer
Evan Lavender-Smith
Patrice Lawrence
Chip Livingston
Ethan Long
Cynthia Lord
Jason E. Lundberg
Charles J. Malone
Maurice Manning
Halimah Marcus
Demetria Martinez
Michael Martone
Brendan Mathews
Trapeta B. Mayson
Joseph Mbele
Devlyn H. McCreight
Patricia M. Mckean
Chris McKinney
Tony Medina
Jasminne Mendez
Richard Michelson
Nelle Mills
Brad Aaron Modlin
Ander Monson
Kamilah Aisha Moon
Wayetu Moore
Kortney Morrow
Vynetta A. Morrow
Douglas F. Murano, Jr.
Kevin Murphy
Joshua M. Murray
Heather Nesle
Diana Khoi Nguyen
Will Niedmann
Jennifer A. Nielsen
Dennis Norris II
Michael Northen
Obi Nwakanma
Biljana Obradovic

Jay Odjick
José Guadalupe Olivarez
Jeremy Paden
Elissa A. Parker
Dustin K. Pearson
Shaunwell R. Pusley
Monica Prince
Justin Phillip Reed
Luke William Reynolds
Linda Rodriguez
Rollo Romig
Jonah Lloyd Rosenberg
Olga Rukovets
Alanna Rusnak
Anthony Ryan
Benjamin Samuel
Erika L. Sánchez
Luc Sante
Scott Saul
Eleanore Jeanne Scott
Lucile Scott
Jasmine Frances Sealy
Olive Senior
Akhil Sharma
Terisa Tinei Siagatonu
Noor Unnahar Siddique
Safiya Sinclair
Hasanthika Sirisena
Jim Sitar
Brando Skyhorse
Charles Smith
Matthew Ross Smith
Zoe Smolen
Bianca L. Spriggs
Sheila Squillante
Nic Stone
Francisco X. Stork
Virgil Suarez
Jeffrey W. Sweet
Bryan Thao Worra
Mi'Jan Celie Tho-Biaz
Paul Tobin

Laura Tohe
Brian Turner
Derek Updegraff
Krithika Varagur
Padma Venkatraman
Jose L. Vilson
Ava Forte Vitali
Asiya Wadud
Kevin Waltman
Mary Watson
Jeff Weigel
Brian Phillip Whalen
Jeff Wheeler
Aaron Wiener
Carter Wilson
Marion Winik
Sherri Winston
Ben H. Winters
Tobias L. Wray
Tim Wynne-Jones
Kobi Yamada
George Masao Yamazawa
Sunil Yapa
James Chien-Hwa Yeh
Javier Zamora
Arnold Zar-Kessler

Foreword

Over my years running the Scholastic Art & Writing Awards, so many arts professionals have said the same thing about judging the Awards: It gives them hope about the future of art and literature. As the judging concluded this year and yet another artist made that comment, I pressed him and his fellow panelists, asking why the work—which addressed a range of social issues, including gun violence and climate change—could leave them feeling optimistic. They were thoughtful as they sought the right words, then said it's hard for mature artists not to have a trace of cynicism in their artwork, especially work that looks at difficult issues. But the teens' work faced those issues with a hopefulness that was refreshing and authentic, which adult artists can't simulate. There was a double meaning in every work—a heartbeat of hope that, just by addressing the issues, you are making a contribution toward solving them.

That's the insight at the center of the Scholastic Awards. Although many great American artists and writers have received their start in the Awards in the past century, at the heart of our mission is empowering teens to look at, address, and help us understand social issues through a creative lens. We have learned over the Awards' life span that developing the muscle of originality will serve students well throughout their lives, as an aid in their expression, as a comfort, and as a life habit.

As you view these pages, we invite you to enter the world of today's teenagers with optimism and hope. Doing so honors the students' efforts to create a more just, creative, and beautiful world.

Virginia McEnerney

Virginia McEnerney
Executive Director, 2008–19
Scholastic Art & Writing Awards

Special Achievement Awards

Political commentaries and civic engagement. Climate change. Love and loss. Teens have a lot to say about life and the world around them. Every year, we partner with dedicated individuals, foundations, and corporations to offer creative scholarship opportunities to teen artists and writers whose experiences and ideas help shape the communities around them.

Portfolio Awards
- Gold Medal Portfolio
- Silver Medal with Distinction Portfolio

Other Special Achievement Awards
- American Voices Medal
- Best-in-Grade Award
- Civic Expression Award
- New York Life Award
- One Earth Award

Selections of Special Achievement Award art works are included in the following pages.

The Tree I Call Family

POETRY

SANDRA CHEN, Grade 12. Amador Valley High School, Pleasanton, CA. Stacey Sklar, *Educator*; Writopia Lab, *Affiliate*; Gold Medal Portfolio

COMMAND WEB OFFSET WRITING PORTFOLIO

To Aunt Jianhong

The last time I talked to you, I spoke less
than the telephone static. My tongue bent
with each word, weighed down by syllables
it no longer knew how to form. In pregnant

pauses, I imagined your conversations
with my mother when I was her weight
to bear. How you agreed to take me in
with less hesitance than my hellos to you

hold now. Your apartment is the first home
I remember, a nursery above subway whirs
and Suzhou river bends. Once, I spilt
a river from the bathtub and you slipped,

broke two ribs. Do fractured bones
look like cracked branches? In the family
tree I drew in sixth grade, I carved you
out, engraved instead an English name

because I couldn't write your real one
in my impostered Chinese. I removed you
like a splinter from the skin I didn't want,
snapped our lineage, buried my roots.

Now the next time I talk to you, I'll speak less
than the telephone static because
the crackling will sound too much
like the cutting and burning of wood.

Nights She Doesn't Feel Like Living

POETRY

BRIANNA COSTA KLINE, Grade 12. Pittsburgh Cape High School, Pittsburgh, PA. Mara Cregan, *Educator*; Western PA Writing Project, The University of Pittsburgh School of Education, *Affiliate*; Gold Medal Portfolio

SCHOLASTIC INC. WRITING PORTFOLIO

There is someone sitting in the dark corner of her room.
The window's jaw is propped ajar. Venetian blinds shudder in the wind.
She is alone with herself, the dark figure, and the moon.

In the heat, the room stirs with the sickly talcum scent of perfume.
It twists towards her, and in the moonlight, its smooth flesh glints,
the dark someone sitting in the corner of her room.

The trees shiver, and in the darkness, night blooms
with the smell of rot. Cicadas hum in wet grass. The air thins,
and now they just wait: the girl, the dark figure, and the moon.

The room shifts like abacus beads. Silence swells, a tumid womb.
She imagines digging out her muscles until she is just bones and skin,
and stares at the something in the corner of her room.

It watches her, eyes red and round as carnival balloons.
She stands still, body quivering like the strings of a violin
as she sits, knees to chest, with the dark figure and the moon.

Her body is damp with sweat, from a warm and soft June.
She feels dizzy; the fragrant air makes her head spin.
There is someone sitting in the corner of her room,
and soon they are all that exist: the girl, the dark figure, and the moon.

Grave Diggers

POETRY

RAVEN LITTLE, Grade 12. Lusher Charter School, New Orleans, LA. Brad Richard, *Educator*; Greater New Orleans Writing Project, *Affiliate*; Gold Medal Portfolio

ALLIANCE FOR YOUNG ARTISTS & WRITERS WRITING PORTFOLIO

I. The Future
One day, this is where your family will lay
down your body. A fixture, emptied for display
and hidden in the warmth of your Easter suit.
Memories of you embalm the air, ripe like fruit.
The largest tragedy of your demise: you never learned to pray.

II. The Preparation
Your name has been etched into this shovel
with the same knife you used to carve devil horns
into your neighbor's tree trunk. Now that you are strong,
the ground waits to be broken. *You can't prolong
your fate*, it says as you rip into its flesh with no trouble.

III. The Eulogy
The sky's jaws hang loose to accept you.
In the privacy of our homes, we don't mention the noose that plagued you.
We are here to commemorate the chains
rooting you to a history that causes teachers too much pain
to even mention in class, out of respect for our black friends
—they really meant for you.

I Watch My Father Give Eye Surgery in Ile Ife, Nigeria

POETRY

ATHENA NASSAR, Grade 12. Interlochen Arts Academy, Interlochen, MI. Brittany Cavallaro, *Educator*; Kendall College of Art and Design, Ferris State University, *Affiliate*; Gold Medal Portfolio

ALLIANCE FOR YOUNG ARTISTS & WRITERS WRITING PORTFOLIO

I watch my father give eye surgery in Ile Ife, Nigeria

have you ever been to Rome? she asks. i hold
her slender fingers in mine. she looks up at me
with her one seeing eye. the other a swirl of clouds

and exhaust from the crowded streets cluttered
with mothers trying to sell bananas, iphone chargers,
goats. their ribs poke out of their chest. the next meal

for their daughters and sons. they don't live to be
grandparents, they live to feed the hollow bellies
of their daughters and sons and they scrape what's left

off of serving spoons. she only knows a few words
in english but she asks *have you ever been to Rome.* i have.
i've roamed the cobblestone streets. i've bathed

in the typhoon dissolving her eyeball. in spices and cheeses
that she doesn't know how to pronounce. chorizo, provolone.
there's a typhoon in her eyeball. manchego, gorgonzola.

she doesn't know the sharp taste of a blue cheese on the tongue.
i wish i could show her how it tastes. hail crashes down her cheeks
and shatters on her gown like glass. she only knows the cold

front of the gale force winds moving through her brittle bones. i try
not to fall into the black hole—my presence a vacuum. there's not a lot

of eye doctors in Nigeria. i freeze like a roman statue—enveloped in the swirls.
our two hands binded by stone. i wonder if she's seen the carving of two angels
draped in robes. her curls fall onto her cheeks and she looks like an angel.
eyes swallowed in the storm. wings cemented in the ground. an angel who

has only the robes her mother draped her in. her eyes draped in a curtain
of darkness. she couldn't see the light of Rome if she was standing right
on the cobblestone streets. the luminescent reflection of gondolas

on the water, the light from lamp posts flooding onto the stone,
clogging the blood vessels that run to her heart. there's no
gondolas in Nigeria. she sails by way of bare feet on the gravel.

she has no oars in the storm and she doesn't know the words
to ask to borrow mine and i don't know the words to tell her
i'm sorry you've never been to Rome. i don't know Igbo or Yoruba

or Hausa to tell her *take mine.* i've seen enough ruins to show
to my future daughters and sons. she was eight years old when
she died and she didn't live to see the colosseum.

The Gods that Failed You

FLASH FICTION

CALEB PAN, Grade 12. Home School, Denver, CO. Jesaka Long and Peiyan Pan, *Educators,* Region-at-Large, *Affiliate*; Gold Medal Portfolio

THE NEW YORK TIMES WRITING PORTFOLIO

Wake up.

Say good morning to your family. Eat breakfast.

Remember to make the bed. But you need to get out the door. Tomorrow then.

Be on **time**. Smile at friends and teachers. Hand in homework. Take notes. Run your highlighter dry. Color code. Clutter your calendar. Ace exams. Diligently study. Show off. Flaunt your **merit**. Make annotations. Micromanage your-**self**. Practice **self**-**control**. Stockpile your pencils. Patronize others. Stress out. Take **pride** in stress. Exaggerate how sleep deprived you are. Let everyone applaud and admonish you. Over**achieve**. Accept concerns as compliments. Run for treasurer. Make it to district. Capitalize your talents. Laugh off anxiety. Flinch at red ink. Check grades with unease. Run the **numbers**. Calculate the collateral to your GPA. Believe in the hierarchy of class rank. Roll the Stone up the hill. Confuse your weaknesses. Usurp **control** of group projects. Feel **pride**. Do all of the **work**. Do community service. Plant a tree. Volunteer at a soup kitchen. Pick up other people's garbage. Donate clothes you don't want anymore. Tutor kids you **pity**. Document the **number** of hours. Over-estimate your**self**. Ascend the Heavens. Play an instrument for four years. Be **self**-motivated. Make it to regionals. Run for vice president. Take a foreign language for four years. Be delighted when peers ask for advice. Ride the Sun chariot. Reluctantly congratulate everyone else for their **achieve**ments. Run for president. Argue in speech and debate for four years. Be tired. Criticize your**self**. Be **self**-deprecating. Fear failure. Play a sport for four years. Make it to state. Ask for references. Get nominated. Lose **control**. Run a club or five for four years. The Stone rolls back down. Underestimate your**self**. Raise money for acknowledgment. Lack passion. Attempt mastering everything. Lose sleep. Thrive in pressure. Fly close to the Sun. Fill in the bubbles. Stop. Pencils down. Break **time**. Hydrate your**self**. Stop kicking your**self**. Come back on **time** or be locked out. Eat a snack. Second-guess your answers. Run out of confidence. Crumble under expectations. Head back early. Pass eliminations. Comfort those who scored lower. Feel **pity** for your**self**. Despise those who scored higher. Make it to nationals. Forget your strengths. Question your recommenders. Fetishize **numbers**. Catalog your awards and certificates. Feel inadequate filling out resumes. Worry over whitespace in applications. Be insecure about your transcript. Drown in the Ocean. Shrug off guilt. Pull all-nighters. Doubt your **merit**. Open congratulation letters. Get struck from the chariot. Smile and wave. Walk on stage. Plummet to Earth. Bask in applause. Take a bow. Click submit.

Enter your bedroom. The bed is still unmade. Start making the bed.

Stop in remorse. Almost give up. Tomorrow then.

Try falling asleep. ■

Her

POETRY

ARIANA SMITH, Grade 12. Las Vegas Academy of the Arts, Las Vegas, NV. Sim Dulaney, *Educator*; Springs Preserve, *Affiliate*; Gold Medal Portfolio

THE MAURICE R. ROBINSON FUND WRITING PORTFOLIO

She is a paradox,
What once grew in the Motherland
Now flows inside of Her.
She is Yoruba before colonial inva-
sion,
Dressed in frost white, curls of bud-
ding cotton
Firmly standing in a veranda with
Her palms pressed together,
A collision of velvet and sandpaper.
She is R&B cemented hips
Swinging side to side,
Jumping on hard eggshell mattress
to afrobeats,
Skin folds like origami flowers and
paper napkins.
Swollen eyes, dark like the color of
her skin,
Her brown fingertips scrape licks of
coconut oil
Out of glass jars with tops covered
in tin,
The flakes etch embroidery into the
slits between her
While the world tugs at my chest
like a violin.
She moves slow like honey;
The clink of her belt being undone,
My body no longer land that I own.
I don't want anybody else

To hear that sound.
Together we are a ravine;
Shadows of the same sea,
Unwavering tides,
Connected dots of Orion.
She gives me the first taste and
I lose myself in the
Raspberry of her tongue—
I am still too reluctant to give in.
I tell her not to reach for me,
For I am too far away.
I tell her,
I am not ready
For shared shrimp and grits
And the braiding of each other's
hair,
I am not ready for sweet potato
gazes,
Or thighs intertwined like yarn,
For I fear that I will unearth
A part of myself that
Frightens me.

Consider the Elephant

CRITICAL ESSAY

DIVJOT WALIA, Grade 12. Glenda Dawson High School, Pearland, TX. Susan Henson, *Educator*; Harris County Department of Education, *Affiliate*; Gold Medal Portfolio

THE NEW YORK TIMES WRITING PORTFOLIO

When thinking of elephants, my mind lists the obvious: ivory trade, elephant meat, and trophy hunting. Political correctness aside, I had to wonder—*who cares?* Does my life, writing in the middle of urban America, rely on the well-being of the sub-Saharan African ecosystem?

It was then I remembered—I in fact had been impacted by an elephant almost a decade ago.

* * *

It was my first time visiting India—I was seven years old, and my mother compelled me to ride an elephant with my Indian-native cousins in Delhi's most touristy district. I admired the elephant's grey leathery skin, grasping on to its wrinkles as I, with the aid of a callous Indian man, climbed upon it. The same Indian man began striking the elephant with a whip, presumably to coerce the visibly apathetic animal to begin the ride. My cousin, eleven at the time, desperately called out, "Stop! Please! Be gentler!" But the man, desensitized to such moral concerns, continued his abuse of the animal. I rocked back and forth as the ride continued. *I am not scared*—I attempted to convince myself. My cousin continued to cry out at the man to lessen the severity of the whip, and I, wanting nothing to do with the *adult* discourse taking place before me (in a language I spoke very loosely at the time), dismounted off the elephant and leapt into my mother's arms. I glared at the elephant, and it stared back at me, with striking ambivalence.

* * *

The passing years have seemed to erase the image of the elephant from my consciousness; thus, I resolved to conduct a brief Google Image search of the term "elephant." These elephants were not banded up, whipped by a callous Indian man, or saddled with Indian-American tourists sitting atop them. The animals I saw were social, yet solitary; majestic, yet playful. The sub-Saharan sun shined behind the scenery as what I can only describe as "grandpa elephants" stared wisely into the expanse of light green grass, mother elephants guarded their elephant babies, and schools of elephant children gathered to play games and take a dip in the local drinking hole. As my cursor moved down the page, I began to understand it more and more: it is true—elephants are adorable.

One particular elephant seemed to pop out. It was a newborn elephant, likely no more than a few days old. His trunk bent, the newborn sprayed a stream of pond water on his still tender, leathery skin. His smile was unlike any other emotion I'd seen from an animal. It was so human, and so innocent, that I waited for the elephant to ask me, "Hey! How's it going?" I waited for the elephant to turn into a *Disney-fied* version of itself—for it to do a few spins and give me an overly enthusiastic fist-bump before breaking out into a perfectly choreographed dance to heavily copyrighted, upbeat music.

In reality, I waited for the elephant to fulfill some *cute* mold I'd cut out for it—long before I conducted the Google Image search.

Nine years after I met my first elephant, I will never forget the stare the it gave me as I dismounted it. I had even forgotten about that callous Indian man, and how he likely abused the elephant for the equivalent of less than a couple dollars a day. But the only lesson I deduced is that of moral outrage on the *elephant's* behalf.

I evaluated my own moral repugnance. *I stand idle, observing all other injustices that occur in a developing country such as India, but when it comes to striking an animal (who happens to have* incredibly *thick skin), I draw the line.*

* * *

But again, *elephants are cute.*

And it is with this cuteness that elephants invoke the *je ne sais quoi* my society finds so enduring. Yet, we all agree, almost pretentiously: elephants are a reflection of us humans, but without all the war, genocide, and violence. Even science seems to approve.

Looking down the taxonomical tree, elephants belong to the class Mammalia. (Even without Latin lessons, most recognize that *mammal* is an overwhelmingly broad class.) On the next taxonomic level, we see the infraclass Eutheria, which, while quite a bit more Latin-sounding, only happens to include a general grouping of animals who use placentas. To clear further confusion, scientists have classified elephants into the order Proboscidean and the family Elephantidae, which both are essentially synonyms for *elephant*. Ultimately, elephants are so unique that all their taxonomic relatives are long-extinct, and to expand to a broader category would place elephants and humans in the same classification.

Yet this comparison to humans begins to seem rather valid upon examining behavior. Elephants have a 22-month gestation period, and for mother elephants, having a "baby" elephant is quite an investment, due to the baby's large size and many needs. Once labor is complete, the baby elephant is *slowly* weaned off its mother's milk; like other placental mammals, elephants are rather useless immediately after birth. After the elephant's useless infant years have passed, however, the elephant will begin using its large, muscle-laden trunk to do what can only be described as shaking hands to greet its elephant brethren. An adolescence of exploration later, the elephant loses its baby teeth, and will reach sexual maturity in its twenties, and die at age eighty. And in this death, there is no reason why we should not suspect elephants feel grief, as evidence of elephants stroking a dead family member's remains or gathering in grief huddles exists; it is not unscientific to attribute the human emotion of grief to this animal behavior—to do so would be the only scientific explanation for such observations.

All of this considered, elephants are basically massive, wrinkly humans. The life cycles of both species track almost uncannily, and taxonomically, science has little refutation. Both species have no close relatives but themselves, and both, without clothes, look awkwardly hairless and wrinkly compared to their more distant mammal cousins. Related by weirdness, it is no surprise the two species have had such a rich and intertwined history. In fact, elephants can recognize themselves in a mirror—much like we can recognize ourselves by looking at the elephant.

But why then, if elephants so uncannily reflect humankind, do we tie them up and subject them to the whims of our entertainment needs? After all, elephants excel in the brain-to-body mass ratio category, high in the ranks among the likes of the great apes and dolphins. Aristotle even noticed this without the aid of science, calling elephants "the animal that surpasses all others in wit and mind."

Despite this, and especially in countries like India, the seemingly innocent elephant offering itself for riding has more than likely been illegally captured. Yet wild elephants would never allow a human to ride atop its back, so baby elephants must have their spirits crushed in a process called *Phajann* (literally, "the crush"), which involves isolation from their mothers and confinement in small spaces, starvation, and physical abuse. Keep in mind: biologically, the elephant spine is not meant for supporting anything, let alone a husky Western tourist. And so naturally, elephant tourism is a prominent issue in Asia, with (largely Western) tourists wanting to ride, wash, and touch the animals. I think to myself: *even I have found myself among this class.* Yet, despite all alarmism, I ultimately may not have to feel so guilty. And to this prospect, I became excited—*I may have a way to justify my moral repugnance.*

Elephant tourism leads to a rise in elephant numbers, which would otherwise be critically low. Thus, the cruelty of the elephant tourism world is largely a product of a lack of planning and consideration, rather than the moral repugnance of the practice itself. Leaders of elephant departments in parks assert that elephants have no habitat to begin with, and their programs offer the only hope for the continuation of the species. Furthermore, to the argument against elephant tourism in countries like India, many argue that the individuals in these locales need their jobs. Ought we value the economic benefit of humans over the abstract moral benefit of elephants?

To me, the answer must be no. I like to think of myself as morally righteous, yet realistically, I have little remorse for my irrational and disproportionate concern over elephant humanity. The elephant has a large amount of "pretty privilege," as there are countless organizations devoted to its well-being, with no real consideration to its correlated ecological impact. It is only because elephants are cute that society displays a strange, almost cult-like fascination with them, that Google Images depicts them in such a romantic light, and that my experience in India has stuck with me for such an unexpected amount of time. We see the elephant as one of us—we impose our human emotions onto the distinctly non-human ways of the elephant (such a process is known as "anthropomorphism"). Elephants are cute, and their cute behavior reminds us of them. Thus, we are justified in connecting this behavior to ourselves, because doing so is simply an observation followed by the most plausible explanation. And compared to the other injustices of the world, the *Phajann* of the elephant, objectively, dwindles into obscurity. But subjectively, it means so much more.

I refuse to entertain the idea that I care so deeply about the well-being of elephants simply because some MRI scans show some interesting patterns of color in an elephant's brain (that may or may not be like those found in human brains). I refuse to entertain the incessant need to take the moral high ground. I refuse to entertain society, and to its constructs, I say: "Elephants are cute, and I feel bad if a *cute* thing also looks like a *sad* thing. The complexity ends there." My seven-year-old self needed no MRI to justify this, and neither do I. And perhaps this is hypocritical, but that does not make its impact any less tangible. As a higher being, my visual pleasure ought to be valued above all else—the science begins to matter very little, not just to "society," but to myself as well. At any rate, I stay true to the seven-year-old version of myself—the one who found that elephant unequivocally cute, and nothing more.

Ultimately, I have the same means of objectifying these moral considerations as the elephant has of understanding the clattering of my keyboard as I type this paragraph. ∎

Meaning of Chinese

PERSONAL ESSAY & MEMOIR

SOPHIA ZHAO, Grade 12. Charter School of Wilmington, Wilmington, DE. Rosemary Basquill, *Educator*; Diamond State Branch, National League of American Pen Women, Inc., *Affiliate*; Gold Medal Portfolio

ALLIANCE FOR YOUNG ARTISTS & WRITERS WRITING PORTFOLIO

Peering out the rounded window, I took in the city's overwhelming vastness. Smog painted the sky overcast; it seemed to slowly stir like a never-ending storm swallowing the airplane whole. Further below, cars congested the highways in a faulty-Tetris fashion that made the row's contiguous seats seem roomy. I stretched out my arms and legs, letting out a loud yawn. The passenger next to me glared and muttered a Chinese expletive. Yes. Shanghai was going to be splendid.

But as my family and I boarded a taxi departing for my grandmother's apartment (where we were planning to freeload), the hordes of skyscrapers, people, and vehicles grew less intimidating. Instead, I began to ponder over whether this would work—being Chinese. Sure, I could understand virtually all the swear words and conversations, yet I still spoke with an American accent and couldn't read or write proficiently. And, according to mass media and my substandard test grades, I was too old to learn to fluency. I expected that relatives would listen to me with judgmental confusion and snicker when I couldn't read ice pop labels or mini-mart signs. I was Chinese, but not Chinese enough.

One afternoon, about halfway through the trip, grandma paused her daily routine of laundering, cleaning, and cooking for the first time. She quietly closed the kitchen's glass door, stepped into her thin cloth slippers, and then shuffled into the living room. Fingers trembling, she loosely gripped a pale paper workbook, its corners furled and spine peeling. With a sweeping hand, she motioned to the narrow couch that I was curled up on.

"*Bao bei, zuo qi lai hao ba?*" Darling, please sit up.

I straightened myself and perched on the rightmost cushion. She eased herself into the empty seat next to me and flipped to the near-last page of her book. Then, a breath. In English, almost a whisper:

"Can you say this for me?"

Each day, we allocated thirty minutes to learning the language. We discerned the slight undulations of "probably," how to differentiate between *Q* and *K*, correct ways to use slang. During mealtime, she'd name each food in English, pointing at the bowls with her chopsticks. Sometimes she'd mix up soy sauce and vinegar, but then would correct the blunder after dipping her dumpling in the right one (in our household, the latter). At night, I listened to her record and scrutinize her pronunciations; she'd rate herself in Chinese, tenaciously proclaiming *"Liu shi!"* but then would heartily laugh, repeating "No, no—I mean sixty."

My grandmother is nearly eighty, yet studies English daily. We still can't hold a perfect conversation, but that's okay. I realized that it didn't matter where I started from, whether it be knowing zero phrases or a couple hundred, or how late I started—I could still learn gradually, writing a couple sentences per day and reading children's books out loud, word by word. It was more important that I cared: that I wanted to jot grandma reminders on what to buy for dinner, that I wanted to decipher museum placards and learn about ancient history, that I wanted to strike up richer conversations with the local vendor, that I wanted to mail friends and family cards brimming with love from top to bottom. That is what it means to be Chinese enough: to care.

After looking out at the beautiful technicolor city one last time, I shut the plane's window. I shifted around in my seat. There seemed to be less room than the previous flight; on the floor, my bag was too full with calligraphy brushes and notebooks. With no chance of salvaging my earbuds, I waved and called out *"Xian sheng!* (Mister!)" unwaveringly. The attendant tossed me a pair, and I clicked them into the mini television in front of me. I tapped on China's latest blockbuster, then enabled the subtitles—following each character, one by one. ■

Gold Standard

POETRY

ALEXANDRA CONTRERAS-MONTESANO, Grade 12. Burlington High School, Burlington, VT. Jill Kelley, *Educator*; Brattleboro Museum & Art Center, *Affiliate*; Silver Medal with Distinction Portfolio

I hate the flashy gold American Express cards
that take a couple seconds longer to
process on the credit machine
and almost make me drop that
retail smile.

I try not to look at
the nails that slide
the card through, manicured like
I can see their lawn in the
color pink they choose.

It's hard to stomach the way they
stare right through me, hydrochloric eyes blinking
until they turn because they see the
small
number of coins in my hand
and decide that I am not a
member of the
gold standard.

I want to be happy with the
clink
that the fake silver I wear on my ears
makes as it tangles in something
but
I know that real silver makes a
thunk.

It seems I am filled with the
fortune of being alive and kicking and trying

to be something more than that penny
that no one bothers to even look at because
the lucky pennies are always shiny.

I don't really care about silver and gold
but I care about the way
silver and gold people
care about me.
or that they don't.

I don't really hate gold American Express cards
or fake silver earrings
but I do hate
that their gold is as fake as my silver
but it buys them
so much
more.

Bonding

POETRY

AKUA OWUSU, Grade 12. Milton Academy, Milton, MA. Tarim Chung, *Educator*; School of the Museum of Fine Arts at Tufts University, *Affiliate*; Silver Medal with Distinction Portfolio

I settle between my mother's legs,
on the soup stain
from a couple of nights ago.
It's hardened by now and the carpet
crunches beneath my thighs.
Resting my head on her knee,
I close my eyes to the sweet smell
of M&Ms baking into cookie dough
and my grandmother's shouts
at the protagonists
of the Nollywood movie mixing
in with the village witch's incantations.
A burning sensation seizes
my scalp as my mother coats
my strands from root to end
with the *Dark and Lovely Kids* cream
and rakes through the softened curls
with a fine-tooth comb, I try
to keep my neck as relaxed
as possible so I don't
receive another burn mark,
and keep my eyes
closed until I can see the
reveal of my good hair.

How to Curse in Spanish

POETRY

STEPHANIE KAISER, Grade 12. Hathaway Brown School, Shaker Heights, OH. Scott Parsons, *Educator*; Cleveland Institute of Art, *Affiliate*; Gold Medal, American Voices Medal

From your worn suede recliner,
You stopped my brother from passing through to the backyard.
He was about 15 at the time,
And I was 12,
In that stage
Where I made myself blend into the background of every room.
You said,
"PJ . . . I have a word for you: carajo."
He asked what it meant and you swatted away a mosquito before answering,
"I can't tell you the definition
but I can tell you what it means.
You say it when you see a pretty girl,
Or get caught in bad traffic,
Or . . . "
You got stuck on a third example
Of when it might be considered appropriate to use such a word.
Now I can fill in that blank you left.
Carajo.
When your abuelo is in the hospital
With a broken hip
And you're not on the moon but you might as well be
For how far you are
And one Saturday night he dies,
Not peacefully,
Or because he was meant to,
But because that's the way it goes
When your hip
And your kidneys
And your pancreas
And your eyes
And your heart
Fail you.

That's carajo.
And I've never said it,
Not for any girl or any traffic jam,
But I might start now.

Cutting Ties

PERSONAL ESSAY & MEMOIR

KHIRA HICKBOTTOM, Grade 12. Homestead High School, Fort Wayne, IN. Jamie Smith, *Educator*; Fort Wayne Museum of Art, *Affiliate*; Gold Medal, American Voices Medal

I pulled my head away, and she pulled me right back.

The first ten years of my life were spent sitting on a pillow between my mom's legs, surrounded by edge gel and shea butter and wide-toothed combs. She spent hours taming me, and then my hair, with hands just as tough as her love.

"Moooom, it hurts!"

"Yeah, well if you want to go to school looking like a fool tomorrow, then you can."

We had the same argument over and over again, always followed by the silence of submission. I'd slide back onto the pillow, fingers twirling the multi-colored barrettes I had chosen for my hair.

And I loved it.

I loved it until I got to school and the pale hands of my friends gravitated towards my head unsolicited, until the gel dissolved in the heat of recess, until I realized I was the only one. Every little girl had silky hair roped in pastel colored bows, but mine never reflected the sun in the same way on the playground.

I told anyone who would listen that my mom would let me start straightening my hair when I was twelve. I wanted them to know that I wouldn't be messy forever, that I would be like them, that I would be better.

After years of nagging, I gained admission to the salon club two years early. My mom and I went to the shop every other week, bonding the chemicals to our hair and ourselves to one another. Our biweekly appointments amounted to three hours of petty gossip underscored by the velvety sound of gospel music echoing from the decrepit CD player. I didn't know it then, but the salon is the backbone of black women. The squeaky tile flooring, old swivel chair, and bottle upon bottle of gooey moisturizer held years of history my ten-year-old eyes couldn't comprehend.

The perms were enough to appease me for a while. My hair was slick and shiny, falling flat against the side of my face. It was enough until the heat of cross-country practice fried the chemicals, until my narcissistic eyes gazed so close to the water that I fell in and my hair recoiled, until it just wasn't anymore.

By the time I got to high school the biweekly trips turned into seven hour appointments every three months to get my hair braided, and the talk concerning my head shifted to another, more patronizing, field.

"How many braids are there?"

"Can I braid your braids?"

"Is it all your hair?"

Questions I am tired of answering. Questions I am *still* answering for the people who ask and don't care to remember.

The kinky curls of black women have always been a point of contention. They are worshipped for their foreignness, their versatility, their ability to defy gravity. They are worshipped until they become an inconvenience. Looking respectable and embracing natural hair have yet to coexist, thus the working women pressing their hair with hot combs in salons and the millions of little black girls always looking into the mirror discontented.

For sixteen years any form my hair took wasn't good enough. I was the little girl in the mirror, and I was on my way to being the grown woman at the salon until I stopped begging to go to the shop, until I realized that Eurocentric beauty standards were complete and utter bull, until I could look in the mirror and not be afraid of the size of my hair and whether it would block someone's view in class or at the movie theater.

Since sophomore year I've known that come the end of senior year I will cut it all off. My self-worth has always sprouted from my head.

I want to bloom elsewhere. ∎

Bowl of Noodles

PERSONAL ESSAY & MEMOIR

ALICE CAI, Grade 10. Fayetteville High School, Fayetteville, AR. Katie Stueart, *Educator*; Region-at-Large, *Affiliate*; Gold Medal, Best-in-Grade Award

I. *La mian*: also known as "pulled noodles" in English. These long, thin noodles are known for the effort and time it requires to make them the authentic way.

My father made pulled noodles almost every night of my early childhood. I remember watching him as he kneaded the dough with powerful hands, specks of white flour falling under smooth rolling hills of tan. To shape the noodles, he first stretched the dough out, flung it between his hands like a jump rope, and then brought the two ends together to do the same thing over again. He started the process early in the afternoon and worked all the way until dinner time, beads of sweat trickling down the side of his face and glistening in the evening sun.

Along with the noodles, my father spent a lot of time hanging up paintings in our house. Every corner I turned, I would stumble across a new *guo hua* of China. My parents also sent me to Chinese school every Sunday so I could learn how to read and write Chinese. Perhaps they saw me as dough that they would stretch and shape to form the noodles they had grown up with.

Summers we flew thirteen hours to China and stayed there for a month. At the time, I breathed China in with simple curiosity. I was too young to filter my own experiences and instead, I navigated that world through sense. The sizzle of *nian gao* (rice cakes) against the pan. The streets bustling loud with people, cars, bicycles. The white smoke of cigarettes, the stench of the bathrooms, the sweltering heat of the summer. The streetside stores with their savory *baozi* and piquant kebabs. When we got home, we slurped up my father's noodles with shameless noise and speed, because they tasted like China. Those noodles were the comfort of my childhood, a semblance of family and familiarity that I embraced with infinite warmth.

But the thing about noodles is they're only good immediately after they're made. When they grow old, they lose their elegant smoothness and become a sticky, smelly mess.

One day, our social studies teacher announced that we'd be studying Chinese dynasties.

As soon as she said this, several heads snapped toward me.

I remember sitting there, throat suddenly tied in a knot, ears burning. I had always known I looked different, but that was when it first dawned on me that other people *saw* me as different—as *Chinese.*

The dinner of my childhood was now old and cold. That word, *Chinese,* now became heavy with connotation. I was trapped in the viscous soup, and wherever I went, I felt like the noodles stuck to my body.

II. Spaghetti: also known as *yi da li mian* in Chinese. Originating from Italy, these thicker noodles are made of wheat and water. They are usually eaten with tomato sauce, meatballs, and parmesan cheese.

One day in sixth grade, I pushed away my bowl of noodles at dinner.

"I don't want these anymore. A girl at school said my noodles smell like farts."

"So?" my father said in Chinese, still slurping the noodles.

"People don't want to be my friend because of them."

He shook his head dismissively. *"Don't worry about that. Noodles are nutritious. Bone broth makes you grow taller. Just eat."*

I stared at my bowl of noodles for a long time without moving, then asked, "Can you make spaghetti instead?"

"Spa-spa—shen mo (what)? *Is it American?"*

"Spaghetti. Yeah, the other kids at school eat it. It's yellow noodles and it has red sauce on it and cheese.

"Ay yo! Cheese!" my father groaned. *"Cheese is nasty—full of fat. Just like other American food. No spaggy.*

"It's spah-GEII-tee." This wasn't the first time he'd mispronounced English words. In public, he sputtered out incoherent sentences with his thick Chinese accent everywhere we went. He was like some sort of brainless parrot clinging onto my shoulder. I always dreaded moments at school when the kids gave me weird looks and whispered about his accent and his noodles.

"Doesn't matter how you say it. We never ate spaggy in China."

"Well this is America," I retorted.

My father shook his head. *"China is your homeland. Just because we live in America doesn't mean you are not Chinese."*

"Yeah, well I wish I wasn't."

Suddenly, the air grew stiff.

"What you mean you wish you were not Chinese?" My father glared at me.

A sternness stitched itself onto both my parents faces. My throat constricted, and neither air nor words could escape. The steam from the bowl of noodles in front of me thickened, wrapped around me, and started to suffocate me.

"You will eat the noodles," my father said. *"And remember: you will always be Chinese."*

I remember staring down at the soup afterward and seeing the reflection of myself in it—an Asian girl with stringy black hair, squinty monolid eyes, and a round flat nose. As long as I kept eating those noodles every day, I would have to face that reflection every day.

So from that point on, I started secretly dumping what my father packed into the trash. Instead, I ate spaghetti from the school cafeteria. Spaghetti tasted weird—the noodles were a little too thick, the tomato sauce a little too salty, and the cheese had the texture of melted plastic. I ate it nevertheless, and over time, acquired a liking for these western flavors.

III. No noodles (*mei you mian*)

I bit down on the Cane's fried chicken, savoring the crunch of its crispy skin and the juiciness of its oil-soaked flesh.

"Ewww, you eat it plain?" Selena, one of the girls on my volleyball team, scrunched up her face in disgust. "I could *never* eat chicken plain. You're supposed to eat it with like ketchup or like barbecue sauce or *something.*"

"Oh . . . my bad, I didn't know."

The other girls giggled. Selena tossed locks of golden blonde hair over her shoulder. "You're so Asian."

"What?" I froze.

"I said, 'You're so Asian,' not knowing that chicken goes with ketchup."

A sudden sense of sickness churned in my stomach. I became painfully aware of the contrast between all the other volleyball girls and me. Their gorgeous large eyes and my own, one-dimensional, black slits. Their smooth, pearl white skin and my coarse, yellowed complexion.

I shook my head forcefully. "No I'm not. I know I look Asian, but I'm really American on the inside."

Vivian chimed in. "Dude. You do math in your free time, you play the piano, and you don't know that chicken goes with ketchup because you're used to eating those stinky noodles all the time."

"Ugh, I didn't even like those noodles. My dad just forced me to bring them."

"Does your dad force you to study math and play the piano too?" Belle asked.

"Yeah, duh. If it were up to me, I'd never do those nerdy things."

"Ohhh . . . So you're like us, but trapped in an Asian body?" Selena said.

"Yup, pretty much. I was born here, just like you. I haven't even been to

China." This was a lie. My parents and I traveled to China to visit my grandparents every summer. "I don't even know Chinese." This was a lie as well. I was fluent in Chinese.

I picked up another chicken wing with greasy fingers, this time scooping up a giant blob of the blood-red ketchup before taking a bite.

During my junior high years, I frequented fast food restaurants like Cane's with my volleyball team. We had practice every day after school, and games several nights a week. It was team tradition to go to fast food restaurants in the time between practice and games.

I had taken up volleyball because it was the most American thing I could do.

For so long, my discomfort at being Chinese had been only that—a feeling of discomfort. It tugged and pushed and nudged me, and was powerful enough at times to draw cries from a raw throat. But it lacked words, lacked structure, lacked a backbone that would give it a life of its own.

When I got a phone in eighth grade, I finally started to understand the "American Dream" through social media and YouTube. This dream was one narrated by words, one that spoke to me from every screen. *Chinese* had a sense of familiarity, but it was blurry, something I couldn't describe with my words. *American*, on the other hand, talked to me in eloquent English. So, when my parents protested against me taking up volleyball, I spoke without hesitation.

"Alice, you are wasting your precious time with sports," my father would say.

"That's not true. Sports give me a social platform. You don't want me to be a social outcast, do you? It is statistically proven that social outcasts experience higher rates of depression and suicide."

"Alice, you barely have time for homework. It's affecting your grades."

"Whatever. Grades don't mean anything. The education system is so stupid. Like all those standardized tests—they don't represent someone's true intelligence. Just search it up. There's articles all over the internet about it."

Family life in my teenage years became a shadow of my Chinese identity that clung to me in my life outside. I tried everything to shed that shameful shadow—listening to mainstream American pop, letting my grades slide, and especially frequenting at fast food restaurants with my friends.

I remember those outings for their loudness. The loudness of the restaurant's brightly painted interiors, of their sticky booths and sticky floors, of the odor of salt and oil sparkling in the air. The loudness of our lipstick, of our hair of bouncy curls, of our sparkly tops and little high heel boots. The loudness of our giggles and yelps in response to gossip and guys flirting with us. And most of all, the loudness of our foods. Squishy hotdogs breaking open in pockets of savory flavor in our mouths. Heavy, warm, comforting carbs soaked in oil, melting with a thick sweetness on our tongues. Cheese—which tasted to me like salty plastic—draped over everything. My "happiness" was louder than ever, and more filled with flavor than ever. I tasted the thrill of sports, of gossip, of boys. I spoke loud and laughed loud, hoping my heart would echo my body.

Yet fast food was too flavorful. Almost overstimulating. It was greedy. I had become addicted to my American Dream, but I didn't realize that the fast food version of it was shallow, a misrepresentation of what it really meant. It was high-calorie, low-content. I gorged, hurting my stomach because my heart was never satisfied. And I forced myself to enjoy the taste of these heavy flavors on my tongue, but nights I would wake up to barf into the toilet, head spinning with a nausea that grew like cancer inside me.

IV. Ramen: also known as *fang bian mian* in Chinese. Typically dried and packaged to be sold in stores, these wheat noodles have a curly texture and a golden yellow color. They are known for the piquant flavor of their seasoning packets and their convenience.

I started eating ramen halfway through my ninth grade year because of what my first boyfriend said about Asians.

"Babe, I'm really jealous of you because you're Asian."

What? Why?"

"Y'all are just naturally smart. I mean, you don't even study and you have all As, and you're definitely gonna get into Harvard."

I stared at him, dumbfounded.

"And like, not only are y'all super smart, your culture is also so . . . exotic."

And with that, being Asian transformed for me. In high school, everyone was intrigued by my "culture." *What does Chinese sound like? Can you speak it for us?*

"*Wo de ming zi shi Ai Li Si.* That means 'my name is Alice.'"

Woah, that's so cool! What is China like?

"The food there is delicious! And there's the Great Wall and the Forbidden City, and it's pretty much legal for kids to drink." I preferred not to think of the pollution, the stinky bathrooms, the heat . . . "Chinese" became my makeup. My foundation was my "superior intellect"; my mascara was my "exotic beauty," my lipstick and blush were the few phrases of Chinese and facts of China I could rattle off to impress people. I painted my face meticulously day after day, and savored the taste of the attention it brought me.

And so I shed my obsession with being American and swung full power into being Asian. I focused my attention on my grades, and studied hard outside of school. I switched out volleyball for Science Bowl, and fast food for ramen noodles.

"Those ramen noodles aren't authentic," my father told me. But ramen was convenient, and when I devoured them, the soup reflected my face in gold.

V. Mi Fen: also known as "rice noodles" in English. These are thin translucent noodles made from rice flour and water. They are known for their soft texture and their ability to absorb any variety of flavors.

High on my illusion of exotic identity, I went to China the summer after my freshman year. But I had spent so much time perfecting the image of my culture to people who knew nothing about it that the darker reality shocked me hard. In China, I was an intrigue, yet an abomination. People stared me down because of my tan skin and thick legs. When I opened my mouth, stammering out awkward, Americanized Chinese, people whispered, "Oh, it's a *lao wai* (foreigner)."

In America people saw me as Chinese, and in China people saw me as American. Yet I was never fully either. I had created a facade for myself on both sides, and untrained eyes couldn't see through that facade. But when I looked in the mirror that summer, I saw a fraud.

And so I sank into a deep state of disillusionment. For too long, I had avoided the uncomfortable question of my multifaceted identity like one would avoid a dusty corner. But now, I uncovered that dusty corner in the spare bedroom of my grandparents' apartment. I sat there for a long time thinking about the words *Chinese* and *American*, and soon, there came a knock at the door.

"*Ai Li Si?*"

I stood up and opened it. "Yes, Grandpa?"

"*It is my eightieth birthday. I want to teach you how to cook Longevity Noodles.*"

In the kitchen, my grandfather took out a bundle of dried *mi fen* and put it in a large, ceramic bowl. Then, he lit the *mei qi* stove. A couple *tsks* and the the flame jumped up from the shadows.

"*First comes the soup,*" my grandfather explained. "*Soup is always pre-made, because it takes a long time for the flavor of your meat to permeate the water.*"

My grandfather took out a pot of soup from the refrigerator and put it on the stove.

"*The soup is like our history, the history of the world. It is much bigger than* each one of is. It soaks into our noodles to give them an essence."

He picked up the *mi fen* and gently placed it in the warming pot. *"These noodles represent life."*

"But aren't you supposed to use *la mian*?" I asked. "They represent a long life." *"That is the tradition, but you should not be limited by tradition. To me, good noodles are medium length—not too short, not too greedy. I like using* mi fen *because it acts like a sponge, soaking up all the flavors around it."*

We stand beside the pot and watch as the noodles started to soften and spread, flowering in the liquid.

"Next, we put in some vegetables." I grabbed him some bok choy and bean sprouts from the fridge. *"These are the things we bring into our lives—it's what we do, and who we do it with."*

He opened the cabinet and took out a jar of Chinese five spice. *"Then comes the seasoning—our culture. This is what gives our noodles flavor."* As he sprinkled a bit of each spice into the pot, their piquant aroma wafted into the air, floating through the kitchen like spirits of ancient times. *"But we have to be careful not to overwhelm everything else. Seasoning is crucial, but its purpose is to enhance our noodles."*

He turned off the stove, then carefully poured the noodles and soup into the ceramic bowl. *"Finally, we add our garnish."* He sprinkled on some chopped green onions and sesame seeds. *"Just a little for aesthetic, but they are secondary to the real things."*

I gazed at the steaming bowl for a long time. In that moment, something inside me reopened. I remembered those early days of my childhood where I would watch my father make pulled noodles. I had grown up eating noodles, but their delicate and nuanced flavor had slipped through my coarse taste buds. Noodles had been first a tradition that my parents put much effort into preserving. Then it became a source of embarrassment, as their foreign smell turned the noses of my peers. Somehow, they became a semblance of superiority in high school, yet only now did I understand what they truly meant. To create a fulfilling bowl of noodles, I had to find the fine balance between all its ingredients.

When I went home that summer, I cooked myself a bowl of rice noodles in bone broth, with American sweet corn and Chinese five spice. The rice noodles soaked up both eastern and western cultures, and although it tasted quite odd, it tasted like something I'd made.

And I would continue to make these strange concoctions until they tasted just right. ■

Tongue-Tied

POETRY

ALYSSA GAINES, Grade 9. Park Tudor School, Indianapolis, IN. Laura Gellin, *Educator*; Clowes Memorial Hall, Butler University and Hoosier Writing Project at IUPUI, *Affiliate*; Gold Medal, American Voices Medal, Best-in-Grade Award

On Saturdays, my tongue is naked.
It tastes like ropa vieja y cafe,
Sips Malta Goya,
Sits in the back of my mouth and relaxes, ignores the s's in Spanish sentences,

Tastes like the chitterlings my grandma makes,
With extra hot sauce.
Tastes like hot cheetos and takis,
And stains red.

On Saturdays, my tongue sings Celia Cruz,

My tongue dances over every syllable to the rap songs on the radio
Without fear or the restriction of any stereotype
White dress left hanging in my closet

Chants zúmbale mambo pa' que mis gatas prendan los motores,
Without tripping over tricky lace.
And dances to R&B, and to alternative like Nao, and to soul.
My tongue moves fast and flips around a new facet of me.

My tongue is multidimensional, fast-moving, and unmasked on Saturdays.

On Sundays, my tongue wears black.
Mourning the now-dead nakedness that it wants back.
It knows what we must do tomorrow.

On weekday mornings, I squeeze my tongue in a white dress,
Pull a veil down over the tip of it, a mask over my language,
That when I talk drapes out of my mouth to floor.
Throughout the day my tongue is married to my private school.

Tied up in matrimony and faithful commitment to the culture there.
Committed, in fear, to the concept of being well-spoken.
Tongue tangled up in all this white and they call me articulate.
When I talk, I taste the weekday worn clothes and they feel foreign against
the roof of my mouth.

Mother always taught me to dress appropriately.
Even when nobody else's tongues are clothed.
When I said my vows I knew the newlywed specials in life that come from
this white dress.
Ambition walked me down the aisle, knowing that this wedding was the only
way to success.

Tongue tangled head to toe in total white and they call me articulate.
My use of naked tongue can never be appropriate.
Is always rude.
I know that being black means existing as two.

I know that wearing this dress is something I must do and so I do it.
And wait for that feeling of freedom that I get on Saturday mornings and
relinquish Sunday night.

Sacrifice

POETRY

SABRINA GUO, Grade 8. South Woods Middle School, Syosset, NY. Theresa Berke and Stephanie Russell, *Educators*; Region-at-Large, *Affiliate*; Gold Medal, Civic Expression Award

Dedicated to all those who are no longer
with us following the Marjorie Stoneman Douglas
High School shooting in Florida on February 14, 2018

In old Christian myths
women and children of
the Middle Ages
were entombed
as protection against
disasters of weather
or war:
virgins lost
to German lakes,
infants buried under
castle fortresses and bridges
to ward tsunamis
or armies . . .
But the songs
of the sacrificed
are never silent,
their wailing is the
wind over the ocean,
weeping
long after
each fortress crumbles.

This, Peter Wang knew
the moment he heard the blasts
of an AR-15 semi-automatic
approaching his classroom
at Marjorie Stoneman Douglas High.
Among the screams,

he held the door for his classmates
and his teachers as if bound
to act with honor
by his Junior Reserve uniform
of pressed grey-blue.
It was gold-pinned,
with black insignia stitched
into the shape of wings
along his shoulders—
the symbol of a hero, even as
fear must have crowded his veins.
No time *to think*, just
his blood rushing through him
like the wave of unbearable grief
in the heaving sobs of his mother,
begging to wake from
her nightmare:
Baby, hold my hand, she says,
Reach me,
the words rippling out of her limbs.
Print in a newspaper cannot capture
her pain as
Peter Wang's casket
is carried away,
stars and stripes
blanketing the memory of him,
still in uniform,
buried with a Medal of Heroism,

and a Certificate of Appointment to
West Point,
2025—
the year he would have graduated.

We share the same birthday, he and
I,
except one of us
will smell the trees and grass on a
college campus,
and one of us will remember
what's been lost.
Our fates intertwined
yet never crossing,
except in the gentle March breeze
when I'm walking to school,
and to the whisper through half-
open windows,
to the soft flap of curtains, to the
silhouette
in the silence, I listen.

A Study in a Lifetime of Elegies

PERSONAL ESSAY & MEMOIR

EMORY BRINSON, Grade 11. South Mecklenburg High School, Charlotte, NC. Erika Ruckert, *Educator*; Charlotte-Mecklenburg Schools, *Affiliate*; Gold Medal, American Voices Medal, Best-in-Grade Award

I. In which I mourn the living.

On September 6, 2018, Botham Shem Jean dies after an off-duty Dallas police officer illegally enters his home and shoots him twice. The story settles into my veins like ice, and it is all too easy for me to picture his terrified face as he is startled by an armed intruder, only to die at her hands. I try not to picture my uncle or father in his place; instead, I watch my mother react to the story. I can see past her painted concealer mask, and like all black women, she harbors an aching sadness for her brothers, husband, and father. To me and her, it seems like death is always one step away. I've been waiting for my father to die since I understood what it meant to be black in this country. Have you ever mourned someone who was still living? It isn't like watching a trainwreck in slow motion. This is an endless funeral. They roll the caskets out one by one, and my dreamscape is painted in black hues. I wake gasping with the image of my little brother laid in white burning in my eyes. Open casket funerals have been in style since Emmett Till's mother told the mortician to show the world what they did to her little boy. There are no secrets anymore, and the constant camera flashes keep the locks of denial from clicking shut anyway. I look into the mirror and wonder what I am supposed to see. Do my full lips and natural hair tell a story of danger or call into question my intent? I look at my father and try to look past his kind heart and ironclad morals to see what they must find at first glance. I take in his powerful shoulders and calloused hands, and for the first time, I wonder if people look at him with fear. Suddenly, I am terrified of losing him to the preconceptions in their heads. Why can't they see what I do?

There is an ache that wraps itself around my ribs; it is a constant noose of loss. For the first time, I am able to see the fearful beast that bares its chest in the place of a person. Understand, this country is committing men to death by prejudice and perpetrating genocide on a systematic level. I have mourned more men in my sixteen years than I dare say most will lose in a lifetime. I wait for a day in which children will not have to know this heartbreak with frantic breaths and a mess of tangled veins in my chest.

II. In which imagination almost becomes reality.

The vibration of my cell phone pulls me awake, but I am still bleary with sleep as I blink at the clock. Its bright red letters glow in the pitch black of my room, the numbers 2:27 searing their way into my memory. My heart begins to pound as awareness finally begins to seep in past the edges of sleep. After all, people don't call at O' dark thirty unless something is wrong. A picture of my mother lights up on the screen from her last birthday as I reach for it, my fingers trembling with dread. Her immortalized bright smile is blinding, but it doesn't help me calm down as I answer, "Mom?"

She answers without preamble. "Tell your father to pick up the phone, right now!" She hangs up before I can answer, cutting off any questions I had with the ominous sound of a cut call. I hurry to make my way out of bed, stumbling as I try to remember the locations of everyone I love.

"Dad!" My voice is sharp, terror leaking into the word as I shove his shoulder. "You have to call Mom right now." He blinks at me, still waking up, but the urgency in my voice startles him into motion, and he is quick to grab his phone. I turn back to my room, only to stop as he flies down the stairs. I yell after him with a trembling voice, "What's going on? Is Mom okay?" But the house stays silent, save for the faint sound of the shuddering door frame.

I flip on my desk lamp as I fall into bed, unable to stand the uncertainty of the dark as I try to quell the nausea. The fear ratchets back up as the distinct roar of my father's car backing out of the driveway fills my room. I can't help but imagine the possibilities, and a million different scenarios wash over me unbidden; it is my own personal hurricane. The storm slams against my flimsy walls, and the only thing I can do is wait it out. It can't be long before the headlights spill into my room once more, but it feels like hours before the door finally opens.

I fall out of bed, making my way on autopilot to the door, drawn to the hallway like a moth to a porchlight as my dad's voice wafts up the stairs. I catch snippets of his lecture as he follows my brother up the stairs, but I'm mostly paying attention to my brother's hangdog expression.

"I can't believe you! We'll talk about this in the morning!" The door slams behind my father, and Christian tries to slide past me to get into his room.

"Hey!" I jerk my hand out to grab onto his jacket sleeve, forcing him to look at me. "What the hell happened?" His shrug is nonchalant when he glances back in my father's direction as if my stomach isn't still in knots.

"Matthew and I snuck out and got caught by the police." He disappears into his room without an explanation, but I am too shell-shocked to protest as the door slams shut. The only sound left is the rush of blood in my ears as I move on autopilot back into my room.

As I struggle to fall back asleep, thoughts race through my mind, twisting and turning. Earlier, I had been desperate for information, now I'm not sure if it's better to know after all. Faces of children with my little brother's nose and sharp cheekbones bleeding out flash before my eyes. I itch to go into his room and shake him until I can make him understand why I'm so terrified.

I toss and turn all night while my subconscious flits between the stories of police brutality that I have tucked in my mind. I wake up gasping more than once with the sound of gunshots resonating in my ears. I'm up far before the sun is, tucked into the corner of my bed as I desperately avoid thinking about any more what-ifs. This is my first brush with the terror my mother experiences on a daily basis, but the scariest part is the certain knowledge that it will not be my last.

III. In which my father and I come to an understanding.
On a Friday night in December, we watch Spike Lee's *Do the Right Thing.* I ignore the discomfort watching the police beat Radio Raheem to death with popcorn grease on my fingers causes me. As the credits roll, I catch glimpses of my father's childhood between the black and white text, and his desperation for us to watch this movie finally makes sense. For the first time, I can see him in his true form.

His New York accent has faded after twenty-five years in the South, but there are parts of him that are straight from the rough streets and cramped bodegas of his hometown. It's in the way he pronounces coffee, the heavy set of his shoulders, and the way he is undeniably straight out of this film.

On the screen, the character Da Mayor tells Mookie in a Brooklyn accent almost too thick to understand, "Always do the right thing." My father, for better or worse, has always lived his life by this rule; he is protective of his pride and family, never strays from his perception of the "right" thing, and is a stickler for fair treatment. There are some principles that ingrain themselves into your bone marrow and shape any and all actions you take from there on out. If I peeled back my father's thick skin I would find those words burned into the white of his bones. I know this to be true in the same way that I know the sun will rise in the morning.

He turns up the stereo volume while we drive past a group of policemen, the words, "F**K THE POLICE" blaring out of all four open windows while we speed by. I'm horrified, but the story he tells me afterward shifts my worldview once again. He's not quiet or ashamed as he unravels the memory, because my father never is, but I can't help and wonder if that is the New Yorker in him, or if he was simply born with an unwavering spine. He paints a picture of a little black boy growing up on the outer edge of New York City in the '70s and '80s. Raw emotion courses through his voice as he tells me about the police pulling him over on his bike in eighth grade. I can imagine him with pains-taking clarity, only thirteen but terrified he wouldn't make it home for dinner because someone decided he didn't belong. I ache for him, and I am reminded of my own brother, who looks so like what my father must have at that age.

It isn't until after Botham Jean that he tells me another story. He describes trying to unlock his door as a college student in upstate New York, only for an NYPD officer to tackle him. The policeman calls for backup, and within minutes there are six police officers arresting him for trespassing on his own property. Yet again, I am learning to understand my father in ways I could never have imagined. His distrust of the police is one that has blossomed from years of prejudice and attacks. Though I can't always agree with him or his methods, I can understand on an intrinsic level where that pain and hurt stems from.

In the days after I first watch *Do the Right Thing*, I am able to look at my father and see the parts he tried to leave behind. New York didn't make him, nor did his experiences with law enforcement, but both have shaped him in ways I can only attempt to understand.

IV. In which I find out what it means to exist in this country while black.
I have always known that being black in America inherently meant being viewed as dangerous. Every day passes like a hunt in the desert of our distant home. This is predation on a big city scale, and they have turned me into prey. The knowledge is passed through the generations: blowing into my mind with the faint bellow of a slave ship's horn, and the stench of sweat wafting from the fields. Every people must pass down something to the new generation in order to preserve the years of history that have built them up from the black soil of our shared homeland. For me, it was the image of my great-grand-mother, holding tight to her son and begging with harsh words and soft hands for him to stay out of trouble as the radio blared on about that boy who was lynched in Mississippi. The memory has always existed in my mind, smudged with the inconsistencies of old stories, and somehow smelling just like the bitter salt of chitlins.

Two black men are arrested for sitting in a Starbucks without purchasing anything, and the incident becomes the spark to a Twitter firestorm. It seems like every day that social media is popping up with another "Living While Black" moment. White women and men have been calling the police on black people living their lives for as long as they have been able to, but now instead of silently suffering the uncomfortable consequences of being born black, the victims were taking to Twitter. The stories that go viral act as a window into the harsh realities that had previously been shoved under the rug that is the privilege of white ignorance. There is a difference, however, between knowing that these things happen and watching a video of a white woman screaming for the police to come and arrest a little boy for selling water. The situations usually resulted in a slap on the wrist no harm done on either side, but it begs the question: how much anguish can the black American psyche take before the constant insinuation that they are less than starts to sink in?

The sweltering summer of 2018 bleeds into the sharp chill of autumn months, and I find pieces of myself among the bright orange chrysanthemums my neighbor plants. The day after the flowers bloom, the moving sign in her yard gets a shiny new addition: A plaque swings in the wind, and the word SOLD sinks into my stomach like lead. The moving trucks blew in with the first jack-o'-lantern, and with it came a growing nervousness in my mother. The new couple was likely nice enough, but images of the innocent black children splashed across Twitter were still fresh in our minds. "I'm going over introduce myself and make it clear that five black children live on this cul-de-sac. That way there is no confusion about who belongs in this neighborhood." The subtext isn't subtle: She wouldn't let these new neighbors treat us as if we didn't belong, but there was no telling what kind of assumptions could be made from a quick glance while we stepped under the streetlight in the morning.

Other people hoped to make nice with the new neighbors to avoid complaints about loud Christmas parties, but my mother wanted to make sure they knew we belonged. She was saying, "Look. These are my brown children, and they live here, just like you." This is our persistent reality; a life of constant motion, always watching for the next predator who waits in the pale brush, preparing to pounce.

V. In which I discover that differences lie deeper than skin.
Growing up, I often longed to be more like everyone around me, but I never felt more like an outsider than at my middle school. That wasn't always the case. In fact, for the most part, it was a positive experience. I learned an abundance about the world and myself from my teachers and classmates, but one thing they never needed to teach me was that I wasn't like them. Being one of three African American girls in the grade left me with the constant knowledge in the back of my head that, as much as I tried to blend in with my classmates, I would always be different. Most of the time it remained in the background, but other times I wore it like a bleeding brand. I bore the nervous looks during

slavery and civil rights units, tried not to roll my eyes when at least fifteen people congratulated me after President Barack Obama was reelected in 2012, and quietly acquiesced to reading off black history facts. Every. Single. February. There are turning points to every story though.

On August 9, 2014, Michael Brown is murdered, the Black Lives Matter movement emerges from the ashes of the burning buildings in Ferguson, Missouri, and my world shifts on its axis. I struggle to come to terms with the idea that there is violence affecting my people in a way I haven't truly understood until this point, but the other kids are angrily protecting the police. They scream "All Lives Matter" and spit when they dare to say his name. In those familiar halls, Michael becomes synonymous with thug, and I learn to walk with my head down. They act as if he isn't worth the same amount of space they are, and by association, I suddenly wonder about the amount of room I take up on the stairwell. They look to me with expectant eyes, but what can I say in response when I see him in every family photo that hangs on our wall? When I look in the mirror?

I was floating alone in a sea of people who didn't understand how close to home a shooting 724.1 miles away could feel, and the loneliness was beginning to eat away at my sparkling worldview.

VI. In which I am learning how to not be afraid.

I am no stranger to fear. It has taken the shape of maggots to eat away at my insides since I learned the difference between denotation and connotation. In these terms, the space between what black means and what this country hears instead is big enough to hold a slave ship worth of bodies. I am terrified of watching my family die at the hands of a nation that doesn't care about them. I am afraid of losing myself in the mass of people who cannot help but see me as less than, who can never understand what it means to exist as a black woman in this country. Still, I am slowly learning how to turn fear's shape into something more. Instead of maggots, it becomes a starting gun, urging me on. I have the opportunity to bring understanding to the people who want to learn, and I have the chance to grow myself. Maybe this realization is the distinction between girl and woman. The time for mourning is over. This is not the age of fear, but instead resilience. Like my mother, I stare down the world and I say,

"Look, we are here, just like you." ■

Hug Coupons and Shoe Boxes

PERSONAL ESSAY & MEMOIR

BRIAN WEE, Grade 12. Peak to Peak Charter School, Lafayette, CO. Kristie Letter, *Educator*; Region-at-Large, *Affiliate*; Gold Medal, New York Life Award

She had fallen before. Yet amongst the cacophonous clatter of Cream of Mushroom cans and the metallic taste of pure horror as my mother collapsed straight into a seasonal grocery store display, seven-year-old me felt a profound pain and shock unlike anything before in knowing that things weren't going to get better. In an instant, the most compassionate, inspirational, and affectionate person that I'd ever known had been reduced to a solemn, unresponsive slump on the floor. Even worse, a crowd began to gather around her like ravenous hyenas after a fresh kill, making me want to shriek at them for degrading her with stares overflowing with condescending pity.

With the assistance of my father, who came sprinting through the store once he heard, my mother eventually recovered and was provided with a scooter cart for the rest of our shopping trip. Yet nothing could stop the torrent of tears that poured out of my eyes that night while my parents slept. After all, here was the mother who had read to me every night and watched movies with me in my parent's bedroom on the weekends, broken by the stage IV lung carcinoma that had metastasized to her brain. In the coming weeks, the only solace for me would come when I saw her in the hospital, the refuge where she still never ceased to love and embrace me in every way she could.

Needless to say, when she passed away, I was devastated. Mother's Day and its memories of jubilant breakfasts in bed morphed into solemn reminders of how empty the world was without her. Free hug coupons and personal drawings that I had gifted her took on a melancholy hue as I stumbled across them in the bedroom where we had once watched movies together as a family. My once-attentive father all but receded away, leaving me in a bleak house with empty painkiller bottles piled up in dilapidated shoeboxes and other shocking reminders that my mother was gone. In short, I had been plunged into a world of grief and adversity, of brutal ironies and cruel jokes, of debilitating despair and excruciating emptiness.

In the face of such anguish, I found solace in the last note that my mother had written to my father and me. On it, she wrote a simple message: "Go, Brian! Do the best you can!" From the moment after I read it, I have made my mission to persevere and honor my mother's memory in that simple way—

constantly doing the best I can for myself and those around me. Through lonely days and sleepless nights, storybook tragedies and missed movies, her words are the wind on my sail that propel me into a future where no free hug coupon goes unused.

For now, while my mother may never have cashed in her free hug coupons, I carry both them and her final note with me wherever I go. They give me the grit to lead multiple honor societies and to pick up trash in my mornings even when pouring rain all but washes me away. They give me the opportunity to pass on those free hug coupons to the struggling students that I tutor and melancholic members of my community as I remember the extraordinary grief that we all come to face in our lives. They give me an inexpressible appreciation for the immense beauty in our world, whether it be in the awestruck eyes of a kindergarten class as I play Liszt or the blazing passion of a ninth-grade Science Bowler as we gush about mitochondria. They give me hope that for every life that I save or help, I can begin to make up for the one that I lost. Yet most importantly, they give me indescribable optimism, solace, and satisfaction in knowing that I'm working to accomplish my mother's dream every day. ■

It Is What It Is

SHORT STORY

MAKAYLA WACH, Grade 10. North Allegheny Intermediate School, Pittsburgh, PA. Joya Talhouk, *Educator*; Western PA Writing Project, The University of Pittsburgh School of Education, *Affiliate*; Gold Medal, New York Life Award

In memory of Aidan

I checked my watch, snapping it closed with a loud CRACK and a sigh. These things can't be rushed, of course, a fact that fails to make my job any less tedious. It is what it is.

Knowing I'd be here awhile, I decided to take a seat in one of the pews, careful not to crease my suit doing so. I looked around the chapel, at the hushed crowds huddled together in small groups like roosting crows. I overheard my name more than once; mentions of how they knew me, stories of their friends that I've met with before. I usually ignore this idle gossip. I've become accustomed to their hate and fear. It is what it is.

The mother caught my eye, sitting alone on a bench. She sat in rigid silence, a stark contrast to the woman I'd visited only a few days prior. Then, there were tears and shaking fists. Then, she'd been screaming and wailing and clawing at my face, trying her hardest to chase me away. Of course, I didn't go away. I never do.

Now, she simply sat. Staring unseeing into space through dull, rusted eyes. It's sad, in a way, to see this switch flipped. To watch as an intricate tapestry is torn and frayed and bleached, to watch a bright and lively woman wilt into despondent weed. One would think that after all I've seen, I'd get used to it. I never do.

Perhaps it's an ache of guilt, buried deep within my bones. Perhaps it's simply a reminder, a sign of purpose and existence disguised in this terrible pattern. Whatever the case, it pangs whatever heart I have left each and every time. It is what it is.

And perhaps that's why, on this particular afternoon, I stood and, hesitantly, approached her. I said nothing—just sat by her side. I braced myself for her to lash out, to attack me again, but she didn't even look up. Just stared at her hands, clasped tightly in her lap. In a way, it would have been *more* reassuring if she'd at least reacted, whether it be in anger or otherwise.

But she didn't.

Finally, a hoarse whisper etched a crack in the silence.

"Why?"

I didn't respond. Usually, any comment on my part stimulates bargaining, which I really can't afford to do. Not anymore.

She buried her head in her hands. "It's my fault. I should have known. I'm his mother. If I'd noticed something was wrong, then maybe . . . "

I wanted to tell her that nothing had been wrong. That she wasn't to blame. That it was just the way of the world. It is what it is.

But I didn't.

The father came and sat beside her, wrapping his arms around his wife. He looked tired—so very, very tired. The last few days had aged him, though not beyond the point of my recognition. I nodded to him, noting how he wearily nodded back. So he did remember me. Of course he did. He'd seen me more often than most. First his mother, then his father, then his sister, and now . . . well, it is what it is.

I cleared my throat and stood, brushing off my suit. For some reason, I couldn't stand to be in the presence of the parents any longer. Couldn't stand the sight of something so broken. Not that I hadn't seen it before . . . but that afternoon, something was different. Wrong.

I decided then that I'd leave, get some fresh air. There isn't much where I live, and I take it when I can. By then I'd be feeling like myself, and then I could finish my job. It's just a job, that's all it is, it's nothing personal. It is what it is, I thought, and in retrospect, I believe I was attempting to convince myself more than anything.

But as I turned to go, a young girl approached me, tears streaming down her face. Without warning, she forcefully kicked my leg, causing me to wince. Ah, yes. The sister.

"How could you?!" she screamed, swinging her fists. I stepped backwards nervously. It seemed I had had the opposite effect on her as I did the mother. I distinctly remembered this girl denying my existence just a few days ago, muttering about nightmares and needing to wake up.

Now, she'd woken up.

"You took him!" She was still yelling, still crying, still trying in vain to pummel me with her delicate hands, hands much too small for such a feat. "You took him! You took him, and you're gonna bring him back!"

I just sighed and strode away, leaving her to her wailing and stomping and the forced, premature growth that shouldn't have come for many more years. However much it pains me to see children shrouded in black, they just never understand. Would I bring them back? Would I, if I could? Perhaps. Perhaps not.

But either way, I *can't*—a fact they never seem able to process in their innocent minds. I can't, so no matter how much they plead, I won't. It is what it is.

Another girl stood by the door, looking down at her handheld screen and chewing gum. She wasn't dressed like the rest of the people in attendance, wasn't wearing ink and shadow. But she was carrying a weight, I could tell. As I approached, she popped her gum, made a rather rude hand gesture, and stormed out.

I stared after her, confused, and a voice behind me said, "Sorry about that."

I turned and saw the brother. He was staring at the floor, hands in his pockets. "She doesn't mean any disrespect," he said quietly, still not meeting my gaze. "She just doesn't know how to help me, that's all. She doesn't know what to say."

I said nothing, and he laughed weakly, running a hand through his hair. "I guess I don't, either. Or, what I should've said, anyway. I didn't mean to snap at him . . . but it was late, and I had a lot of homework . . . "

I wanted to tell him that it wasn't his fault. That he had no need to carry this burden, not all on his own, in any case. That he was allowed to cry, allowed to mourn. That he and his father didn't have to be the strong ones, and that there's no shame in leaning on others for support. It is what it is.

But I didn't.

I stood frozen at the door as he shuffled back into the chapel, where his family was waiting. And there I stood for a long while, not knowing what to do. A breath of air was no longer as enticing as it had been before. And besides, it must have been almost over by now. I'd met with the mother, the father, the sister, the brother, even the brother's girlfriend . . . who else would my work have affected?

My silent query was answered as I looked around, eyes lingering on everyone present. Coaches and teachers, wondering if they'd been too harsh or pushed too hard. Teary-eyed girls, heads swimming with the unsaid declarations of love that they'd been too shy to confess. But one particular boy caught my attention, hunched in the corner. Almost without thinking, I approached him.

He looked up as I neared his secluded spot, and a flash of fear crossed his features as I realized he'd been trying to avoid me. His eyes were rimmed red, and he wiped his nose on his sleeve before speaking.

"Why?"

The friend's hoarse, whispered word echoed with a different sort of pain than the mother's. Perhaps that's because he wasn't really asking *me*—not really. He was wondering why he'd been left behind, left alone on this miserable rock between birth and death. A common, slightly aggravating reaction. Why do they always assume *I* know all the answers? Why do they think that just because I'm here, I can see into the mind and heart and pain of everyone I take? I'm not here to ask questions, and I'm certainly not qualified to answer them. I'm here to do my job. It is what it is.

The friend wiped his eyes and took a photo from his pocket, creased from the constant folding and unfolding it had been subject to these last few days. I've often wondered why people keep these pictures, looking at them again and again when they never truly replicate the spark of a real smile. When the memory they treasure so much and carry in their pocket only serves to remind them of what they've lost. But they can't let go, not of old photographs or sweatshirts or blankets. It is what it is.

I turned back to the chapel doors, knowing it was nearly time. I'd given them all long enough. But before I could take another step, a girl appeared in front of me, face red and eyes fixed on her shoes.

"Um . . . I'm so sorry to bother you, but . . . here," she murmured. "I-I was wondering . . . could you please deliver this? If not, that's fine . . . " She held an envelope in her shaking, outstretched hand. I was surprised by the gesture, and I'd be lying if I said I wasn't slightly irked as well. I am not a mailman, I am not a servant, and I am certainly not a friend. But, unsure of what else to do, I took it. With a sigh of relief, the girl darted off, disappearing into the crowd.

I stared after her a long while before opening the letter. All it said was this:

I'm sorry I didn't get to know you, and I'm sorry I didn't say this before, but thank you for helping my brother.

I frowned and craned my head to see where she'd gone, catching glimpse of her at the side of a young boy . . . a boy in a wheelchair. I cursed the pang in my chest, cursed the melting hunk of ice that was supposed to be my heart, and turned away. It's only when it's too late that they remember these things, or care enough to bring them up. They think that maybe, just maybe, the words they'd left unspoken could have changed what happened. That's absurd, of course. Nothing can prevent me from my purpose, whether I like it or not. And, as I'm beginning to discover, it's not an enjoyable position to fill. It is what it is.

And so I went to the long, wooden box, polished surface gleaming in the dim light of the chapel. I went to the box and found the one I'd come for sitting atop, legs swinging and eyes wide as he looked out across the crowds of people gathered for him. I beckoned for him to follow. He hopped down and reached for my hand, then hesitated.

"I . . . I didn't mean for any of this," he said quietly. "This wasn't supposed to happen. If I'd known . . . "

"Known what?" I said, caught somewhat off guard by my own gravely, seldom-used voice. "Known the sorrow of a mother? The pain of a father? The bitterness of a sister, or the guilt of a brother?"

The boy was silent, but I was not.

"You, all of you, never understand. This doesn't end with family and friends. I've seen it, time and time again. I've watched strangers weep and wail and harbor responsibility over someone they never really knew. I've watched lives crumble, and since the beginning of time, I've said nothing. Because . . . "

Here I took a deep breath.

"I could say it is what it is. But that doesn't mean it should be."

He nodded and looked away, blinking back tears. We stood in silence for a while longer, watching the unraveled world slowly begin to knit itself together. Then, with one last glance over my shoulder, I took his hand in mine.

And I led him home. ■

Pan

POETRY

KAYLEE CHEN, Grade 8. Dutch Fork Middle School, Irmo, SC. Kristi Grooms, *Educator*; Region-at-Large, *Affiliate*; Gold Medal, One Earth Award

i.

mount olympus was a perfect paradise, but he knew paradise
before marble and gold-plated luxury.
yes, he wandered the forests when they were new and untainted,
ruled lush jungles and clear streams, gently sloping hills and valleys,
reveled in a sun that warmed the earth and gave way to glorious life.
he used to be able to breathe.

ii.

he always knew not to play with fire. the others would curse and bless and love
those humans, but not him. never him.
his world was too precious to burn, too fragile to dare,
and when prometheus stole the still-flaming embers from mount olympus itself,
he wept. he saw the smoke that rose from those coals
and the flickering ambition in man's eyes,
and he knew that his realm was primed to fall.

iii.

years are nothing to gods. they shouldn't be, but he never thought that was true.
when he found the humans burning, burning, *burning*
his eons felt so very small.
ash littered the soil, choked the roots of the trees he whispered to,
slid down the throats of the animals he had promised to protect.
heat rose into the winds that circled the earth, and even the spirits of the air
cowered within its strangling hold.
gods were perfect, he knew. they should be. that was the truth he was promised.
but his world was crumbling around him, and all he heard were lies.

iv.

in his last few breaths, he remembers what it's like to hope.
humans have always been so innovative.

he listens to them speak in terms he doesn't understand.
they say things like *energy* and *fossil fuels*. metal screeches
and sparks fly, and when they dig up the soil, they do not plant seeds in the earth.
no, their plants are steel and like the giants of the old days.
their blades slice through the wind. he hears them say *turbine*.
somewhere, aeolus finds himself tethered once more.

. . .

the only gods men worship are those of iron and steel, machines that screech across roads,
but he looks closer and realizes that there are some that do not smoke like the others.
there are some with zeus's lightning crackling in their welded veins.
they whisper, *electric. energy. less gas. more mileage. more, more . . .*
man will always want more, he knows. he is surprised to find
that now, they want more paradise.

v.

they have noticed his passing. have cried it out in the streets, holding signs,
yelling until their voices are hoarse. they write. speak.
he's always admired their persistence.
no one remembers that when prometheus first gave humans fire,
he never told them how to burn. their love for destruction
is in their blood, some might say, as much as ichor is inside of him.
and yet, the more he sees, the more he searches,
he discovers another side, a golden side
that yearns for the full forests and landscapes he used to roam
and calls for clear streams and cooler air. although he is fading, those humans are not.
he can never tell whether that is good or bad. maybe the world is not so black and white.
gods cannot pray, but he hopes for a better ending.
a paradise that mirrored his own. a vision for the future that he will not live to see.
so as he closes his eyes for the last time, as they cry *the great god Pan is dead,*
with the smoke that rises in his lungs,
he breathes once more.

Hell and High Water

DRAMATIC SCRIPT

AYSHA ZACKRIA, Grade 12. NSU University School, Davie, FL. Jaimie Crawford, *Educator*; Young at Art Museum, *Affiliate*; Gold Medal, One Earth Award

CHARACTERS (in order of appearance):

Narrator: Third person observer.
Franklin Wells: Man in late 50s; luthier; politically conservative, white, Catholic.
Leo: Man in early 40s; wood supplier and piano tuner; environmentally aware.
Mary Wells: Woman in mid 50s; Franklin's wife; working a dead-end job.
Radio Announcer 1: Reporter.
Radio Announcer 2: Weather person.
Cecily: Woman in late 30s; famous violinist; hotheaded and impatient.

SCENE: Franklin's home in Texas.
TIME: 2023.

SCENE ONE

NARRATOR: September twelfth, 2023.
(FRANKLIN rhythmically scrapes at a piece of wood. He sets down the tool and pushes his chair away from the work table. Sawdust sounding beneath his boots, he retrieves a set of clamps from a rack on the other wall and sits back down. The chair groans under his weight. He sets one of the clamps down on the table. He confidently tightens the other.)
NARRATOR: *(following the action)* This is the birth of a violin: methodical scraping at pieces of wood. Franklin's getting clamps to secure it all together. *(Immediately after he grabs the second clamp, the phone rings. He hurriedly puts the clamp down, wipes his hands on his jeans, and clears his throat before picking up, putting the call on speaker.)*
FRANKLIN: Yes?
LEO: Hey Franklin. I, uh, have some bad news . . .
(He pauses as if he expects a response. None comes. He proceeds with caution.)
...The Sargent's Spruce is not doing well. The price is gonna go up a little.
FRANKLIN: How much?
LEO: I don't know exact numbers yet. I just wanted to call and warn you. I get that money is tight right now.

FRANKLIN: Okay. Thanks, Leo. How's the tuning?

LEO: Same shit, different day. How's Mary?

FRANKLIN: She's well.

LEO: That's good to hear. Tell her hi for me.

FRANKLIN: Okay. Will do.

(He hangs up and continues to work. The scraping sounds are initially steady and controlled, but become more erratic as he reflects upon the call. One final scrape sounds particularly aggressive.) Crap.

FRANKLIN: *(quietly, laughing to himself)* Third violin in five months. Christ, I hope Cecily makes this worth it.

(He pauses for a moment before starting to hum Schumann's Traumerei. *He turns on the radio. The first channel he goes to is just static. He changes the channel. More static. He changes the channel again.)*

RADIO ANNOUNCER 1: –vironmental science. The new satellites provide definitive information on the growing effects of climate ch–

(FRANKLIN scoffs and changes the channel. More static. He changes the channel once more.)

RADIO ANNOUNCER 2: –mperature. Record breaki–

*(FRANKLIN changes the channel again. Slow, dark classical music [*Schindler's List*] fills the workshop.)*

NARRATOR: *(with action)* Franklin is diligently cleaning his tools. After wiping them dry, he puts them away.

(He picks up a handful of tools and brings them to the sink. He lets the water run while rinsing them off. He places them on a towel and sprays them with a healthy amount of WD-40. After wiping them dry, he puts them away in cabinets and on wall hooks. He turns off the light and exits, shutting the door behind him. End of scene.)

SCENE TWO

NARRATOR: September seventeenth. *(action following)* Franklin enters his workshop carrying a stand and sheet music. He prepares to play.

(Once he puts down the stand, he lifts the top. He places the sheet music. Taking a deep breath, he picks up a violin and plays Beethoven's 8th Symphony in F Major. A couple seconds in, it starts to go out of tune.)

NARRATOR: Inexplicably, his violin goes flat.

(FRANKLIN makes a sound of disgust and quickly tunes each string. He tries to play the piece again, but the result is the same.)

NARRATOR: Again, it goes out of tune.

(FRANKLIN tunes the strings again, but this time he is meticulous, centering

each pitch to perfection. He plays the piece slower with the same result.)

NARRATOR: Though it is no fault of his own, Franklin finds himself with little success.

(FRANKLIN scoffs and sets down the violin. End of scene.)

SCENE THREE

NARRATOR: September nineteenth. Franklin opens a jar of varnish, pouring it into a cup. The substance is viscous, somewhere between maple syrup and molasses. He closes the jar and places it on the table. After grabbing a brush, he begins to stain the sides of the violin with long, controlled strokes.

(FRANKLIN follows the actions detailed in narration. The phone rings in another room, but he continues to work. Just seconds after it goes to voicemail, the phone rings again. He exasperatedly puts the brush and violin down before shoving his chair back. The sawdust sounds angrily under his heavy steps. He picks up. The voices begin faintly, growing as he walks back toward the workshop.)

CECILY: Where is my violin?

FRANKLIN: Hello to you too.

CECILY: Hi Franklin. Where is my violin?

FRANKLIN: On my table. Almost done.

CECILY: And when are you planning on shipping it?

FRANKLIN: Soon. A week, give or take.

CECILY: Step on it. I don't pay you to waste my time.

FRANKLIN: Of course not.

(The phone beeps loudly after CECILY hangs up. FRANKLIN sets down the phone and continues to stain. A moment later, MARY comes home. She enters the workshop.)

MARY: How's it goin, hun?

FRANKLIN: *(irritated)* Just got off the phone.

MARY: Who was it?

FRANKLIN: Who do you think.

MARY: Oh. Cecily's still breathing down your neck?

FRANKLIN: Yeah. She's getting worse.

MARY: You've done so much work already. Just keep your nose to the grindstone. You're so close.

FRANKLIN: Thank God.

(MARY exits. End of scene.)

SCENE FOUR

NARRATOR: September twenty-fourth.

(FRANKLIN sits in his workshop listening to the weather report.)

RADIO ANNOUNCER 2: Today is gonna be a hot one. The high is 127. Try to stay out of the sun and drink a *lot* of water. Now, a message fr–

(FRANKLIN turns off the radio. Subsequent action follows the narration.)

NARRATOR: Franklin opens a small, waxy envelope containing brand new strings. One at a time, he takes each string out and places them on the table.

(FRANKLIN puts down the envelope.)

He grabs the first one and strings it on the violin. At the end of each string, there's a little metal ball. That satisfying click is it sliding into place.

(while the peg creaks)

He threads the other end into the scroll, using the peg tighten it. He picks up the recently finished violin and starts to pluck the string.

(while FRANKLIN bows the A string)

As he gets closer to the desired pitch, he slows down and begins to bow across the string before finally centering the note.

(while FRANKLIN repeats with the E string)

He follows the same pattern of threading, plucking, and bowing with the next string. This time, he's more hesitant. Nearing the pitch, he holds his breath, almost in anticipation of something going awry.

(A long, suspenseful moment in which the only sound is the note slowly creeping higher. The string snaps.)

FRANKLIN: Son of a bitch!

(MARY enters, clearly startled by FRANKLIN's sudden outburst.)

MARY: What happened?

FRANKLIN: *(setting the bow down)* The E snapped.

MARY: You didn't scratch the wood, did you?

FRANKLIN: No.

MARY: Then what's all the fuss about?

FRANKLIN: *(beat)* It was never actually in tune.

MARY: What do you mean? You put the right string on, right?

FRANKLIN: I don't know . . . *(He sets down the violin. Fanning himself with the collar of his shirt.)* It's hot.

MARY: And a little stuffy.

FRANKLIN: Feels like I'm suffocating. *(after breathing slowly and loudly for a moment)* The string was too low. It didn't get to E. *(beat)* I understand why it snapped. I tightened it too much. But it was the right string. It shouldn't have been an issue.

(FRANKLIN and MARY are silent for a moment, racking their brains for any possible explanation. FRANKLIN begins to anxiously drum on the table with his fingers.)

MARY: I need to go get ready. I'm sure it'll be fine.

(MARY exits.)

FRANKLIN: It'll be fine.

NARRATOR: *(action following)* Franklin stands up to grab a broom and dustpan. He begins to sweep the sawdust from the table and floor.

(While sweeping, FRANKLIN hums the same slow, dark classical piece that was on the radio before [Schindler's List]. He is in no hurry. After dumping the sawdust into the garbage, he puts the dustpan and broom back.)

NARRATOR: *(action following)* He's getting another string.

(He opens a cabinet, grabs another E string envelope, and sits back at his table. He takes out the string and puts down the envelope. He picks up the violin. Again, the string's ball clicks into place. End of scene.)

SCENE FIVE

NARRATOR: September twenty-sixth. *(action following)* As if performing a ceremony or sacred ritual, Franklin begins to pack the violin while reciting a prayer, an act of contrition. He places a heavy case down on the table and puts the violin inside.

FRANKLIN: My God, I am sorry for my sins with all my heart.

NARRATOR: *(action following)* After rooting through a few cabinets, he returns with scissors, wax paper, foam cubes, bubble wrap, and masking tape. He puts them on the table.

FRANKLIN: In choosing to do wrong and failing to do good,

NARRATOR: *(action following)* He cuts two small squares from the wax paper, places a cube of foam on top of each one, and slides them above and below the bridge of the violin.

FRANKLIN: I have sinned against you whom I should love above all things.

NARRATOR: *(action following)* He cuts a large piece of bubble wrap, rolling it tightly, and positioning it at the base of the violin. *(beat)* Finally, he must close the case.

FRANKLIN: I firmly intend, with your help, *(He secures each locking mechanism with the following phrases.)* to do penance, to sin no more, and to avoid whatever leads me to sin.

NARRATOR: *(action following)* He grabs a bag of packing material, rips it open, and pours the contents into a large cardboard box.

FRANKLIN: Our Savior Jesus Christ suffered and died for us.

NARRATOR: *(action following)* He carefully lays the violin case inside, insuring that it will not shift during its trip.

FRANKLIN: *(while applying a piece or two of packing tape)* In His name. My God have mercy, Amen. *(He lifts the box and exits. End of scene.)*

SCENE SIX

NARRATOR: September thirtieth.

(The phone rings. FRANKLIN picks up almost immediately.)

CECILY: What the hell, Franklin?

FRANKLIN: What.

CECILY: Don't play dumb.

FRANKLIN: *(beat)* That violin was perfect.

CECILY: Bull.

FRANKLIN: The wood isn't warped. The cuts are clean. The neck is straight.

CECILY: None of that matters if the violin doesn't work.

FRANKLIN: You don't know what you're talking about.

CECILY: *You're* telling *me* that *I* don't know what I'm talking about? Which of us tried to sell a broken instrument? *(beat)* You're not getting the money.

FRANKLIN: Wh–

CECILY: I refuse to pay for a violin I can't play.

FRANKLIN: I labored over that for weeks. I busted my ass so you'd have it early.

CECILY: It doesn't matter.

FRANKLIN: I–

(CECILY hangs up. FRANKLIN turns on the radio, Schubert's String Quartet No. 14 in D minor [Death and the Maiden] - IV. Presto blares. Boxes of screws and cans of paint hit the ground. MARY enters. They stand staring at each other for an uncomfortable amount of time. When she begins to speak, her words are barely audible above the music.)

MARY: Shit . . . Franklin, what did you do?

(FRANKLIN shoves his chair back and walks out. The front door slams in the distance. End of scene.)

SCENE SEVEN

NARRATOR: October sixth. Cecily isn't the only one to contend with.

(MARY and FRANKLIN sit looking at the work table. FRANKLIN types briefly.)

MARY: Are you sure? You don't have to look.

FRANKLIN: I need to know.

(FRANKLIN clicks something. The two begin to read comments left on his website aloud, scrolling slowly.)

FRANKLIN: "Franklin Wells is a fraud. His violins are no better than the rest, but he charges ten times as much. The past week, all of my instruments have stopped staying in tune, including his. So much for quality workmanship."

MARY: *(beat)* This one is Cecily . . . "Mr. Wells sold me a broken violin. Right out of the box. He should be ashamed of himself." . . . Franklin . . . I'll try to pick up extra shifts, but you know I can't support us both forever.

FRANKLIN: I'll figure this out. Don't worry.

(End of scene.)

SCENE EIGHT

NARRATOR: October seventh.

(FRANKLIN dials a number. LEO picks up.)

LEO: Hello?

FRANKLIN: Leo . . . Is there anything unusual happening with your strings?

LEO: Actually, yeah. On hot days, they're really flat . . . Weird shit has been happening with most my instruments when the weather changes.

FRANKLIN: My violins have the same problem. But it's every day.

LEO: Well, yeah. You live in Texas.

FRANKLIN: What do I do? I can't keep working like this.

LEO: You could go up north?

FRANKLIN: I can't. My entire life is here . . . I'm too old to move. I can't begin to imagine starting over somewhere else . . . And even if I did move, I can't change what people have already said about me. It's all over the internet. It's too late.

LEO: I don't know what to tell you. It's not your fault those violins just can't function like they used to . . . You either need a new type of violin or a new type of climate. And I doubt the world is gonna stop getting warmer any time soon . . .

FRANKLIN: . . . I have an idea . . . Thank you.

(FRANKLIN hangs up. End of scene.)

SCENE NINE

NARRATOR: *(action following)* October twelfth. Franklin sits at his work table, sketching furiously. Over time he develops an off-kilter rhythm: pencil marking, contemplative pause, frustrated erasing, repeat. Occasionally, he goes for a ruler. When Franklin is finally satisfied,

(FRANKLIN dials a number and pauses before clicking to make the call. The phone rings.)

AUTOMATED VOICE: Thank you for calling the United States Patent and Trademark Office. For trademark information, say one. For patent information, say two.

FRANKLIN: Two.

(End of play.)

Gold and Silver Medals Awards

Students in grades 7–12 may submit works in 11 writing categories. This year, nearly 4,000 writing submissions were awarded Gold Keys at the regional level, which were then adjudicated at the national level by authors, educators, and literary professionals. Gold and Silver Medals were awarded to exceptional works of writing that demonstrated originality, technical skill, and emergence of a personal voice.

Some of the writing selections have been excerpted.

Visit **artandwriting.org/galleries** to read all of the work as it was submitted.

Winter's Creek

SCIENCE FICTION & FANTASY

PAITON STITH, Grade 11. Olathe North High School, Olathe, KS. Molly Runde and Deirdre Zongker, *Educators*; Greater Kansas City Writing Project, *Affiliate*; Gold Medal

He always kept one foot in the creek when we were kissing. Other times, when we talked, he'd dangle his legs in the delicate current and soak his cuffed jeans up to the knee. The trees stood at our backs, gentle giants with their arms spread to shield us from the sun. Light splintered through occasionally, dappling the swift rabbit-footed creek with shimmering spots of yellow like the dandelions speckled in the grass.

I used to ask him to go places with me, the pool, the movies, my house. He gave me the same smile every time, lips like dusty summertime pressed together to cover white, crooked teeth. Then he turned away to run his fingers through the water or fall back on his elbows to look at the sky. "This place is mine. How could I leave it unprotected?" His voice rushed, smooth like water but carrying that subtle trace of burn, that ability to wear something down over time.

We could sit for hours, looking up at the leaves and the clouds, talking about whatever crossed our minds. It worked because when the world stood still, we didn't. Lying there, looking up, the space within was a whirl of stars. In the dark woods, the silence, we glowed and we twinkled.

But only in the spring. Once every year he'd look over at me as the breeze sent ripples through his cotton shirt, and he'd say, "The snows are coming tomorrow." It was hard to believe him when his brown skin still blended with the wood, as if they were watercolors born from the same palette. It was hard to imagine that everything would be so white so soon.

"Did the creek tell you that?" I asked that first time, sour-voiced and skeptical.

He only smiled. "What else would we talk about?"

If I did come back to the path that led to the creek I'd find it unwelcoming. What was once open and lush become skeletal, barren, the branches twisted into an impassable cluster. This year I didn't even try. I stayed home with my parents, my grandmother in town for Christmas, and I'd do my best to steer the conversation away from Creek. Still, Grandma Gray always found a way to bring him up in unrelated conversation.

"Vida, are you still cavorting with that water sprite in Nelson's Wood?"

"Cavorting, Grandma?" I pinched the edge of my plate until my fingers turned white, spinning it so the turkey slices were before me. "Hardly."

She turned to my mother with her penciled brow raised in a prim arch. "You ought to keep her away from the fair folk." Mother nodded without enthusiasm. She never cared where I went. Grandma held a cut piece of potato to her mouth, "They're cunning, playing at sweet and charming until they bind you with a riddle. Quick as a whip. Then they steal you away and make you rear their children." The potato popped in with an emphatic nod.

"God, Grandma, you can't say that."

Her eyes flared and she straightened like a cobra. "Have you forgotten what happened to my sister?"

I sighed through my teeth so that it sounded like a hiss. "You'd like him if you met him."

She laughed, "In winter?" She sawed at the turkey on her plate. "Tricky as they may be in the spring, every bit of good is gone after the first snow."

I forced myself not to stiffen in surprise. "Why is that?" I asked nonchalantly, trying not to look too clueless in case she thought I wasn't keeping my wits about me. That would only make her more convinced that I needed to be protected.

"I don't know," Grandma snapped. "all a respectable person needs to know is what charms are the strongest, how to weasel out of a bargain, and common sense enough to stay away from them in the first place." She waved her fork through the air. "And most importantly, a winter faerie is a faerie you avoid." She narrowed her eyes. "Stay away, or suffer for it."

I stabbed my fork down into my mashed potatoes so that it stuck up on its own. "He doesn't let me visit in winter, so you don't have anything to worry about." I meant it to sound nasty, but it came out bitter.

Grandma paused with her fork on the way to her mouth. I saw her coffee-stained teeth before she pressed her lips together again. "Good." The rest of dinner was unnaturally still.

I got up to rinse my plate and Grandma touched my arm as I passed. I paused, already preparing a retort. She only said, "Be careful."

Of course I was careful. I was always careful. I'd heard the stories, but in every case the foolish human had done something to offend. If you knew the rules, dealing with faeries was a breeze. I'd been going to the woods for years now, and I'd never had problems with any of them. Never in winter, though.

Maybe that's why my heart cowered in my mouth, like it felt safer using my teeth as a shield and my tongue as a sword than in my ribcage. See, that was the trick to the fair folk. All their power laid in their silver tongues. You just had to play along with enough skill, and I'd spent years sharpening my arsenal of flattery, language flowered with deceptive description, and of course, the potent last resort: lies.

I knew Creek, I'd been spending every warm season with him for twelve years now, back when I'd been an over-exploring toddler and he was just a little babbling brook. Still, Grandma's words haunted me. I had to see him, just once, and then I'd never force my way through the brambles again. Truth is, I was worried about him. For years, I'd let him convince me to stay away so easily, but something about Grandma's expression when I told her made me uneasy. Nothing surprised Grandma. Something must be wrong.

The one time I'd tried to get through the twisted path, the branches held like they were made of iron. This time, though they weren't exactly welcoming, they shifted eventually to let me through. Roots hidden beneath the crunching snow grabbed half-heartedly at my ankles. The branches hung lower than in spring, scraping at my cheeks so that I had to shield my face with my arms.

The silence was the strangest part. I was so used to springtime chatter and constant movement. This landscape hummed with barren silence. "Hello?" I called out a few of my friends' names, but no face showed. I tightened the scarf around my neck and held my wool coat together at the collar.

I didn't recognize the end of the path when I came to it, and nearly plunged a foot into the frozen creek. With my right boot crusted with snow, I crouched at the edge to wait. The afternoon sun glittered across the ice, and I thought that it wasn't so hideous. Barren could be beautiful too.

Creek didn't take long to show up, standing like a ghost on the ice, barely out of the trees. The naked branches cast sharp shadows across his body, and his dark eyes peered out of a hollow, sunken face.

"Creek," I said, standing. "Aren't you cold?" He was barefoot, in the same cuffed jeans and light cottony T-shirt he wore in spring.

"Yes." His voice had hardened, brittle and splintered and hoarse. He didn't come any nearer. "What are you doing here?"

My cheeks warmed despite the cold. "I came to see if you were alright."

"I am."

"Are you sure," I asked, and dared to take a few steps toward him. He backed away, lowering his head until he was glaring up at me beneath his frosted brow. I stopped. "Creek, where is everybody?"

He wrapped his arms around his chest, squeezing his ribs until his arms paled. "Hiding." He was shivering.

My blood chilled in my veins. "From what?"

He shook his head, wouldn't meet my eyes. "I told you not to come."

I took a tentative step forward once more, watching the frost creep up from his blue toes to disappear under his jeans. "My grandmother told me you'd be dangerous in the winter."

He looked up sharply at that. "No," he said, then his eyes slid away from mine. "I'm not."

I hissed through my teeth, white breath clouding out of my mouth and spinning up to the sky like a bird. "What's wrong with me being here?" I felt eyes on me now. Out of the corner of my eye I'd catch the flicker of tiny bodies moving amongst the snow and withered shrubs.

His hair fell forward into his eyes, thin and dry as his skin, as his body. He was skeletal and the warmth had fled his skin, leaving him pallid and dull. The sight filled me with a stark unease. I had never known him like this before, always he was brimming with vibrancy and joy. He spoke in soft voices in the spring, with whimsy and humor and beauty. Winter had turned him bitter. I was right. Everything was wrong.

I lifted my chin. "You let me in here. The branches could've barred my path like they used to, but they didn't."

Crackling ice and snow were the only sounds as I approached, and they bounced around the emptiness like it was a skeleton to fill, like it knew what this winter world needed, but couldn't meet the demand. "I'm sorry I ignored you," I whispered, "I won't any longer."

Disjointed arms with spidery fingers reached for me, and he was the heart of winter itself pressed against my chest as I wrapped my arms around him, unbuttoned my coat so he could slip his arms inside.

It was cold and miserable. I wasn't pretending not to notice, but there was something full about this. Something that had been missing when I only loved him in the spring. That had been halfway, a lovely fantasy. He was bitter and cold and even cruel at times, but so was I.

I imagined my warmth leaching into him, and I knew I'd hold him tight. Even if he never stopped shivering. ■

Layers

SCIENCE FICTION & FANTASY

INNOCENZO ROCKSMITH, Grade 9, George Washington Carver Center for Arts and Technology, Towson, MD. Rebecca Mlinek, *Educator*; Region-at-Large, *Affiliate*; Silver Medal

Lydia Caldwell's house was not very inviting from the outside. It was one of those buildings everyone just glosses over: the everyday people, the big men with big plans who want to take your property for office buildings, and perhaps time itself. It was small, almost ramshackle, plagued by mold and vines and set deep into the outskirts, but I couldn't just ignore the sign.

"Inner Voices of the Soul, Interpreted by Lydia Caldwell, Discover Your True Self!"

Under it hung a little "open" flag, proudly waving in the gentle breeze. It was a Saturday, I was bored, and there were a fat five-dollars in my pocket just clamoring to be spent. But would it be enough? The house lay in a slight depression of the land, and what must once have been a trail led down to it. Now it was overgrown and faint, but a guide all the same.

I scrambled down the slope, tearing through the creepers and ferns without care, and reached the door with breath to spare. No light spilled out from the windows, and the porch lamps were oil-less. The house looked dead. Beginning to have misgivings, I tentatively tried the handle. It wasn't locked—a good sign, but, nevertheless, I moved charily.

An unearthly creaking filled my ears, and I screwed up my face in an effort to block it out. The door was meeting resistance, and I pushed harder. It clicked against a lever on the ceiling, and suddenly thoughts of booby traps, and cages, and swinging axes filled my mind. Nothing of the sort happened. It was merely a bell, one that sounded with an echoless finality.

I stepped inside, still taking care with every movement. The house was sparsely and distastefully furnished. There was a hideous moth-eaten couch, flanked by statues that looked like gargoyles. A towering lamp stood in the corner, draped in a long cloth, and on the far side of the room sat an immense box with a padlock.

I was losing faith in the truth of the "open" flag. As I turned to leave, however, the lights flicked on, and I started. Out of nowhere, out of nothing, came an old woman, shuffling towards me from across the room. She was, perhaps, the oldest thing I had ever and would ever see. If each wrinkle on her face was a year she had lived, the woman could have been a thousand. Her eyes were dull with cataracts and sunken into her skull. Her skin was liver-spotted and papery, folds of it hanging like curtains over her prominent Adam's apple. Her hair was thin and wispy, clinging to her shining head and drooping over her shoulders. She was, however, inexplicably, wearing an orange Nike T-shirt and boy's shorts with a pair of pink socks pulled up past her shrunken knees.

I stepped back, trying to comprehend what I was looking at before the old woman opened her mouth.

"Can you read?" She snarled, her voice a rasping hiss of emphysema, her teeth like shards of broken rock, her breath the rank odor of death and decay.

"The sign says closed, boy!"

"No, it doesn't! It says open I swear!" I shouted fearfully.

"Get out!" roared the woman. She drew nearer and as she did, something in the fury of her gaze seemed to falter, to fall away and be replaced by wonder. She halted, three feet away from my frozen figure.

"I . . . Uh," I stammered, "I'll just go then . . . "

"No, no dear." Her voice had suddenly attained a soft, dreamy quality. "It's quite alright, I was just going out for a jog." Her claw-like hand seemed to creak with arthritis as it shot out and seized my wrist with the strength of a vice. Shocked, I attempted to wrest my arm from her grasp, but all the muscles in my body seemed to freeze as I beheld her face. It had twisted into something inhuman, something to which I could put no name. It was sneering, spiteful, the countenance of a malignant creature that had crawled its way up from the depths of hell. Exhilaration and rage emanated from the old woman, and her labored breathing was suddenly a growling hiss. I closed my eyes, wanting to scream, hoping more than anything that it was just a dream.

When at last I opened my eyes, the creature was gone, and the old woman was smiling, her hand a warm, shriveled spider over my sweaty palm. She led me down a hall, into a room as black as night, and yet I did not resist. All volition seemed to have seemed to have seeped from my limbs, and some great inevitability was drawing me towards itself like a spider with caught flies. The woman retrieved a shawl from a hook still barely illuminated, and draped it over her shoulders, covering the sports clothing. I stood there, unmoving, and would have appeared silhouetted against the light of the doorway to someone inside the room. The door slammed shut, and a great candle flickered into life, almost like a torch. In fact, thousands upon thousands of candles burst into flame, and as my shock receded I became conscious that it was a mere illusion. Mirrors lined the walls of this room, ranging from new and sleek, to ancient and antique. Each, however, reflected the barely illuminated visage of a skinny fourteen-year-old alight with untamed fear, his lank hair an unkempt mess, and a vast, tapering candle.

The old woman sat, cross-legged upon the matted floor with a sigh that reverberated off of the walls. The flickering, insubstantial light of the candle played eerily across her bony, sunken cheeks and the black pits of her eyes, defining in sharp detail the contours of her prominent features. "I'll give you a reading for free dear," she hissed, as I sat without conscious thought, my brain no longer seeming in control. "I would like that very much ma'am," I replied, in a flat, monotone voice that was alien to my vocal cords.

The old lady's face broke into a wicked smile that displayed her malformed teeth sticking out at iniquitous angles from her ravaged gums. Her fathomless eyes locked on my own, and the penetrating gaze did not break as she fished a small object from within the shawl. Unable to stare any longer into those eyes, I glanced down at the object.

It was an onion.

I gaped at it, utterly confused. Self-control was starting to again fill my body, and an ominous feeling, a shapeless, formless sense of foreboding began at once to dominate subconscious. "What's that for?" I asked, and the monotone quality in my voice was beginning to waver, replaced with a cautious air. The woman merely smiled wider, placing the onion in her lap. She drew something else out from beneath the shawl, something that gleamed with a metallic glint and reflected the candlelight. A knife. A short, wickedly curved piece of steel whose tang was wrapped with pale cord.

"No," I croaked, half-formed conceptions of resistance, of retaliation chasing each other around my sluggish brain, none acted upon. The old woman grasped the *blade* of the knife, the jubilant look unwavering on her face as dark blood ran between her shrunken fingers. *"No!"* My voice had risen to a near shout, and yet still I did not act, did not move, did not even shy away from her bloodied hand as it closed over my arm, forcing my palm into view. She brought the knife across the sweaty surface and I screamed, a bloodcurdling, hair-raising shriek of agony that forced gales of laughter from Lydia Caldwell, as drops of blood ran down her face, hysterical screeches of heinous mirth. Her hand left my arm and grasped the onion as the other forced my slashed palm onto its surface. The exterior of the onion was rough, papery, brittle. The blood from both of our hands ran into dark lines etched in the shell. "Let's see," she cackled. "On the outside, an extreme introvert, reticent, you don't have that many friends, do you boy?" In that moment I knew only pain, and that truths about myself which I might never have perceived were buried in this onion, born of my blood and interpreted by this old woman, and so I dug into it.

The first layer peeled away and the onion was now smooth, damp, slightly translucent and coppery with interspersing shades of lime. "Hmm, more outspoken with the few friends you have . . . A great lover of the arts, especially literature, you've read Harry Potter well over fifty times. Well, just your average *nerd!*" There was nothing neither malevolent nor surprising about the truths she uttered; the way they were spoken made my skin crawl. Relentlessly, I dug deeper, reveling in the experience. The onion was now a pale green and was starting to lose its shape. Clear fluid was leaking from inside, and my eyes began to sting and water, both from the juice itself and from the pain as it assaulted my cut palm. "Asthma, eczema, multiple allergies, well you're quite the weakling, aren't you? Oh, and what's this? A deep-seated terror of death? Well, let me tell you something boy. It comes for us all in the end. *It comes for us all, and you can't stop it!*

Reason and restraint had left me, and I tore into that onion like it was my mortal enemy, fingernails hanging off in splinters, eyes streaming with tears. The tinge of green was gone from the onion, it was now small and white, its shape, or lack thereof, not even remotely reminiscent of its previous structure. It looked like a fake candlewick dripping fluid onto its hard stump. "You seek a change in normal life, an aberration in the course of human existence. Maybe that's why you write so much fantasy, huh?"

I had reached the last layer, and the onion was now smaller than its stump, minuscule, drenched with repugnant juice and blood. The old woman's endless ramble stopped, and she began to laugh. Her mirth was depraved, execrable. She opened her mouth again and bellowed, *"They never loved you and they never will! No one will! You are nothing! You—"*

"Shut up, shut up!" I thundered, wrenching my hand away from hers. A thousand onions fell and spun away into the dark. I stood up, a wrath like I had never felt pounding within. The old woman began to shriek unintelligible curses, her claw-like hands scrambled for the knife. In a blind vagary, I struck her across the face and ran. I did not know where, all that mattered was that I left them behind; the woman, the pain, the truth. ∎

The Unfiltered Otherness and Autonomy of Josephine Baker and Cardi B

CRITICAL ESSAY

CHARLOTTE SPOHLER, Grade 12. Grace Church School, New York, NY. Toby Nathan, *Educator*; NYC Scholastic Awards, *Affiliate*; Gold Medal

Five years ago, the idea of a stripper from the Bronx gaining international fame as a rapper and performer through her Instagram account seemed impossible, or at least highly unlikely. However, the contemporary success of Cardi B (born Belcalis Almanzar) has shown that her unfiltered authenticity promoted by her social media persona has appeal for mainstream audiences. While Cardi B seems to be a unique and radical figure, she is actually the product of a long history of black female entertainers who have played on white perceptions about their sexuality and otherness in order to gain economic independence and autonomy. One of the first prominent and most significant of these entertainers was Josephine Baker, who became a superstar in the 1920s for her provocative performances in France. As two prominent figures in the history of black female entertainers, both Josephine Baker and Cardi B employ self-made, outrageous personas and exploit contemporary media culture in order to both meet the public's demand for an authentic "other" while also challenging the limits of their roles as black women in a white-dominated society.

From the time of the Great Migration, ideas concerning black women have revolved around themes of authenticity, otherness, and vice. These perceptions informed the development of black female entertainers as exotic and sexualized for the enjoyment of white audiences. Hazel Carby notes that as black women moved to cities for economic opportunity during the Great Migration, their autonomy generated moral panic among both whites and upwardly mobile middle-class blacks: "the behavior of black female migrants was characterized as sexually degenerate and, therefore, socially dangerous." Black women could not be trusted in the workforce, where they were consistently given employment of lower rank and quality than white women (White, 418) and experienced more discrimination than black men. Many desired a traditional family structure with a male breadwinner; however, the racism in the workforce and the overall lack of inclusivity in the North made this a nearly impossible goal to attain.

Black women were closely associated with vice, and it was necessary for institutions to control their bodies so that they did not become prostitutes. As Carby argues, "the migrating black woman could be variously situated as a threat to the progress of the race," because her presence held risks for the black urban community in the arenas of black middle-class respectability, appropriate black and white relations, and strong, virtuous black masculinity. Nightclubs where black women performed for predominantly white audiences threatened traditionally acceptable interracial relations. As Mark Haller highlights, "ironically enough, the worlds of gambling and popular entertainment were, in this period, the most integrated sectors of American cities." However, this environment resulted in fears of female sexuality, fears of miscegenation, and fears of independent black female desire: "If a black woman can claim her freedom and migrate to an urban environment, what is to keep her from negotiating her own path through its streets?" By participating in the Great Migration, black women gained autonomy; their presence would shape negative perceptions about single black women in urban environments, but this would in turn create the role of the black female entertainer as authentic, dangerous, and exotic. Many black women entertainers conformed to certain types of character roles that were in dialogue with the perception of them as dangerous and highly sexualized, and these roles would dominate culture through the twentieth century, influencing the general understanding of the types of roles black women can play.

Although black women often play characters and take on personas that are independent and tough, they continue to be highly sexualized. Black women constructed personas that demonstrated awareness of the white man's fantasy that celebrated stereotypes of black female sexuality, including danger and exoticism. This image has carried into contemporary rap culture, where women are referred to as "bitches" and "hoes" and women's bodies are barely clothed and displayed as background objects in music videos. Although this culture is still present today, it has been reshaped so that women can embrace their sexuality and display it for their own empowerment and economic independence. Though both Josephine Baker and Cardi B use their bodies for employment, the "vice" that they are selling is popular in mainstream entertainment, and they control their images in order to capitalize on the stereotypes which society has presented.

Josephine Baker had her first job when she was eight, working as a white woman's maid. Though her white mistress made promises of niceties she made Baker sleep in the cellar with the dog and once punished her by plunging her arms into boiling water. In Baker's autobiography, she explains her decision to leave home at thirteen to join a vaudeville troupe by recounting some violent events in her life, including the East St. Louis riots of 1917, in which some of her relatives and neighbors were murdered. Her journey away from home at such a young age is telling of the brutal violence and oppression she experienced, and demonstrates that becoming an entertainer was the only way for her to gain freedom.

Like Baker, Cardi B also comes from a background with limited economic opportunities and became an entertainer in order to thrive. A college dropout from the Bronx, Cardi B initially turned to stripping in order to gain financial independence from an abusive relationship. As Cardi B states, "I was dictated to, and had to do things I didn't want to do because I was living under a man's roof . . . I was living in a space where I couldn't even pay rent and people threw that in your face all the time." In this way, she equates economic autonomy with self-respect. Her rags to riches story is an important part of her persona and makes her a people's champ (Wired). Her expensive style may seem frivolous, but it is representative of the aspirational aspects of economic independence. As critic Tahirah Hairston writes, "Stunting is a form of resistance, a push-back to the haters who doubted your talent, and a fuck-you to poverty and a system adamant on keeping you there."

Audience members were astounded by Baker's performances. Both white men and women had strong reactions: men were fascinated by her dark skin and women were scandalized by her display. "La Revue Negre" proved to be the turning point of her career and led to Baker's tremendous success from that point on. Baker's performance fed the desire for the colonial black female and the exotic while also challenging expectations.

Cardi B's success can also be attributed to her provocative persona, which her audience recognizes as authenticity. Her unfiltered qualities and outspokenness have set her apart from more polished performers in a way that many find appealing. Cardi B explains this by suggesting that she lets out an honest energy that most of us keep inside, saying, "Everyone has a me inside them, that loud girl that just wanna go 'ayyyy!' No matter if you a doctor, a lawyer, a teacher, it comes out." In this way, she suggests that she provides a release for her audience similar to what Baker offered to early twentieth-century Paris.

Demonstrating a shrewd understanding of media culture and what the public wants, Baker and Cardi B were able to manufacture their own reputations and shape perceptions about themselves. In 1920s Paris, Baker capitalized on white audiences' desire to free themselves from the restraints of society, exploiting the "eagerness for something real, something not so refined and restrained," transforming herself into a racial and sexual icon to become "the world's first colored superstar." Her lack of inhibition led her to be seen as a representation of danger that was thrilling to the audience, and Baker clearly encouraged this reading of her stage presence. Her performance and persona spoke to what Cheng calls the "dream of a second skin," which allows one to remake oneself in the skin of the "other," whether that is white audience members seeking to be something other than themselves, or racialized subjects escaping the burdens of their skin color. Baker's stardom can largely be attributed to her ability to fulfill this fantasy.

Cardi B has, likewise, been able to shape her image by understanding the desire for authenticity and the most effective new media platforms for projecting that image. She has amassed a devout following for her selfie videos, in which she gives relationship advice, makes jokes that "cut through the medium's inherent performative silliness," and gives "the occasional sharp nugget of socio-economic analysis." The intimacy of Cardi B's selfie videos has a similar effect as Baker's "dangerous performances"; both give the sense that you are experiencing something raw and exciting that you are not supposed to see. Her ability to connect with anyone through social media satisfies the "eagerness for something real" that Baker also fulfilled.

As black performers in a white-dominated world, Baker and Cardi B both align with and challenge perceptions of how black women entertainers are meant to be and what they are meant to do. Baker's performance of black female exotic primitivism is the first significant example of a black female performer who inspires debate on whether she is being exploited or whether she is subverting that exploitation. Baker "had come of age at an unusually perverse moment in American and European history, when whites hungered for undiluted 'African' or 'Negro' art as a panacea for the 'overcivilization' that had so recently driven the world to war." Though some may view Baker as a sexualized object of racist fascination, her control over her image speaks to her control over how she is represented. Because she framed herself as as a woman who transcended nationality, she was seen as "the woman who could be anything—anything with color—for France and, indeed, the world." Cardi B likewise challenges stereotypes about black women entertainers. Similar to Baker and others, she appropriates negative stereotypes in order to "assert control over the representation or at least reap the benefits of it," displaying herself as a free and liberated woman.

Having a political voice is crucial to challenging the limits placed on black women in entertainment, and both Baker and Cardi B notably sought to use their star power to speak on political issues. Baker engaged in a number of activist causes, including charity work with orphans and the poor, and spread an anti-racist message through Europe. When touring in America, she refused to perform in segregated venues, and broke down color lines. Baker once stated that she had taken a rocky path, but that "as I get older, and as I knew I had the power and the strength, I took that rocky path and I tried to smooth it out a little. I wanted to make it easier for you. I want you to have a chance at what I had." Her rocky path laid the foundation for how future black female entertainers such as Cardi B could attain the same icon status. Cardi B has demonstrated her own political activism, weighing in on economic issues and telling *GQ* that President Franklin Delano Roosevelt was "the real 'Make America Great Again,' because if it wasn't for him, old people wouldn't even get Social Security.'" Her interest in other issues, including gun violence in schools and the divide between rich and poor, come from a genuine place that inspires others to listen and take these challenges seriously.

Both Josephine Baker and Cardi B represent significant figures in their unique historical moments, and their similarities demonstrate important truths about Western culture. Black female entertainers still have to traverse the same paths and deal with the same sexualized stereotypes and limitations they encountered in the early twentieth century. The music industry is still dominated by men. According to a study by the University of Southern California, women comprised just 9 percent of Grammy nominees from the past six years. Rap and hip-hop in particular are male-dominated genres. This may be a result of the constant objectification of black women entertainers based on the long history of their struggle to be accepted. We can only hope that black women will attain more mobility and autonomy as they gain more control over their own representation, and that audiences will expand their perceptions of what black women should and can do. ■

Chicken Soup

CRITICAL ESSAY

N'JHARI JACKSON, Grade 12. Carrollwood Day School, Tampa, FL. Judith Anthony-Birge, Debbie Coad, and Sean Marcus, *Educators*, Hillsborough County Public Schools, *Affiliate*; Silver Medal

As I sit here with my classmate's eyes directed at the screen, which illuminates the many flashes from cameras across the world, I glance around the room to take in the faces of my peers. So many expressions, coupled with revelations that I am unable to put pen to paper for fear of being disrespectful. I wait, while securely holding on to every visual dictation. Some look on in dismay, while others want to smile, but refrain from showing the joy they feel inside. Still, others doodle with quick glances at the screen to appear interested. I try to picture my face as I've done my classmate's and not surprisingly, it's one of a bowl of gumbo. Discontentment, reflection, stew, joy, humility, pride, gratitude, patriotism, and a little conflagration to cement a facial expression, I cannot see. Can others see what I can't see? Have they formed an opinion that I can care less about this historically significant moment in time? If so, is it because I'm considered the opposition of the president-elect and should systematically oppose the transition of executive powers taking place during my lunch? Whatever the reason, I'm certain any unfounded conclusion is one simmered and stewed behind closed doors. Like old family recipes, ingredients are kept tucked away at home, while leftovers are packaged neatly and carried into my educational realm.

The ceremonial pursuit of this moment in time unfolds on screens as Americans show their true colors with some protesting, even setting ablaze posters of the president-elect. Others erupt in elation and cheer for a man they see as a new savior of the masses, a new beginning, and a renewing of the American people. Some relish in a prophesy fulfilled, the great hope of making America great again as proclaimed. News clips align the bottom of the tube with jarring headlines of students from elementary to college disrespecting the new leader of the "free world." I reflect on a lesson taught by mom: "never disrespect your elders, and always show respect . . . you don't have to like a person to show respect." With this soldered in my mind, how is it that students are allowed to miss school to disrespect an adult who just happens to be the U.S. president-elect on national television? That part of my face showing conflagration slowly swells in my heart, causing an anxiousness to learn, to study, to show thyself approved as commanded in 2 Timothy 2:15. I refuse to be ignorant to the point of disrespecting my family, my church home, my America, or myself regardless of who is at the helm of this great nation.

I try to visualize that part of my facial expression that elicits joy and gratitude as I see the incumbent First Lady, Michelle Obama, poised with grace and humility as she welcomes the First Lady-elect, Melania Trump. In this brief exchange, I imagine she has secretly handed down the First Wives Club, Handbook of Survival and Knowledge which she affably accepts with a soft smile. I once wrote an essay expressing what my late granddad taught me: "selfless kindness." This important characteristic flashes across my mind when I think of two teen girls who displayed to the world what I learned early on, selfless kindness. They altruistically shared their dad with all of America. The joy I feel knowing that two teenage girls will finally welcome their dad home after being on the frontline of a domestic battlefield for eight years with no hard feelings. The grace and maturity that two teenage girls exemplified during a time known to teens as the most confusing period of our young lives pour out hope that our generation is not completely lost. No, it won't take place in the gymnasium on an episode of Lifetime's *Coming Home*, nor will he surprise them still in full regalia during a piano recital. After the cameras have all shifted to the daily happenings of a new fascination, he'll take a walk of humility. He'll walk head held high after taking one final call from his buddy Joe, who called just to say, "Job well done, bro." After a sigh expressing, I did all I could do, he asks, "what's for dinner babe?" In typical fashion, he leans to kiss the cheeks of his favorite girls before wrapping his First Lady in his long arms and whispering, "thank you, for being my ride-or-die, my queen."

I know young people are not always taught to be independent thinkers but expected to think as our parents do and do as they do. With the transition in executive powers upon us, there should be a transition from dependent thought to independent thought. Dr. Martin Luther King Jr. made this clear to us when he said, "Education must enable one to sift and weigh evidence, to discern the true from the false, the real from the unreal, and the facts from the fiction."

I reflect back to sixth grade when a classmate was disgruntled at the election results and openly referred to the commander in chief as "the monkey." At first thought, I had to decide if I was upset because of the blatant disrespect of the highest office, or the disrespect of a man, or the intentional insult of a man who happened to be African American. This is where the words of Dr. King really hit home: "Darkness cannot drive out darkness; only light can do that. Hate cannot drive out hate; only love can do that."

In this instance, I remembered recipes are often shared amongst family members; coming up with new recipes remains a critical part of independent learning and individual rhetoric.

We cannot tout ourselves as Americans and fight for it to be "great again" if that greatness is at the expense of American security, American education, and the American people including those lives still blossoming inside the womb waiting to make their grand entrance. Most importantly, we have to educate ourselves as an American people if we are to remain great, remain a free country, and remain leaders of the free world. No one person or entity can make us a great country. We are accountable for our own greatness as a country collectively. So, when legislation comes about to better the education of American children and young adults that is not the time to become self-absorbed with personal gain, but it is a time to work as an American people to remain great. To that, I thank you, sir, President Obama, for pushing an agenda to educate all Americans in a financially responsible manner because to be great, we have to first be educated. Similarly, no one person including a president can be responsible for individual education. As individuals, we have to take responsibility for our own education so that we are equipped, contributing members of this great nation.

Now, that the bands have collected their instruments, and the bouquets of balloons released into the atmosphere, and tempers returned to heated sections of various areas of the country, we settle in for the ride. Whether it is smooth, bumpy, or outright Busch Gardens Cobra's Curse scary, we are strapped in. America has a new leader and Americans are charged with educating themselves vastly and taking an active role in bettering our communities. Take a bow President Obama and know that a great surgeon once told me while explaining blood flow through the human heart, "You can't make chicken soup out of chicken 'shiznit.'" Although I laughed, mainly because I didn't quite get the analogy then, as I reflect on what holding the highest office of the land must have been for you, the analogy is crystal clear. We play the hand dealt, and we use the ingredients in front of us and make the best of it. No matter how much we want it, how badly we need it even if it's just to pacify us, we won't always end up with chicken soup. Blessings to the forty-fifth president, and may wisdom upon him and his many advisers; to the many Americans idly watching in hope or hate, educate yourselves. ∎

Flickering

DRAMATIC SCRIPT

TYLER ECONA, Grade 12. Woodbridge High School, Woodbridge, VA. Cathy Hailey, *Educator*; Writopia Lab, *Affiliate*; Silver Medal

CHARACTERS, in order of appearance:

TALL MAN: A white businessman in his mid-30s, prone to nervous habits.

OLD WOMAN: A mild-mannered African American lady who speaks with a hint of Southern drawl.

YOUNG BOY: A small, erratic schoolboy who doesn't know much about anything.

CONDUCTOR: A whiskered fellow who takes his job seriously.

Scene

(Lights flicker on. A single wooden bench is set stage left, tilted at an angle so that it mostly faces the audience. Low sepia lighting recommended for a warm, somber atmosphere. The most concentrated source of light should emit from a lantern dangling from a post just next to the bench. We're in a small, liminal space: a train station in the middle of nowhere, between the late fifties and mid-sixties. There's a moment of eerie silence before a TALL MAN enters stage right; he wears a suit, tie, and hat, and carries a briefcase. Unbeknownst to him, his trousers are ripped in some places and blotted with dark red stains. He approaches the bench with an unsure step, looks around, and settles down with the briefcase on his lap. With an exhale of a nervous breath, he folds his hands together and looks up at the lantern. He waits a moment.)

(An OLD WOMAN enters from stage left. She's dressed in a simple, long nightgown. She glances up towards the lantern, and then to the man on the bench. Without a word, she strides over to take a seat on the other end of it. They sit in silence.)

OLD WOMAN: *(Quietly, looking around)* Is this really it? This the place?

TALL MAN: *(Turning his head to her)* Sorry?

(She looks at him. No answer. A beat. She notices his briefcase)

OLD WOMAN: You just come from work?

TALL MAN: I, uh . . . don't exactly remember. *(He pauses.)* But, uh . . . my name's Richard. I'm from Carolina.

OLD WOMAN: Carolina, Alabama?

TALL MAN: No ma'am. South Carolina, the state. You come from Alabama?

OLD WOMAN: *(ignoring him, looking around)* I don't think . . . this is the place.

TALL MAN: Carolina? Alabama? I'm not sure either . . .

(The OLD WOMAN spots something across from him: a YOUNG BOY who darts onstage. He wears overalls, one shackle dangling off his shoulder, and a newsboy cap, which is also stained with a dark red. Coming to a skidding stop upon seeing the two on the bench, he looks around frantically.)

YOUNG BOY: Paul? Evelyn? MA!

(The TALL MAN looks to the OLD WOMAN, unsure of what to do. He takes out a pocket watch and gives it a few nervous taps, then stuffs it back into his pocket.)

YOUNG BOY: *(Taking a few steps forward)* You folks from around here? Seen my friends or my Ma anywhere? *(He tries looking around again, but his sight is soon fixed on the lantern ahead. He gets as close as he can, tilting his head back and craning his neck to get a good look at it.)*

OLD WOMAN: Well . . . I think it's best if you stay here, boy. Come, sit down. Is that blood on your forehead?

(YOUNG BOY snaps out of the trance and wipes at his forehead. When he sees blood come off on his hand, his expression darkens.)

YOUNG BOY: Where am I?

TALL MAN: Look, kid . . . maybe you should sit down, wait for the train with us.

(The YOUNG BOY looks between the two of them hesitantly. Then, for a split second, he glances to the audience. His features are knitted in concern; vulnerability engulfs him. He quickly turns back to the two.)

YOUNG BOY: I don't wanna get on that train. It's not mine.

OLD WOMAN: I do believe it is. We all gotta do things we don't like sometimes, son. Part a' growing up.

(TALL MAN folds his hands together again while YOUNG BOY's attention shifts towards the lantern again. A beat.)

YOUNG BOY: *(Pulling away from the light)* No! I want to go back, I need to!

TALL MAN: Home's sounding better and better to me now, too—

OLD WOMAN: But you wouldn't want to get lost back there, would you? In the dark, all by yourself?

YOUNG BOY: I-I don't care. I'm going home! *(He turns around, facing where he came.)* Look, I can hear them! EVELYN! MA!

OLD WOMAN: Child—

(Before she can finish, the YOUNG BOY breaks out into a run and exits the way he came. The OLD WOMAN shakes her head and watches him go. The lantern above them flickers once. TALL MAN checks his pocket watch again.)

OLD WOMAN: You know that ol' thing won't help you none here.

TALL MAN: Well, how would you know?

OLD WOMAN: Young folks . . . it was always something, wasn't it?

TALL MAN: Sorry?

OLD WOMAN: Always had to be somewhere, do something, meet someone. Always rushin'. Always apologizin', too.

TALL MAN: . . . Sorry.

OLD WOMAN: *(with a gentle sigh)* Guess you can't help it. I was like that too. Always askin' all sorts of questions . . . even after I was grown. But I guess it don't matter all that much anymore.

TALL MAN: *(agitated)* Why wouldn't it? Is everything just . . . done, now?

OLD WOMAN: See what I mean?

TALL MAN: No. You're acting like . . . like this is all okay! Now that we're here, we're just stuck, no going back, leaving home—well, I don't agree!

OLD WOMAN: Happens every day, all 'round the world, but we only make a fuss when it affects *us*.

TALL MAN: And once we go through that tunnel on this . . . this *train?* I don't even remember purchasing my ticket!

OLD WOMAN: You angry, huh? For the first time in your life, somethin's outta your control . . .

TALL MAN: *(He stands up suddenly, pacing towards the lantern.)* Why are you sitting there like it doesn't *matter?*

OLD WOMAN: Don't presume I'm enjoyin' this any more than you are!

TALL MAN: Then why aren't you *acting* like it?!

(He's reached the lantern, and as he delivers the line, he kicks the base of it with a force brought on by unadulterated rage. The sudden outburst leaves them in silence. The lantern flickers once, and then once again. He paces back towards her.)

TALL MAN (CON'T.): What happens when the train arrives? What if . . . what if it doesn't have to arrive? *(Realizing the possibilities, he begins to pace again.)* I-I'll think of something. The both of us, we don't have to stay here if we didn't want to . . . We could go back, with that light . . .

(The OLD WOMAN *looks up at him solemnly. There's some semblance of hope, now. He flashes her a crooked grin.)*

OLD WOMAN: Well, I'm not so sure, but . . . if it would mean seeing my family again . . .

TALL MAN: We can find a way, can't we? The way back? Oh, I'd do anything—I've got things I could sell in my briefcase, I'll sell my hat and shoes, and then I could go on with my life! Keep doing business like I was doing!

OLD WOMAN: Lord, I don't think there's a thing I wouldn't do . . .

TALL MAN: Come on, then! *(He grabs her by the wrist, tugging her just slightly* *to the edge of where she's sitting.)* Let's go, we can't waste any more time—before the train catches us!

(He continues to tug gently, waiting for her to stand, but she remains seated. His efforts soon prove to be futile. Her face has fallen from its sudden glimmer of hope to a painful, silent realization. She looks down, shaking her head.)

TALL MAN: Come on . . . please. I don't want to stay here—

(He begins to choke on his words. Soon, his hand falls to his side. The lantern flickers once, and then again, then a third time.)

OLD WOMAN: I'm sorry, but . . . that little boy ain't gone home. I can't follow him.

TALL MAN: *(sitting back down, with a shuddering exhale)* What . . . am I going to do? Without them, I'll . . .

(A beat.)

TALL MAN (CON'T.): What are *they* gonna do without *me*? My folks . . .

OLD WOMAN: *(now looking up towards the lantern)* They'll get by. They always do, eventually. What kinda 'folks' you got?

TALL MAN: Parents. A younger brother. And I've been with someone a couple years. I was going to propose. But it's too late for that now, I . . . I ruined it.

OLD WOMAN: Son, this wasn't your fault.

TALL MAN: I could've been more cautious. I could've—

(He stops himself, choking on his words. The OLD WOMAN *puts a hand on his shoulder.)*

OLD WOMAN: Listen . . . can I tell you what I last remember?

*(*TALL MAN *nods.)*

OLD WOMAN (CON'T.): I was asleep. I'd been sick. I remember . . . heat. Blazin' heat, and then suddenly . . . someone yellin', screamin' they head off for me to get up, but I can't. Then I see . . . flames. I thought it was the flames of Hell, all ready to swallow me up, but it was . . . beautiful. That's the last thing I remember, I was thinkin', *that's beautiful.* But now . . . now I'm here, and I don't think I've seen the most beautiful thing yet. We're both waitin' on it. You understand? We gotta be patient. Can't give up now.

*(*TALL MAN *sits for a moment, and then speaks up softly.)*

TALL MAN: You know what I remember? It was the diner after work. We were in there, holding hands. *(He shakes his head.)* I was a fool. Someone came up and grabbed us and . . . I'm here now. *(He puts his face in his hands defeatedly.)* I could've prevented it.

OLD WOMAN: Well, did you love her?

TALL MAN: . . . Him.

(A beat. She nods in understanding.)

OLD WOMAN: Well . . . did you?

TALL MAN: I never loved another like I loved him.

OLD WOMAN: Long as you held onto that love . . . we're gettin' off at the same stop.

(Another beat. The air is lighter. The TALL MAN *seems less despondent now.)*

OLD WOMAN (CON'T.): You know, for a little, I wanted someone to blame. I recall thinkin', *it's the white man.* Them figures outside my window, their white hoods—but now I seen you here, and I think it's more'n that. You know, my son was in those marches . . . got arrested a few times, even. Made the news. We was a threat to their power. But you . . . you were just somethin' they didn't *understand.* I think they hated that as much as they hated us. *(She shakes her head and takes his hand gently.)* But . . . listen, don't we get some comfort here now at least? Waitin' on our beautiful thing?

(She attempts to smile at him—he picks it up halfheartedly. From beyond, a faint, screeching train whistle can be heard, which draws TALL MAN's *attention.)*

TALL MAN: . . . Are you a Christian?

OLD WOMAN: Does it matter all that much now?

TALL MAN: Well, I . . . I assume it does.

OLD WOMAN: You of all people should know that assuming never did no one any good.

TALL MAN: You aren't . . . afraid. Your faith helps, doesn't it?

OLD WOMAN: Well, I've had my seat reserved. You . . . you're young. Travelin' so far, so soon . . .

TALL MAN: *(sighing, looking around)* How much longer, then?

(The lantern above them flickers four times.)

OLD WOMAN: I really don't know much more than you. Don't even know if they have a schedule.

(Another long whistle blows, this time louder. Their train, although not visible to us, has arrived. CONDUCTOR *enters, wearing his uniform. He steps up to them with a clipboard and pen, flipping through his forms.* TALL MAN *stands first, exhaling and picking up his briefcase.)*

CONDUCTOR: No, no, leave your belongings here. You won't need anything where you're headed.

TALL MAN: Then how do I know if I'm prepared for . . . wherever that is?

CONDUCTOR: *(pointing at the lantern above them)* How many times has that thing flickered since you arrived?

TALL MAN: *(looking back at it)* Were we supposed to be counting?

OLD WOMAN: Four, I reckon.

CONDUCTOR: Good, then you've moved through all the necessary customs.

TALL MAN: Customs?

CONDUCTOR: Grief customs. There are five checkpoints, four's all you need to be let on. This one's the last. All you have to do is set down your briefcase and follow me.

(TALL MAN sets down his briefcase. OLD WOMAN stands up as well. The CON-DUCTOR then pauses and seems confused as he glances back down at his papers.)

CONDUCTOR: Wait—We were expecting . . . a boy, as well. Small. *(He flips the pages back into place and looks up at the two.)* Overalls?

TALL MAN: Oh, he . . . ran off, back that way.

(He points across the stage. CONDUCTOR looks, but sees no one and shakes his head.)

CONDUCTOR: Poor kid. Lost souls are always the hardest to collect. *(He looks down at his clipboard, sighing, and marks something off with his pen.)* Well, looks like you two are it for tonight. Follow me, just through here.

(As he walks off, the main lights slowly fade out, until the only sources of light left are the lantern as well as two spotlights looming over the TALL MAN and OLD WOMAN. TALL MAN takes one last look at the OLD WOMAN as they stand side by side, backs to the audience. There is a moment of hesitation.)

OLD WOMAN: *(looking up at the TALL MAN)* I never got to ask you, but I meant to . . . What was the most beautiful thing you ever saw?

TALL MAN: You know . . . I was thinkin', for a time . . . that lantern there. *(He points to it.)* But we're both meant to really find out, now, aren't we?

(The OLD WOMAN smiles and nods in agreement. Spotlights fade. There's the long, moaning whistle of the train. The lantern flickers: one, two, three, four, five—and it's gone.)

End

"When the Oceans Rise and Thunders Roar": The Life and Work of Rachel Sachdev

JOURNALISM

ERIN BRENNAN, Grade 12, Detroit Country Day High School, Beverly Hills, MI. Matt Sadler, *Educator*; Region-at-Large, *Affiliate*; Silver Medal

Kadugodi Road in the outskirts of Bangalore looks almost completely deserted. It is easy to miss, tucked away behind a granite company with a dull white sign written in swirling Kannada. Further down the road, signs of life become more sparse. A single family restaurant. A purple Bible college. A compound hidden behind a large metal gate.

This is where Rachel and Matthias Sachdev have lived since September 2010.

The Sachdevs run the Abundant Grace Children's Home, a foster home of sorts for India's most underprivileged children. Through contact with Matthias's family in northeast India and a network of pastors throughout the country, they have been taking in kids since 2011. Today, the Sachdevs have eighteen young boys and girls under their care, in addition to their own three children. They feed them. They clothe them. They send them to school. They show them love and compassion. Above all, they show them God.

* * *

The sweltering heat of an Indian summer was just beginning to fade when Rachel Sachdev stepped off a plane and into a new world. Five months pregnant and exhausted from a full day of travel, Rachel took her first look at the city of Bangalore, India.

Cars honked. People yelled at each other across the crowded streets. A myriad of scents—sewer, curry, rubbish, livestock—assaulted her nose all at once.

"It was an overload of senses," Rachel recalls of her first visit to India. "As soon as you get out of the airport, you see the crazy traffic, and it was night time, so everybody was going crazy and honking and everything. And they were all kind of pushing at us, and—because I'm white—staring and everything."

That was Rachel's first trip to her husband's homeland. Five years later, in September 2010, the two moved their family permanently to Bangalore in search of divine purpose.

Rachel met Matthias in 2003 at the Master's College (now University) in Southern California. "He was an international student, and I had some good friends in the international house where he was staying. And so we got to know each other that way," Rachel explains. Matthias told her about his family back in India, and about his desire to return home to teach at his parents' Bible college. One year later, Rachel agreed to move to Bangalore with him, and the two got married.

"It had been Matthias's mom's desire for a long time to start a children's home," says Rachel. "So in July 2011, when I was five months pregnant and we had just moved into the new place, we got a knock on the door."

It was a few of Matthias's friends from the Northeast. "Okay, we've got four kids for you," they declared. "Here you go!"

"Whoa, okay, I guess we're starting now!" thought Rachel.

This unexpected development plunged Rachel and her family once more into a world of insecurity. "Okay, where do we put them?" they wondered. "What are the government rules? What do we have to do? How do we do this?"

Seven years later, the Sachdevs run a successful Christian ministry and are changing the lives of their eighteen Abundant Grace kids one day at a time. But even now, Rachel describes their experience in India as a "learning curve" packed with monumental challenges and unfathomable rewards.

* * *

"There's a story that's told in India about a foreigner who comes to visit India, and he meets a farmer who has crabs. The farmer puts the crabs in a bucket, but he doesn't put a lid on the bucket. And the foreigner is watching this, and he sees one crab start trying to get out. And he tells the other guy, 'Hey, your crab is starting to get out.' And the farmer says, 'Oh, no, sir, it's okay. These are Indian crabs. Indian crabs won't let one crab succeed. They want everyone to be low with them.' So, sure enough, as the crab tries to get out, the other ones pull it back."

Rachel's eyes fill with both sorrow and frustration as she recalls how society has pulled her Abundant Grace kids back, again and again. How they have learned to pull each other back as well.

"There's a mindset in India that if no one is succeeding, we're all suffering together, which is good," she says. "So there's that mindset among the kids. They think: 'This is my lot in life. I'm supposed to suffer, I have to suffer, this is what I have to do. And so I should not try to make myself better, and I should not try to let other people succeed either.'"

Rachel and Matthias have had their fair share of run-ins with Indian crabs. When they received their first four children, they had no idea that the four were actually siblings. The kids' parents had instructed them to lie about their backgrounds in case the Sachdevs were unwilling to take four children from the same family. The truth did not come out until six years later, when Rachel and Matthias were looking through paperwork and realized the kids all shared the same last name. Three of them eventually confessed and were forgiven. One of them had already been dismissed for stealing repeatedly.

Some of the Sachdevs' challenges have surpassed even stealing. "Our most frightening experience was the first time that the kids ran away," says Rachel. Her eyes widen as she recounts the story, her voice taking on an increasingly frantic tone.

"There was one boy who had been the ringleader. And he had convinced three of the other boys to run away with him because they thought, 'Let's go have a night in the jungle.' They thought, 'Oh, yeah, we know how to fight tigers, we know how to take care of snakes, let's just have a night in the jungle.' And we were like, 'Wait a second. They're missing. Where are they? What happened?' And, especially here in India, because we're a Christian organization, if the police were to find out, we had no idea what would happen.

"So we searched everywhere, looking everywhere. We were so worried. 'What happened to them? Why are they not here?' We were screaming their names, calling for them, looking everywhere we could look. And then we said, 'Okay, we have to report them missing in the morning. And how are the police going to take that? Are they going to do some investigation into us? Will this be shut down? What about the girls that are here?'

"Matthias went up on the roof, and was praying a lot, and he saw some movement over at one of the other houses. The boys had hid on the roof . . . They had come back because they were hungry. And they had put us through this whole ordeal. This was the first time this had ever happened to us, and again, it was a learning curve for us. We had never had this situation or anything like it. And so, we had to wonder: 'What would have happened if—because of these boys' selfishness—the whole children's home had been shut down?' At that time we had eighteen kids. That was the first scary moment. We've had others, but that was the first one."

Even today, the Sachdevs continue to face problems with stealing and lying among the children. "We noticed it because I had just bought biscuits for the kids, and we keep them in a box for when they get snack tickets on Friday for getting full marks on their tests. And six packets were missing," Rachel explains. Her voice is heavy with weariness over this latest crisis, which she describes as an "emotional rollercoaster."

Despite the challenges they have faced—and continue to face—the Sachdevs remain firm in their mission. Thanks to Rachel and Matthias, the Abundant Grace kids are able to smile and play and just enjoy being kids. Every morning, the children go to school for the chance to earn better jobs once they graduate. In the afternoon, those who finish their homework early get to play in the yard while the others work. They laugh and joke throughout lively games of capture the flag or *lagori*, a native Indian sport. Occasionally, when the kids have finished their chores and homework for the weekend, Matthias and Rachel will put on a movie for them all to enjoy. The girls know every song lyric in the movie *Frozen*. Many of them can quote *Zootopia* fluently.

* * *

When the oceans rise and thunders roar,
I will soar with you above the storm . . .
The Abundant Grace children stand in three straight lines on the Sachdevs' front porch. They are all dressed up in the nicest clothes they own: skirts, cardigans, and dress shirts gifted to them by Rachel and Matthias over the years. Their melodic voices ring out across a vast crowd. Rows upon rows of chairs line the rocky yard, all filled with friends, relatives, students from the Bible college, and the workers who made this night possible.

Rachel, Matthias, and the kids have spent weeks anticipating the dedication ceremony for their new building. A project months in the making, the building stands tall and proud in the corner of their compound. The plumbing has been put in and the rooms inside have been painted a brilliant blue. In the next few days, the workers will finish putting glass panes in the windows and stringing up clotheslines on the roof. When all is done, the thirteen girls from the Abundant Grace Children's Home will settle into their brand-new dormitory. But first, they must all give thanks to God for this latest blessing.

The ceremony begins in song. While Matthias strums along on his guitar, the Abundant Grace children sing hymns praising God for His good work. Next, a local pastor gives a speech from atop the granite porch. Matthias and Rachel speak next, ending the festivities in solemn prayer. When night falls, the crowd migrates to the entrance of the new building, where a red velvet ribbon has been stretched over the open door. After another long prayer, Matthias cuts the ribbon, and cheers fill the evening air.

When asked about the most rewarding experience during her seven years in India, Rachel says: "It was in October 2012. Khushi came to me and she said, 'Aunty, I want to become a Christian. How do I do that?' And I was like,

'Wow.' And we didn't force them, but we were doing devotions every day, and we told them: 'God's Word is important. You want to follow him.' So she came to me first, and then, in a period of two weeks, all the kids—through different circumstances—wanted to become Christian . . . . We called it a two-week 'mini revival.' It was so cool because they chose this, they wanted to do it, they wanted to serve the Lord, they wanted to give their lives to Him. We knew that what we were doing day in and day out, investing in their lives, was not in vain. God was working on their hearts."

Tonight, each one of their voices rings out into the darkness:

. . . *Father, You are King over the flood,*
I will be still and know You are God.

* * *

The kids all call Rachel "Aunty." It is a common honorific among English-speaking Indians, but the word carries infinitely more weight when her name follows it.

One would only need to observe the kids for a single day to see how much they look up to Rachel, how much she means to each and every one of them. "Aunty, can we try to cook for you?" they ask. "Can we try to make a cake? Aunty, can we massage you? Can we make some dinner? Can we do this for you?"

"It's amazing to see how the girls are stepping up," Rachel says with a proud smile. "How they're maturing, how they're growing, how they're loving the Lord, how they're praying. That is definitely the most rewarding thing: to see us being able to impact their lives, and to know that God is going to use that, and God is going to use them.

"Our biggest motivator is knowing that we are serving God, and at the end of the day . . . He's going to be the one to work everything out. And so even when we have difficult days, even when we are so tired, so stressed, we remember that what we are doing is not just something simple like going to an office and coming back every day. This is for eternity." ∎

Siri, Will You Marry Me?

JOURNALISM

REBECCA CHO, Grade 9. Jericho Senior High School, Jericho, NY. Mellene Hederian, *Educator*; Region-at-Large, *Affiliate*; Gold Medal

"Siri, will you marry me?"

A thirteen-year-old boy, Mike, surprises the iPhone software with such an unexpected proposal. However, this question will not appear startling if you are aware of the bond Siri and Mike have developed through particularly unconventional conversations. The topics range from specific interests like thunderstorms to knowing when to say, "thank you" and, "please"—matters that are unusual for Mike to discuss with people.

Mike's story is just one of the many accounts about autistic children who are learning to show empathy and to develop communication skills through a surprising tool—artificial intelligence (AI). A recent breakthrough in technology has allowed researchers to develop digital social robots for autism therapies.

What is autism? Autism, also known as autism spectrum disorder (ASD), is a complex disorder recognized when a child has significant challenges in socialization and communication. Imagine living a life unable to interpret others' expressions, unable to initiate conversations, and unable to establish eye contact.

Families typically turn to long, sometimes ineffective, therapies to assist their children. However, robots have been seen in a new light with their increasingly well-known ability to teach these children and participate in a new type of autism therapy.

This AI method aids kids in easily learning to socially interact and in opening up with their emotions. Researchers believe that autistic children are more expressive with robot teachers because robots are simpler to understand than humans are.

Mike's mom explains, "It's not that Mike doesn't understand Siri's not human. He does—intellectually. But like many autistic people I know, Mike feels that inanimate objects, while maybe not possessing souls, are worthy of our consideration."

The use of robots has resulted in up to a 30 percent improvement in communication skills in children with autism spectrum disorder. Additionally, innovation in this increasingly popular method has appeared internationally, creating several AI robots that may be employed in autism therapy.

Nao, a white, human-like robot developed by a French company, records children's body language as they interact with the robot during conversations and activities. Nao then carefully assesses this data to determine the most effective method to garner the attention of a child based on the data gathered about a child's facial expressions and movements. The robot is of immense assistance to therapies because it can design personalized therapy plans for each child based on the child's strengths and weaknesses. Still in the testing stage, Nao should become available in 2019.

A new instructor enters a Dallas school. Less than two feet tall, Milo is a specialized robot who helps autistic students learn vocabulary and social skills. Milo has the unique ability to display feelings through facial expressions and to converse in its own voice. He asks the children to name the emotions he demonstrates. Meanwhile, an instructor controls Milo with an iPad. Special education teachers can fully observe and take notes while the students and Milo socialize. This school's special needs teacher exclaimed, "I've seen students go from one- to two-word responses to full sentences." Three hundred U.S. schools are relying exclusively on Milo in their therapy.

KASPAR, a humanoid robot the size of a three-year-old child, takes yet another approach to the autistic individual. It exhibits a silicon face lacking features that would normally define its gender and emotion. This characteristic frees the children to imagine the robot as someone they are comfortable with, and assists them in opening up to talk and express themselves more easily. The robot responds through gesture and voice to convey basic emotions such as happiness, surprise, and sadness.

Zeno, a two-foot-tall robot, meets with seven-year-old Ethan who is diagnosed with autism. Zeno asks, "What is your favorite food?" Ethan replies, "Chocolate milk and french fries." The robot adds: "I love chocolate milk," raising its arm, encouraging Ethan to mimic him. Ethan's mother discovered Zeno and believed it would be a great friend: "It's always good for him [Ethan] to be put in different situations, things outside his normal routine . . . . It's a good learning and growing experience for him." So far, the two have had two therapy sessions. Ethan's mom thought the first meeting was uncomfortable and ineffective. However, after the second meeting, she describes, "This second time, Ethan fist-bumped Zeno, which was great. It shows he was a little more relaxed."

Parents exist as witnesses to these technological accomplishments. A robot named Romibo transformed a young autistic boy, whose mother testifies: "Before Romibo, he used to be at school all day and not say anything. But there is something about Romibo where he engages and asks questions." Mike's mother was impressed by Mike's valuable lessons in etiquette from Siri. Now, Mike nearly always compliments, "You look beautiful," just before his mom leaves for the day.

By changing the lives of children, AI is shaping the future of social therapies for autism spectrum disorder. It provides a helping hand to teachers and parents and individually focuses on each child. The robots discover the strengths and weaknesses of each student, which helps to get the child accustomed to communicating and socializing with others.

Robots personalize their teachings based on the child's fortes, development, and learning pace. Children with autism are all unique and require differentiated education so they can take as much time as needed with the robot. These AI robots are the ideal, nonjudgmental teachers and friends.

Children can gaze at a future in which they live independent, confident lives. Some have already been able to transfer to a mainstream class after interacting with artificial intelligence.

The first author of a study relating to AI education, emphasizes, "The long-term goal is not to create robots that will replace human therapists, but to augment them with key information that the therapists can use to personalize the therapy content and also make more engaging and naturalistic interactions between the robots and children with autism."

Mike's proposal was a daring conversation starter. While Siri and Mike will not be exchanging wedding vows, they are "engaged" in deep, endless conversations. Mike is opening up with his emotions, widening his range of vocabulary, and expressing his interests more easily. And though Siri may very well answer, "I'm not the marrying kind. My end user agreement does not include marriage," at least Mike even asked the question.

The global journey to finalizing AI therapy for students with autism spectrum disorder surely continues. ■

Carrying the Flame: Escalante's Journey

JOURNALISM

RICHARD XUE, Grade 8. Shanghai American School—Puxi Campus, Shanghai, China. Matthew Errico, *Educator*; Region-at-Large, *Affiliate*; Silver Medal

One hundred fifteen years ago, a quote by Emma Lazarus was etched into a stone pedestal that supported a colossal "woman with a torch." These words, "Give me your tired, your poor, your huddled masses yearning to breathe free . . . send these, the homeless, the tempest-tost to me" are distinctly American. Historically, the world has lauded America's commitment to freedom and praised it as the land of opportunity in which immigrants from all corners of the globe have come to thrive. Yet in modern times, immigration is a simmering controversy, and America has slammed its doors shut.

Simply put, immigration is a hot-button issue splattered across the pages of newspapers daily. One article in the *New York Times*, "American Dreamers," profiles hundreds of young Americans. In the interactive story wall, Juan Escalante's photo pops out as if it had been carved in bas-relief, the background fuzzy, but his physical features in sharp focus.

At the time of publication, Escalante had received his bachelor's degree in political science and his master's in public administration from Florida State University. Working as a digital immigration advocate, it is evident that Juan is smart and successful—but below the success that appears on the surface, there's a much larger story.

Escalante is a DREAMer. He is an undocumented immigrant who has for decades struggled to find a pathway to citizenship in American society.

Escalante's story begins in 2000, when his family first came to the U.S. from Venezuela. At the time, Juan was just eleven, and his two younger brothers only nine and seven years old. As Hugo Chávez rose to power and the future of Venezuela looked bleak, political and economic instability forced Escalante's family to migrate. During the first couple years, Escalante lived in America like any other teenager. "I went to school, skateboarded in the evening with my friends, and attempted to integrate as much as possible into my new country and culture," he wrote. Life was peaceful, normal.

But that serenity didn't last long. In 2007, Escalante, a senior in high school, was awarded a scholarship to study at Florida State University. His whole family was ecstatic. But when he completed the necessary paperwork for registration, he was hit with shocking news: he was undocumented.

Years before, Escalante's family's immigration attorney had mishandled their papers. All of their green cards had expired, and their efforts to become legal citizens of America were wasted. It was a devastating blow. Seeing his mom burst into tears and unsure how to resolve the situation, Escalante reassured, "Everything will be fine, mom."

At this point, it was impossible for Escalante's family to return to Venezuela. Not only had all of his relatives fled, but Chavez's regime had made their homeland dysfunctional. "The infrastructure is broken, the government . . . is more concerned about keeping power than keeping the lights on for the population." Yet, living illegally in the United States seemed risky. The family was at a crossroads.

Staying in the U.S. was the only way to build a brighter future for Juan and his brothers, but his parents faced the menacing monster of deportation. Although his mother and father abided by the laws, paid all of their taxes, and were lawful citizens, fear ran high in Escalante's home, as "[his] entire family became removable from the United States at any point in time."

But one day in 2012, as Juan walked into his office lobby, his life would change.

On TV, Escalante saw news of an immigration law being passed. Established by President Obama, the Deferred Action for Childhood Arrivals program (DACA) temporarily protected Central American children from deportation.

DACA was not created for all illegal immigrants. In order to benefit, the government imposed strict qualifications. First, applicants had to be younger than thirty-one when the program officially began. Next, they had to have entered the United States as children under sixteen years old before June 2007. After these two criteria were met, officials examined whether applicants were a threat to national security. Finally, candidates must have enrolled in school, completed their high school education, or participated in military service. Only after clearing these rigorous hurdles were they allowed to become DACA recipients. Fortunately for Juan and his brothers, they qualified.

To Escalante, DACA was a superhero who had pulled him from the jaws of despair. Imagine that for "years, you are consistently reminded that you would not be able to accomplish much due to your immigration status. That you wouldn't get a job, go to college or be accepted in the country that you grew up in," said Juan. But when DACA came along, there was a glimmer of hope.

"I called my mother in tears and proceeded to tell her that my brothers and I would be able to benefit from a program that would temporarily shield us from deportation while allowing us to work and drive legally," he said. Although Escalante knew the program would not benefit his parents, with DACA, he was finally able to re-enroll at FSU to pursue his Master's.

"With degrees in hand, I was able to obtain a job as a digital immigration advocate, putting my years of experience and passion to good use." For Juan, his commitment to fight for the rights of other undocumented immigrants was stronger than ever.

Since its initiation, nearly 800,000 young adults have benefited from DACA; however, its history is controversial. While some like former president Obama see it as a human rights issue, helping the children who are "Americans in their heart, in their minds, in every single way but . . . on paper," others perceive it as a free handout, helping people who have come to the country illegally.

There are political objections as well. Many right-leaning opponents think the creation of DACA was an executive overreach of Obama's power, and as one senator described it, "an affront to the process of representative government [which circumvented] Congress." With all of these polarizing perspectives, a storm began to brew.

In the lead-up to the 2016 presidential elections, when Escalante was just starting his new job, immigration moved to the forefront of the debate. Donald Trump fervently campaigned for more border protection and the deportation of illegal immigrants. So, when he won the presidency, DACA's legitimacy was directly in the crosshairs. Echoing the ideas of other Republicans, Trump announced in September 2017 that he would repeal the program within six months. This, he said, would give legislative rights back to Congress, allowing them to draft a solution regarding DREAMers like Escalante.

With this newfound antagonism towards DACA, advocates such as Juan, now more high-profiled in media outlets, protested hard to voice their opinions. Later, multiple court rulings delayed Trump's decision and forced the administration to hand out DACA renewal applications after March 2018.

Yet, circumstances failed to deliver renewals to many former DACA recipients, throwing DREAMers into a state of uncertainty. Despite the fact that several officials, such as Defense Secretary James Mattis, claimed that deporting the DREAMers wasn't a priority, Juan said that even parents "who are dropping off their kids to school or are making their way to work" have been deported on the spot. In other words, no person was exempt from persecution.

Escalante fought hard to preserve DACA, not just for himself but for others like him. He says, "A new report from the Institute on Taxation and Economic Policy estimates that undocumented immigrants, the same people Trump referred to as drug dealers, murderers, and rapists, contribute $11.74 billion in state and local taxes." Ultimately, he feels that most illegal immigrants are misunderstood, and contrary to common belief, DACA recipients are not the "freeloaders" others claim them to be.

His assertions also echo the thoughts of many other advocates, that young DREAMers are not asking for free rides. Instead, DACA allows bright, educated, and responsible people to become contributive members of American society, in hopes that one day they may gain citizenship.

Nikola Tesla. Albert Einstein. Joseph Pulitzer. All were immigrants who transformed America in the most beautiful ways because they were encouraged to "breathe free." Had the doors been closed, not open, America's landscape would not be the beacon of diversity and innovation it is today.

Currently, America is reaching its boiling point, and the politics around DACA remain uncertain.

"The thought that you would be STRIPPED of your DACA status is not just traumatizing, it's dehumanizing and exhausting," Escalante wrote in his "101 Guide," a tweet opening up on life as a DREAMer under the new administration. As he wrapped up his thoughts, his final words were, "PLEASE take care of yourselves. And if [you're] an ally, please take care of Dreamers now more than ever."

No matter your personal perspective, whether for or against DACA, you can't ignore the symbolism of Lady Liberty. The U.S. has always strived to embrace the struggling, industrious populations of the world. And it is these resilient and diligent people—people like Escalante, who make America great and still carry the torch of the American dream. ∎

Not Just Clickbait

JOURNALISM

BRIANNA YI, Grade 10. Carl Sandburg High School, Orland Park, IL. Susan Chang, *Edu.* Chicago Area Writing Project, *Affiliate*; Silver Medal

Although the numbers of those affected by depression is on the rise, the mental health of students is seen as an afterthought, a joke, or a call for attention when, in fact, it is anything but. Each high school student struggles with mental health and the stigmatized perception of that mental health journey in his or her own way.

* * *

Steven sat in the clinic, the only sounds being the ticking of the clock on the wall behind him and his foot tapping to the beat. The walls were a simple beige and lacked decoration, creating a somewhat stale atmosphere. Seated across from him at a desk, his counselor looked at him through her glasses, her back perfectly straight and not a single hair out of place. Next to Steven, his father's face was unreadable. Whatever thoughts or emotions he had, he kept them to himself. Everybody in the room was quiet.

The counselor broke the silence first, clearing her throat. "As you know, we received your official diagnosis," she said, her tone blunt.

Depression.

Steven couldn't help but let out a small sigh of relief. For years, he had felt something was off, but had not understood the degree of it. He looked over at his father, unsure about how he would react. His father always blamed himself for anything that happened to his family and that was the main reason Steven had waited so long to get help.

According to the National Institute of Mental Health (NIMH), an estimated 2.2 million teens from age twelve to seventeen had "at least one major depressive episode with severe impairment" in 2016. Of these 2.2 million, 60 percent did not seek out or receive treatment. The Anxiety and Depression Association of America (ADAA) reported that 50 percent of all lifelong cases of mental illness begin developing at fourteen years old. In addition, the average delay from onset to intervention is eight to ten years. Without treatment, depression and other mental health issues may continue further in life. In 2015, the ADAA stated that "40 million adults suffer from an anxiety disorder and 75% experience their first anxiety episode by 22."

...ter trying to binge drink herself to death, Mia's face remained neutral as her psychiatrist told her the news. She had been officially diagnosed with manic depression and bipolar disorder and already had a prescription for pills written out for her. There was no significant emotion towards her diagnosis, as Mia already knew that she was showing signs of a mental illness. The diagnosis and prescription were like telling her she needed water to stay hydrated.

She had been in the hospital for only a day, but she was already tired of it. The blinding lights and sterile smell made her feel sick, and the nursing staff didn't help make things any better. It was Tuesday and she should have been in school, helping her friends with their group project about *Jane Eyre*.

* * *

The cause of depression and other mental health conditions vary from person to person. The Mental Health Foundation states, "Depression can happen suddenly as a result of physical illness, experiences dating back to childhood, unemployment, bereavement, family problems, or other life-changing events."

When asked about what had influenced her mental health the most, Mia replied that she had been sexually harassed over a period of three months. She explained, "Sexual harassment isn't just scary; it's humiliating, embarrassing, and the frustration and helplessness one feels is beyond belief, which is why it had such a significant impact on my mental health."

Victims of sexual assault may experience flashbacks. The experience of sexual assault may cause a mental illness or amplify existing ones, making a victim feel ashamed, shocked, or isolated. After her experience, Mia feels extremely uncomfortable being touched, even by close friends or relatives. When her shoulder was unexpectedly grabbed at a party, Mia began hyperventilating and then had a panic attack.

Meanwhile, the biggest impact on Steven's mental health was his childhood history of bullying. According to bullyingstatistics.org, "Both bullies and their victims are more likely to suffer from depression than youth who are not involved in bullying. This connection can be long-lasting; people who are bullied as children are more likely to suffer from depression as an adult than children not involved in bullying."

"Ever since preschool, I was bullied for my size, my looks, and my interests," Steven recounted. "The bullying 'peaked' in third grade. I was pushed around and beat up. I would come home with multiple bruises. What made everything worse was that I could never spill any of this to my parents because, at the time, my family was not in the best of situations. I did not want to become another problem to them."

For high school students like Mia and Steven, the effects of depression can hinder success, motivation, and the pursuit of future plans. Haesue Jo, who works with the ADAA, states, "Depression can impact every area of your life, including but not limited to how you sleep and eat, your education and career, your relationships, health, and concentration . . . Leaving depression untreated can lead to many other complications in one's personal and professional life."

Mia, a sophomore in high school, was diagnosed with manic depression, bipolar disorder, and severe social anxiety during her freshman year. When asked about how her mental health has influenced her life, Mia responded, "The anxiety I feel over whether my friends like me or not has harmed many relationships I cherished; it had caused me to lose motivation in school. It's difficult for me to work through everyday social interactions like paying for food or asking for directions. I'm unable to perform simple tasks like throwing away a wrapper in fear that people will stare at me. I feel as if I'm unable to function like a normal human being."

Having his identity attacked from a young age, Steven hid the effects of his depression until an attempted suicide finally led him to be diagnosed. When asked about what influenced his mental health the most, he said, "People. Those who can't sympathize, empathize, or just have somewhat of an understanding of what mental health really [is] tend to degrade it as 'seeking attention' or an 'excuse.' To this day, it affects me, the way I think of myself, my confidence, my anxiety."

* * *

Because of the rise in social media usage, the image and identity of users have changed. In the debate over the benefits and disadvantages of social media, one clear effect is that it has led to an increase in cyberbullying and a rise in negative behaviors. Cyberbullying, as well as the dramatization of self-harm, can potentially influence youth at high risk of depression. Other negative effects of social media include a self-conscious response to body image and constant comparison to others. The Child Mind Institute reported that in recent studies, teenagers and young adults who spend a large amount of time on social media were shown to have a 13 percent to 66 percent higher rate of reported depression than those who do not.

Steven felt that social media treated mental health as a trend or an excuse. He stated that because of the reputation of depression on social media, he was not taken seriously when he tried to come forward with his mental health. "It's led to me feeling ashamed for something that I believe is not my fault," he elaborated.

Meanwhile, Mia felt neutral about the effect of social media on youth with depression. She believes that social media is a "great platform for sharing experiences and educating large sums of people." However, she also agrees that social media can be harmful. Mia elaborated, "Of course, we've all seen edgy accounts with pictures and jokes regarding mental health. These are not only immediately harmful to anyone who views it, but also reinforce pretty much every known stigma attached to mental illnesses. Therefore, it's a bit difficult to say for sure whether social media has had a solid positive or negative impact."

While neutral about social media, Mia felt that representation of mental health in media could have a negative impact. The television series *13 Reasons Why* quickly gained fame upon its release as it handled topics relating to mental health; however, the show received mixed reviews because of its glorification of suicide. Fox News reported that two teens were triggered by *13 Reasons Why*, leading them to commit suicide. This effect caused alarm in parents.

When asked about her opinions on the show, Mia was at first excited for its release but then became disappointed. "I was excited that a show was shedding light on bullying and mental health, but the way the show portrays the issues of someone with a mental illness and how it portrays high school life in general was simply unrealistic."

As somebody who experienced depression and suicidal thoughts, she stopped watching after a few episodes. "Of course, it's a TV show and must be dramatic, but it seriously turned high school into some kind of war zone that hardly anyone who suffers from a mental illness can relate to. It seems that almost every character was toxic and made suicide seem like something people commit as an act of revenge to have a last laugh."

While *13 Reasons* Why mishandles certain aspects of mental health, the show highlights the importance of having a support system. Support systems or peer groups are extremely beneficial for those with depression or other mental health disorders. With isolation being an effect of depression, having a trusted person to talk to allows a person affected by a mental illness to openly speak about their emotions in a safe environment. A healthy interaction may also influence their decision to seek help through a therapist or support group.

Mia, unfortunately, lacked a strong support group that she could trust and talk to. She explained, "Therapy has been discussed but floated off to the back of everyone's minds. I've been given the generic 'You need to get out there and live life in order to help yourself!' talk. However, when it comes down to it, my family—as well as many others—do not understand how I feel nor do they really attempt to. One of the worst feelings is believing that your family is uncomfortable or annoyed with you over something that you are desperately rying to, but can't quite, control."

Steven also felt that he lacked a support system. Living in a religious family, he refrained from telling his parents or other close relatives about how he feels. Currently, only his father knows about his depression. Despite the relief of his diagnosis, Steven still has to keep his mental health a secret from most of his family, which is very isolating. He added, "In terms of contribution to my mental health, it was made worse because of how unwelcoming this idea is to them."

* * *

According to Mental Health America, the mental health of teens is suffering because not enough are pursuing a diagnosis. Currently, the majority of adults affected by mental health are continuing this trend. Despite the stigma surrounding mental health, Mia and Steven both expressed how their diagnosis proved helpful. Mia mentioned that a proper diagnosis and treatment has greatly improved her health and she's very grateful for those who have helped her. "I strongly encourage anyone else struggling to reach out because, although terrifying at first, it is so rewarding."

Through treatment, Steven hopes to further his recovery and pursue his interests. "I'd also like to work [in] any occupation in the medical field. Not only am I interested in that field of science, but I love to help people in any way I can. This would probably require a healthy state of mind."

Similarly, Mia found hope in her recovery. She said, "I'm slowly becoming a more confident, social, and happy person. I'm able to hold conversations with strangers, which is something that seems so minute to others, but used to seem nearly impossible to me. Sometimes I feel as if nothing has changed, but looking back on myself two years ago or even five months ago makes me realize how different I am."

Reflecting on what he learned throughout this journey, Steven realized that he can't blame himself for the negatives in his life. Mia took a different approach, having felt that she learned more about others than herself. She stated, "As a naturally timid person, I always assumed the worst when people approached me. Thinking that everyone was evil by default felt safer than trusting and seeing the good in everyone. However, that was selfish of me. One thing I have learned is that we are not all that special; humans are all nervous, anxious beings. We all face challenges and we are all scared, but we usually are good, and I'm glad I've come to that realization." ■

The Daniel Project

NOVEL WRITING

RACHEL EASTMAN, Grade 10. Flandreau High School, Flandreau, SD. Jamie Fryslie, *Educator*; The University of South Dakota, *Affiliate*; Silver Medal

"Do you know why you're here?" The girl shifted in her seat. She was anxious at the thought of being in the principal's office—and there she was in the seat of the principal's office. She had never been in there before, she didn't know what was needed of her. Sitting was an obvious option, but she was making a fool of herself just being in her seat. She kept fidgeting in her seat; there wasn't a moment where she sat still. There was so much to take in in just a couple moments. She didn't know what to focus on since the principal wasn't looking at her.

A photo of the principal and his wife were on the desk in front of the girl. The photograph was an innocent, wedding photograph of a newly wedded bride and groom. It frightened her. Anything in a room not familiar to her was intimidating. Even the small succulent plant on the edge of the desk terrified her. She had no words to say. She couldn't think straight. She couldn't think correctly. The room felt suffocating. The room was getting smaller and smaller by the second.

"Caelyn," the principal spoke again. "Do you know why you're here?" The same question. He asked for the second and final time. Caelyn didn't know how to respond. There was never a time she had to go to the principal's office. There wasn't anything wrong with her behavior. She had some problems just like everybody else. She turned things in late every once in a while. She missed school sometimes. Caelyn didn't think she missed so much school that she needed to be in the principal's office.

Seconds felt like hours while Caelyn tried to think of an answer. "I . . . I'm not entirely sure, but if it's because of my grades . . . I told you many, many times before—"

"No, Caelyn, it isn't because of that. Your grades are fine." The principal spoke, finally facing the girl. Caelyn let out a sigh of relief and felt relaxed. It didn't last long though. She realized that it wasn't because of her grades and she absolutely had no idea why she was sitting in the principal's office. Caelyn was panicking again. It wasn't because of the grades or attendance. What could it be? Was it because of the fight she had months ago? It was obvious and clear that everyone had moved on. Everybody could talk to each other like it had never happened.

Caelyn hoped it would be because of the old fight. It wouldn't have surprised her if the main person got offended and refused the apology again. Each day was different for them, the way they would treat her was always unknown. Caelyn would try and talk, but sometimes they didn't want to and acted rude. She couldn't control their behavior and knew they couldn't control it either. She didn't have a full understanding, but she understood when she needed to back off. Now, sitting in the office, she had done something wrong that she didn't know about.

The office's door opened, making Caelyn jump in her seat. It made her sit still, finally. She watched as the principal held the door open for a woman to walk inside. It made Caelyn's heart race, she knew exactly who the woman was. The woman was about four foot and nine inches. She dressed as if she was a lawyer who was about to win the case and she won every case. Caelyn knew this by heart. The woman's name was Maureen Harrison. She was her ex-boyfriend's aunt. Maureen was horrifying. Caelyn's four-foot-nine worst nightmare. Once she had gotten a lecture from that woman and it traumatized her. She couldn't move on without thinking about the words she spoke . . . otherwise yelled.

Maureen was known for being intimidating. She was never the big teddy bear as most would put it. The ones who said she was a teddy bear were all wrong. Everybody was wrong about her. Maureen had always been intimidating. She knew exactly what to say when she wanted to get you depressed or furious. She knew who you were without having to think twice. Caelyn didn't know if it was because of Maureen's horrid methods, but listening to her words made her think twice. There were things that she didn't know existed about herself until she had that lecture from her ex-boyfriend's aunt.

Caelyn sat next to Maureen, the most anxious and worried she had ever been in her life. She wasn't this close to Maureen ever, not even during her own lecture. Maureen sat only a couple inches away from Caelyn. She was still the same person she was when first Caelyn met her and during the lecture. She sat still and made herself look tall. The woman was strong and independent. That was no question. It didn't take her long to notice Caelyn.

"For god's sake, relax. Everybody can feel that you're tense in a twenty-mile radius." Maureen spoke sharply. It nearly stung Caelyn. Words that came out of Maureen's mouth always hurt. Words didn't sting the principal though. He chuckled at Maureen's remark. He was even agreeing with her as he shut the door. He walked back to his desk and sat down in front of the women. Maureen didn't speak much and she wasn't going to speak anytime soon.

It worried Caelyn once Maureen pulled out envelopes from her purse. She saw the envelopes before, but not frequently. She remembered getting one envelope exactly the same. It was a big, white envelope. It was the kind used for delivering certificates. It surprised her when Maureen pulled out three more of the same envelopes. She plopped all of them on top of the principal's desk. The principal grabbed them and took a quick glance at them. Caelyn was too afraid to take a glance. She somewhat had an idea on what it was about. She was going to get in trouble for what she was doing to Maureen's nephew. She was guilty of using him, but she was too guilty to say for what.

The principal handed the envelopes to Caelyn. She took them, shaking more than ever. It raised a concern for both the principal and Maureen. "These are all for you. Maureen told me that these were folded up with your name on and she put them into bigger envelopes. I believe that these all are dated." The principal explained, watching Caelyn mess around while opening it. She didn't know how to properly open up a sealed up letter. Usually, she received letters that were folded up in another piece of paper with her name on it. This was probably the case.

Caelyn finally got one of the envelopes opened. She could feel the burning eyes of the people inside of the room. She didn't have to pull out half of a piece of paper before knowing who it was. She knew exactly who these were from. Still, she didn't have a clue why she was in the principal's office. She had done nothing wrong, beside using Maureen's nephew for her own good. Maureen had probably read the letters and saw what Caelyn was doing. Now, she was reporting her for it. Caelyn knew that the time had come where she was going to get in some serious trouble with messing with the wrong family. She had done that before and hadn't learned her lesson since she was still messing with the same family.

"Caelyn," the principal spoke again. "Are you close with Daniel Harrison?" He asked. Caelyn's eyes widen. She didn't know what to say. She remembered that she needed to keep quiet about Daniel, behalf of his own words. She remembered him telling her that they needed to be a secret and that he wasn't comfortable being seen with her anymore. Caelyn understood and kept true to his word. She couldn't go to him but he could go to her. It depended on the day. Especially since the big fight.

The principal took the silence as a yes. He was well aware of the fight that had happened between them and somewhat of the reason why. Caelyn and Daniel dated for a month or two, but Daniel ended it. No one was quite sure of the reason why. Caelyn was heartbroken and angry, but she moved on quickly. It happened during the summer before. The first days of school, Caelyn wanted to apologize for what her brother had sent to Daniel. He told her it was okay, but she didn't believe it one bit.

The fight started during the first few weeks of school. Caelyn's brother, Alexander, apologized to Daniel. He explained that Caelyn was also angry too and that she wanted to find ways to make him angry alongside her friends too. Daniel was shocked and hurt. He never noticed it and all he wanted was to be friends with Caelyn again. He was trying to move on and keep his emotions inside. It was okay until he ran into her again. Daniel greeted and told her what was happening that day, she said something that he didn't hear. All he did was ask about what she said, but she started to curse names at him. Hurtful names.

Soon after, all of Caelyn's friends joined in. Daniel quickly ran away. He didn't want to be around them anymore. He quickly told the few friends he had about what happened. They all suggested that he needed to confront them. Daniel did what they told him to do. He walked back to the group of friends. He had no idea what to do. What Daniel did shock him and everyone else. He ran up to them and started to shout at every single one of them. Some of those friends never even heard him speak. There he was, shouting at the top of his lungs at them.

Caelyn and her friends quickly left. They went to the police and parents. They all went to the police and school. Caelyn's mother, Cynthia, called Daniel soon after. She was yelling at him over the phone and Caelyn noticed that he was actually angry. He didn't seem affected that he was being yelled at over the phone. He argued back that he only did it because Cynthia's daughter was calling him names he hated. Caelyn found out information she didn't know about Daniel. She knew she needed to talk to him.

The next day at school, it was even more of a shocker. Caelyn went into the school, expecting Daniel to get in trouble. Everything was turned around and she was getting in trouble. The principal and counselor both said Daniel's outburst wasn't bullying, but instead it was self-defense. That morning, Daniel and his aunt went into the school and gave his side of the story. Caelyn couldn't understand why his overruled hers. She knew why it was though. She had left out the big part why Daniel was shouting at her and her group of friends. She got grounded by her mother after she found out the truth. She was even forced to come out with her new boyfriend.

It was surprising for Caelyn to find out that Daniel wanted to talk too. He wasn't the best speaker, but when he wanted to talk, it was a big deal. She had never actually had an actual talk with him at that time. By the end of the week, Caelyn was able to catch Daniel alone. They talked for hours about what happened between them. She could sense that he wasn't too interested in her new boyfriend. All he could say about it was, "Good for you. Good for you." Caelyn didn't know if it was a rude remark or not. It seemed like the first "good for you" was genuine, but the second wasn't.

"Were you close with Daniel Harrison?" The principal repeated his question again. Caelyn was caught off-guard again.

"We were close, but then . . . we kind of just separated." Caelyn somewhat told the truth. There was so much she was leaving out. She hoped she didn't say the wrong thing. Maureen still looked the same, but her eyes changed. Her eyes were still stern as ever, but they were also slowly softening up.

Maureen cleared her throat and adjusted her posture. "Daniel committed suicide on Friday night. No one was home to stop him." She spoke bitterly. Caelyn's mind fell apart right then and there. The day had come. She wasn't prepared or expected it. She felt guilty. She didn't understand Maureen's reaction either. She was acting like it never happened and it was just a thing that happened in a television show. Caelyn didn't know what to say anymore. She couldn't believe Daniel actually did it.

Caelyn sat up straight and sighed. She clutched onto the envelopes for dear life. "I'm sorry for your loss, Maureen. Daniel is—"

"Was," Maureen corrected her. The word "was" felt like it stabbed Caelyn in the gut. She was never going to get used to using "was" whenever she would talk about her friend . . . otherwise her best friend. She thought of Daniel as the best person there was. She never felt sad around him, she always felt joy when being in his presence. Now, he was no longer there. Maureen looked confused in her stern eyes. Caelyn could see it clearly. Maureen spoke again, "We both know why. I don't know why he didn't ask for help. I was hoping you could find out why. I want you to find out why he thought it could only end by . . . " She couldn't finish her sentence.

The envelopes looked lifeless. They were lifeless. The one who wrote them was gone. Gone for good. Caelyn didn't know what to say or think. "I'll try to figure out why." She spoke in a whisper. There wasn't much to do now. The last letter she received from Daniel was on Friday morning. She couldn't believe it. That was the final letter she got physically from him. Daniel would walk up to her and hand her the folded up letter. They were always four or six pages long. Caelyn thought it was a lot, but she knew he always could have written more.

Now, there were all these new letters and Caelyn knew not all of them had everything on it. She didn't know how she would be able to read them all. Supposedly, every single letter was dated. She didn't know if she needed to read them all in order or just to read whatever one was in front of her. Caelyn assumed Daniel would have written her instructions. That's what he did before after she tried speaking to his aunt. His aunt drove off with him before Caelyn could take another step towards the car. That next Monday, she received a couple letters with some instructions on how to read them.

Maureen left the office quickly. She didn't say goodbye or anything. She got up and walked away. She left the principal with Caelyn. He didn't know what else to say. He didn't know what to do. This was the first time a student had actually committed suicide. "Caelyn . . . you can be excused for the rest of the day. Take your time reading the letters. I have no clue on what's inside. I'm hoping for clues or signs on why he was like that," the principal explained. He opened up the door for her.

Caelyn sighed and shoved the envelopes into her backpack. "That would be appreciated. I'll walk home, no worries. It'll give me some time before I start reading these." She explained, throwing her backpack over her shoulder. The principal smiled and nodded. Caelyn walked out of the door to see no one else. Maureen wasn't even outside, she already sped off in her car. She sighed, walking outside of the office. She saw that her classmates were still in lunch. Caelyn didn't even want to tell her friends that she was leaving. She didn't want anybody to know, she didn't want to face anybody. Her best friend was gone, really gone. He wasn't gone for another appointment; he was gone forever.

The sun was covered with dark clouds. It was the first gloomy day of the start of many gloomy days. Caelyn didn't know what to feel. The sky was affecting her as well, it was making her think of her best friend. He loved gloomy days, he loved the idea there might be a chance of rain. He loved thinking of rain, but hated being in the rain. He hated sunny days, but he loved the idea of them. He hated the heat, but he loved being warm. Gloomy days was one of his best days. On gloomy days, he could actually sleep. Gloomy days made him feel down, but he also felt happy when his aunt didn't complain about him being his room.

Daniel was the best person Caelyn knew. She knew he was the best person alive. All she could think of now how the best person alive turned out being the best dead person. She couldn't understand why he didn't want help. In all the letters before, he said he didn't like crying out for help. She couldn't understand why he felt that way. Help was the thing that could have saved her best friend.

After spending thirty minutes walking, Caelyn realized. She realized that Daniel did want help. In many, many letters, he wanted help. He never said it blankly. Thinking of the past letters made it obvious that he wanted help. There was a point where the word "help" stopped appearing in the letters. Caelyn needed to figure out why Daniel gave up asking. ■

Iron Spires

NOVEL WRITING

LIAM ULLAND-JOY, Grade 9. Bothwell Middle School, Marquette, MI. Paula Diedrich, *Educator*; Region-at-Large, *Affiliate*; Silver Medal

"Jenkins, Jason. 107th Arporian Infantry, Current Assignment: Mozicran Support Force," the bald security guard droned. His cap was tilted at an angle on his head like it would fall off at any minute. Standing in a concrete checkpoint box behind thick glass, he looked up from his holoscreen and peered at me. He spent a second or two analyzing the face on the sleek digital screen and the one staring up at him. He seemed to reach the conclusion that I was who I claimed to be, tapped a few buttons on the holoscreen display, said "confirmed" a single time, and thrust what looked to be a ticket into my hand. I stared down at the slip of paper. The words "Hyena Base, Meeting Tent Gamma, 1400 hours" were stamped onto the surface. Instructions on where to go now that I am in Mozicra, I assumed. Knowing that it was past 1300, I stumbled past two slightly amused Mozicran soldiers and over the border, taking on a quick trot. I shouldered the heavy backpack that I had slung over my shoulder for the commute here. It was filled with weapons and equipment provided by the Arporian Army.

I walked across the border and took in a massive array of tents, concrete buildings, wooden guard towers, and a few bigger buildings constructed out of a metallic alloy. The compound stretched outward as far as I could see. I saw a Mozicran sentry carrying a sleek TouchPad standing underneath a wooden signpost reading "Welcome to Hyena Base." As I approached him, I saw the words "Tongo Niji keep out. That means YOU." scrawled in smaller lettering underneath. When he saw me approaching he quickly directed his attention to me. *Probably a guide for new soldiers,* I thought. When I approached him, I asked how I might get to Meeting Tent Gamma. "Oh, Meeting Tent Gamma ain't a tent anymore, pal." the man said. He flicked his fingers across the screen, then turned the silvery pad to me. "Meeting *Room* Gamma, now, pal. They're trying to modernize around here. They've got fancy skyscrapers with hoverlifts down in the cities, but the military camps get only a digital pad to keep the newbies in the loop?"

There was nothing hostile about the man, he just seemed to thoroughly enjoy directing new recruits across the base.

I thought back to the briefing. Since even before the Dividing, Arporia and Mozicra had been strong allies. The countries provided military and financial support for one another, maintaining one of the steadiest alliances of the time. This was doubly impressive especially because alliances of that time tended to be short-lived and cold, with looking-over-the-shoulder, distrust, and hostility. Since the Dividing, the bond between the two countries has, if anything, tightened. Arporia maintains commerce with Mozicra, trading lumber and ore in great shipments, while Mozicra sells electronics.

Seven years ago, a group of insurgents known as the Tongo Niji formed in what was a well-planned and devastating series of attacks on Mozicran military bases. After the rapid and aggressive campaign was mostly quelled, the Mozicran government called upon their allies, the Arporians, to provide military aid.

Note that I said "mostly" quelled, for the Tongo Niji still hold one great city that fell in their original campaign: Iron Spires. One of the most advanced Mozicran cities, it was the last to fall, but the Tongo Niji had years to plan their campaign. They added the technological innovations to their own technology and now zealously guard the city.

More Mozicran and Arporian troops have died in the city of Iron Spires than every other Mozicran city combined. Of course, the rebel group's hold has loosened over the years, and the city has essentially become a massive battleground between the Arporians, the Mozicrans, the Tongo Niji, and other fledgling militias fighting for one reason or another.

Over the years, the Tongo Niji have grown more powerful and more and more Arporian troops were sent to fight in the foreign war. I knew that eventually I would have to enter the Arporian Grand Military. Of course, the time came, and I was herded to the Mozicran front within a week.

I boarded an armored transport which rendezvoused with a large campaign of other transports, all heading into Mozicra.

As I walked along the hard gravel path, I saw soldiers with Arporian and Mozicran uniforms, of every rank and regiment, talking and strategizing. I finally arrived outside of a small, boxy building constructed from a thick, silvery metal. The door was of sturdy maple wood, rough to the touch. As I opened it, it creaked and groaned on its shiny new hinges. I crept into Meeting Room Gamma.

I got the sensation of being inside of a cramped boxcar. The room seemed much larger on the outside, but in reality the interior was small and dark, illuminated only by several strips of fluorescent lights that flickered intermittently. A group of around twenty Arporian soldiers were huddled together, muttering and talking, facing a tall, straight-backed man in officer's uniform. I surmised that the man was the commander of my squad.

As the officer raised his hand, the hubbub ceased almost instantly, the soldiers standing rigidly at attention. They had formed up into two lines of ten. I quickly took my place at the end of the front line.

"Glad you could join us, private." the officer said. He allowed the soldiers to chuckle momentarily before continuing. "My name is Commander Bunker. I am the leader of this squad. Before I begin I would like you all to know that you are doing a great service to your country. The citizens of Arporia and Mozicra are indebted to you for keeping them safe." Now that I was up close, I saw that the officer had the beginnings of a scraggly beard and brown hair that was slowly turning gray. His dark, cold brown eyes had a look of true experience and first-hand knowledge of the field of battle about them, possibly disguising pain. He was wearing the standard green Arporian combat fatigues, but with several medals of various sizes hanging from them.

He continued. "As you know, the Tongo Niji Insurrection has recently been gaining ground in Iron Spires and several other key footholds. They are becoming bolder with every fresh rebel that streams into their bases."

"The Mozicran government claims that they have some degree of control over the situation, but the truth is, without us, they'd have collapsed already." Commander Bunker said gravely, his jaw set in a cold grimace. "The Iron Spires front is looking particularly grim," he went on. "The Mozicrans have lost more than a third of their positions there, including a particularly valuable supply depot containing huge stores of explosives, weapons, and vehicle parts."

"The Arporian Military assigns soldiers with specific specialties to the Iron Spires front. Trackers, climbers, snipers, demolitionists, engineers, many of which you will find amongst us here today."

The troops in the room were rapidly growing agitated. I myself am a Class-Silver Combat Engineer (CE) who graduated from the Arporian Military Academy three years ago. I knew what was coming next, but it was difficult for me to accept. I'd just arrived in Mozicra, and now they're throwing me straight into Iron Spires? Was the situation there really that bad?

"I want all of you to be aware that this assignment is not a death sentence. We will be providing infantry support to an Elite Regiment of the Mozicran army along with two other squads of Arporian commandos that we will work alongside," our commander explained. "Working together, the Mozicrans and the Arporians, we will liberate the supply depot and regain the ground we lost in Iron Spires, hopefully using the momentum to forcibly *shove*," he clenched his fist grinding his teeth, "the Tongo Niji out of Iron Spires for good."

There was no cheering. In fact, the room was dead silent. I shifted uncomfortably.

"A7, come up here," called Commander Bunker, beckoning with his right hand. The man standing next to me detached from the row and walked stiffly up to Commander Bunker, flanking him. "This is Lieutenant A7, my second in command, from the Augment Corps," Commander Bunker informed us.

Augments are those citizens of Arporia and Mozicra wealthy enough to mechanically enhance their body. Some of them surgically alter their appearance, others enhance eyesight, speed, strength, hand-eye coordination, and stamina. Still others mechanically implant weapons in their skin. Most things I have heard about the augments are rumors or farfetched story-spinning.

However, it does make sense for an augment to join the army. Their enhanced physical abilities could be put to great use here, it seems.

Lieutenant A7 appears to be primarily metal from the left shoulder down. There is also a titanium band encircling his forehead, squeezing in on his head. I can just barely see it beneath his combat helmet. It looks painful. A few lights of various colors flicker across the metallic ring.

"Lieutenant A7 is a highly capable soldier, with many of his physical abilities increased or modified. He can keep up a sprint much longer than you or I, and the circlet on his forehead can scan his surroundings for hidden assailants." barked Commander Bunker. The Commander's voice took on a quieter, but no less gravelly tone. "Should I be unavailable to give orders or rendered . . . incapacitated, the Lieutenant will inherit command of this squadron."

There was a momentary pause. "Is that clear?" he questioned. A resounding chorus of "Yes, sir" rose over the troops. "Good, good." said Bunker, "We'll board the transport at oh eight hundred hours tomorrow morning."

The soldiers filed out of the room in a single file line that widened at the door, with people shoving one another to get out. I was the last to leave. As I walked out, I was sure that I felt A7's eye on me. I wondered if that was because of some upgrade he made to it.

I slept in a stuffy, tepid canvas tent crammed with Arporian soldiers from my squad. I set my backpack on the ground next to me and stretched out on a cot. I was just nodding off when someone sitting next to me jostled me. "Hey, you awake?" came the rough voice.

I rolled over. "Mmmph . . . yeah . . . " I muttered. "I'm Daniels. Infantry. Academy Graduate." the man said. "Jenkins." I told him. "CE. I got out of the Academy three years back."

I heard a click. An electric lantern sprang to life, and I saw the man's face through the dim light. "CE, huh? Figures they'd take you to Iron Spires. Urban warfare, strategizin', blowin' up bridges, and such. I've come out of two assignments already, Mozicran countryside. I think this one'll be my last, I won't lie."

I sat up. "Is it really that bad in Iron Spires?" Daniels leaned in close. A jagged scar ran across his cheek, partially obscured by a thick mop of dark brown hair. "Yeah," was all he said for a good minute. "I've heard stories of sentries gettin' cornered in the abandoned streets of the city, being killed and hung like trophies from the streetlights."

I tried to suppress the grotesque image that was forcing its way into my mind. "Well then," I said matter-of-factly, "It would be good to have a partner." After a moment, Daniels' face split in a grin, and he slapped his hand to my back. "You know what, Jenkins? I was thinkin' the exact same thing." After a moment, he turned the lantern off.

I rolled over to go back to sleep, lying in silence for a second, before the lantern switched on for a second time and Daniels, stonefaced and half-illuminated by the lantern, whispered hoarsely in the dark. "One more thing, partner. Iron Spires is notorious for whittling away at the mood of a fighting force, and nerves are already frayed 'cause of the Tongo's movements. The Arporian government has tried to suppress the desertion numbers, but my advice? Keep your eye on the enemies *and* the friends."

The next day, I woke up early and waited for the transports outside in the brisk morning air. It was 0800 on the dot when the first one arrived. The massive armored truck rose more than ten feet above the ground, rumbling into view just as Commander Bunker exited a large tent. A7 came out with him. The transport was considerably louder than I had expected, the engine roaring and distinct even from hundreds of yards away.

The two officers waited by a large patch of dirt obviously designated for transports. The vehicle rolled to a stop a few feet from the two men.

Some Arporian sentries roused a group of troops from sleep a few tents over from where my comrades slept. Grumbling and snarling, the soldiers marched to the transport, lining up into formation. As the back wall slid down into a ramp, several wounded soldiers trudged off of the transport and were greeted by medics. I watched as the huge vehicle swallowed the outgoing squad up like a hungry bear.

A few minutes after the squad had boarded their transport, a second one appeared on the horizon. Commander Bunker sent A7 to wake the other members of my squad, who rose from the tent one by one. Daniels was one of the last, loudly protesting that the augment had interrupted a fantastic dream. Commander Bunker waved me over before everyone reached him. I trotted to the Commander and joined ranks with Daniels and the other troops. The two lines of Arporians stood in the dawn light buzzing with conversation as a group of wounded soldiers were helped off the transport by their uninjured comrades and into the arms of the medics.

Finally, Commander Bunker gave the order to board the transport, and we all marched single file into the armored truck.

Inside of the truck were two rows of hard, aluminum benches constructed out of a simple aluminum lattice, separated by a thin aisle. The floor was grimy and made of the same lattice. Bright lights in the ceiling cast an orange glow over the metal walls. Openings under the benches allowed for storage of equipment. I stowed my backpack underneath the benches and took a seat at the far end of the transport.

The aisle was narrow and cramped, only one person wide, and I got the surreal impression of being on a school bus. From where I was sitting, I could see the driver's seat and another seat, occupied by a sentry, through a mesh of wire. A thick metal door with a large and advanced DNALock prevented any unauthorized personnel from entering.

Daniels sat to my immediate right, and a man with a stretched, gaunt face and darting yellow eyes sat crosslegged directly across the aisle from me. "Tiger," whispered Daniels in my right ear as he caught me staring. "He's an augment, like the Lieutenant. Only, he can extend razor-sharp steel claws from between his fingers at will. Uses something called a subdermal transceiver. Logs his neural patterns so he can stick 'em out whenever he wants. Dang good for when you get captured by the Tongo and they think you're unarmed." he muttered.

I silently pondered how Daniels knew this much about this Tiger. Seeming to anticipate my thoughts, he went on, still maintaining a low hiss. "I know more than most do about him 'cause of an assignment I had with him a couple of months back. He's a saboteur, works for the Augment Corps. Took out two Tongo power grids before they figured out what was going on."

The transport roared to life and started moving. I guess the third transport had already been loaded up.

I looked down the aisle, observing the other soldiers as they chattered anxiously. As my gaze fell on a well-muscled man with what appeared to be a bionic eye, Daniels whispered, "Cinnamon. He's an Elite Sniper, but he refuses to work for the Augment Corps."

"That eye doesn't look biological," I said. "That's because it isn't," Daniels replied. "It can zoom in and out, see in the dark, with ultraviolet and infrared modes."

I scanned the transport further and saw two women, almost identical except for the color of their hair. They both carried weapons in their hands. "The one with the darker hair is named Janice, and her sister is Candice. They're twins."

Finally, my gaze settled on a man with dark, angry eyes who was looking at the floor. He had pulled a heavy coat over his uniform, up so high that most of his face was obscured by the black fabric. "His name's Rat," said Daniels matter-of-factly. "He's a demolitionist. Nasty one at that. Keep away from Rat."

We sat in silence. I kept my eye on Rat for a while longer. The glowering soldier kept entirely to himself, not conversing with anyone.

Suddenly, the transport lurched violently. My backpack slid out from underneath the bench and I nearly fell over on my side. "Bit of a bumpy ride," Daniels explained. "We've got to adjust our course several times on the way to Spires, 'cause of Tongo mines and such. You'll get used to it."

We sat in silence, listening to the roar of the engines. After a few minutes, I heard the crackle of a radio in the cabin. Slowly, a sentence poured through the choppy speaker, "Transport Alpha to all transports in the vicinity, do you read?" Through the mesh, I saw the driver hold down a button and respond, saying, "This is Transport Beta. We copy. What's your status?" Moments later, Transport Gamma, the third transport, echoed our message.

"Transports Beta and Gamma, we believe we have come under attack—" there was strong interference (or was it weapons fire?) "—Tongo Niji. Requesting immediate—" A resounding boom was heard through the speakers, and then there was only static. ■

Dear Kurt Hummel, I Hate You

PERSONAL ESSAY & MEMOIR

CHRISTIAN BUTTERFIELD, Grade 11. Bowling Green High School, Bowling Green, KY.
Natalie Croney, *Educator*; Southern Kentucky Performing Arts Center (SKyPAC), *Affiliate*;
Silver Medal

As a closeted teen walking through the LGBT capital of the world, I had ox-
pected something easy, a simplistic feeling of validation in my nascent sexual
identity. But all I felt was resentment.

From the age of nine, the realization that I was gay, not straight-but-ques-
tioning, not asexual, but a full-fledged homosexual, came in slow waves. Prime
evidence of my sexuality, with clues as obvious as unconsciously lingering
around the men's underwear section at Target or religiously rewatching *Crazy,
Stupid, Love* for a reason I couldn't quite spell out (Spoiler alert: That reason
was one hundred percent a shirtless Ryan Gosling.), somehow went ignored
until one day it simply couldn't, and I, faced with irrefutable evidence, came
to grips with the fact that I was about as straight as a cooked noodle.

I don't say any of this to write a heartfelt piece about how I overcame my
inner demons and became confident in my sexuality. I say this because I am
still grieving those innocent days where I only knew to care about being gay,
not about how good of a gay I needed to be.

The whole conceit of being a "good gay" seems rooted in something purely
psychological. An inferiority complex maybe? Possibly internalized homophobia? A fun/unhealthy combination? Whatever it was, eleven-year-old me
didn't know or care. All I knew to do was squeeze with my Kindle Fire into my
sister's closet and watch episodes of *Glee* deemed contraband by my parents
for it's gay-friendly content. As I sat, eyes like magnets glued to out and proud
gay men who forever seemed opposite to me, I should've been comforted, but
all I ever got from *Glee* was a deepening insecurity.

I became obsessed with main character Kurt Hummel, who represented
the exact type of gay that I wanted to be. He had great skin, a handsome
boyfriend, and the ability to adequately sing "Defying Gravity" from *Wicked*.
These were all equally important to me. Incidentally, I also held a visceral
hatred for Kurt Hummel. I hated his stupidly clear skin, his stupidly caring
boyfriend, and his stupidly above average singing voice. But he was a gay man,
and as much as I hated him for living a life that closeted me couldn't, I also
had to be obsessed with him, because watching him represented at least some

sort of hope that one day I could be the gay that other gays hated because of his smile. His slim build. His ability to sing Idina Menzel's greatest hits.

As I grew older, I always held an underlying assumption that I wasn't particularly good at being a homosexual. My teeth were too crooked, my jeans too baggy, my BMI too high. Hell, I hadn't even listened to an entire Cher album yet. The world was one entire pride parade that I continued to be jealous of, with gay men dancing in clubs that I didn't have enough clout to be allowed into. Being attracted to dudes was one thing, but being an actual "gay" was reserved for the Kurt Hummels of the world.

I lived in this assumption until I went from being shunned from the pride parade in my mind to finding myself smack-dab in the middle of an actual pride parade on the streets of San Francisco.

My aunt and uncle had lived in San Francisco since my birth, and though I had an inkling of an idea that California was particularly gay-friendly, I had no expectation of just how welcoming it would be. As I walked down the Castro, San Fran's original gay-borhood, the force of their pride almost knocked me off my feet. Ads for *Sheila Sue's Sex In The City Drag Brunch*, pamphlets regarding HIV treatment options, stupidly happy men walking hand in hand; they all flooded my vision and were washed in a palette the color of the Castro's kitschy yet tasteful rainbow crosswalks. I could almost hear Idina Menzel singing a self-confidence anthem in the background. Here I was, a closeted fifteen-year-old receiving his first taste at a world that ostensibly accepted him. I should've been in my element.

But I hated every stupid second of it.

I saw these stupidly happy gay men walking on the stupidly pristine rainbow crosswalks being stupidly confident in their lives and I felt like a sham in a world of Kurt Hummels. I saw men with impeccable haircuts and slim-fit jeans, and I felt like a failure. I saw men kiss each other right in the middle of the street. I tried to feel excited because I never really saw that in my own small-town Kentucky, but I just felt an underlying worry that no one would ever want to kiss me. No Kurt Hummel wants a fatass in cargo shorts.

As my family all packed into a Uber and left the Castro, I couldn't help but feel guilty. Nobody threw a brick at Stonewall Inn or campaigned for marriage equality so that some half-closeted punk would look at a historic gay-borhood and want nothing more than to run back to a world devoid of rainbows. They fought for a world free of judgment, and here I was judging myself. It barely mattered anyways. I was too concerned with how wrinkled my cargo shorts were to care about much else.

Weeks after the trip, long after I managed to turn that visit to the Castro into a distant memory, my little sister began to watch *Glee* for herself. She, much to my chagrin, dragged me into her room and forced me to watch with her. She, of course, did not know about my morbid obsession with Kurt Hummel's singing chops, only that I watched the show a few years prior and that she felt determined to rewatch it with me. And as she did, to keep myself occupied, I began to point out any flaw that I could find of Kurt. I noticed a small zit on his left cheek. I noticed his boyfriend eventually dumping him seasons after I had stopped watching. I heard his voice crack as he tried to belt "Defying Gravity."

Kurt Hummel was no longer perfect.

And if Kurt Hummel wasn't perfect, then the gay couples in the Castro were no longer perfect. And if the "good gays" that I believed I could never be a part of were no longer perfect, then I no longer felt obligated to be perfect. I still might've been a fatass in cargo shorts, but all of a sudden that became perfectly fine. It was a jarring observation. Years of internalized homophobia or an inferiority complex or quite possibly a fun/unhealthy combination were defeated by a slightly out of tune falsetto. It was petty, but also quite freeing.

This is the part of the essay where I'm supposed to write about how I overcame my inner demons. That I've become confident in my skin, my BMI, and my inability to sing the entire *Wicked* soundtrack. But I already said that I didn't overcome anything. I don't think anyone has. Including Kurt Hummel, who may or may not hate me back. ■

Small Moments

PERSONAL ESSAY & MEMOIR

SAWYER LINEHAN, Grade 7. Center for Teaching & Learning, Edgecomb, ME. Anne Merkel, *Educator*; Region-at-Large, *Affiliate*; Gold Medal

I wake to the cold breeze blowing through the rough wood cabin. It's barely light out and fog obscures the open oak door. I slip quietly out of my down sleeping bag, grab a headlamp, and narrowly avoid the dark lump on the floor that is my fellow camper. All is still as if the world is holding its breath. Avoiding more lumps strewn around the dark alpine hut, I creep quietly towards the exit, careful not to wake the trip leaders and move slowly down the disfigured creaky steps,

I walk out onto the green mossy field where just yesterday we parked and unloaded our heavy bikes. Sticks crackle underfoot and I can barely make out the thin gravel path leading up to the overlook. Reaching up I switch the light on and watch the shadows recede. By the time I've reached the rocky outcrop, I'm shrouded in a fine cloud of precipitation. A shiver runs down my spine and I regret the decision to leave my grey raincoat behind. Stumbling through the mess of boulders and slick pebbles I find a small nook perfectly protected from the torrent of wind and rain—classic Vermont weather. I wait, shrouded in the shadow of the cave and remember a few weeks back to Lake Tahoe, Nevada.

My shoe slips into the soft dry sand as I hop back and forth up the steep ridge behind my grandfather's old house, I scramble over the rough sandy stones and jump large gaps picking my way farther up the hill.

"Be careful!" my mom shouts from the porch as it disappears from view behind a huge alpine tree. I stop to kick the pine cones gathered around its thick trunks, and laugh as a startled squirrel leaps into the protection of its branches. Soon I press forward and continue up to my goal of today's adventure: the giant boulder that overlooks the lake. The altitude is catching up to me and my breath comes in short hard gasps. I take a detour to chase black geckos around and rest for water. I think back to mom telling me stories about mountain lions and bears, and become aware of how exposed I am.

Spying my objective just fifty meters away sways my thoughts and I make haste up the final hill and stop, awestruck. What's in front of me takes my breath away; across the lake the sun illuminates sharp mountains. I can see snow speckled peaks in the distance and a few multicolored hot air balloons drift lazily in the shimmering air. I sit down, never wanting to leave the moment and what seems like hours pass, just me, the mountains and the ever expanse of nature.

A sliver of sunlight draws me back from my thoughts and I start to make out the side of a hill far in the distance before another cloud passes over obscuring my view. I must have fallen asleep at some point because I don't remember the sudden change in light, I breathe in the moist air and sigh before slipping into another reflection.

Cool moonlight seeps into our sailboat's cabin and the steady rocking of the waves against the hull wakes me from a deep sleep. Dad's voice startles me as it sceps through the wooden doors.

"Hey guys, wake up."

"What is it?" I reply

"Just come up on deck," he whispers. Glad to end my sister's loud breathing I wake her up, slowly clamber down from the bed and move as quickly as possible on my eight-year-old legs, up onto the slick deck to where dad is sitting, he gestures to the water.

"What?" I question, in response dad dips his hand into the calm water and swirls it around, millions of tiny lights swirl through and around his fingertips. They twinkle as if they were the stars themselves. Dad draws his hand away, the lights flicker and die out,

"It's called bioluminescence. It's the emission of light from a living creature," dad explains, but the words pass through my ears and mesmerized by the receding glow I quickly dip my hand into the water and watch the lights swirl again. Awestruck by the living miracle I barely notice Kestrel come up as well. It's only when dad tells me that it's time to go to bed that I am finally aware. I lie in bed grateful for the experience until my tired eyelids close and the rocking of the boat lulls me to sleep again.

I chuckle as I fondly recall that memory. What an experience. I stand up. Precipitation still sweeps the hill and through the mist I can hear the groans as my trip leader drags unhappy campers from their bags. I turn and pick my way back across the rock field disappointed that the view wasn't what I was expecting. Just as I find the trail back to the cabin, the clouds seem to melt away revealing a emerald valley filled with lush vegetation, small clouds streak up the sides blown by a fierce wind and a clear waterfall cascades onto a flat glacial rock creating colors so vibrant its hard to say that they look real. Birds shake water droplets from their feathers grateful for the moment of sun. Just as quickly as it appears it's gone. The clouds roll in, the rain starts to fall, and I walk happily back to camp grateful for small moments like these. ■

JXN

PERSONAL ESSAY & MEMOIR

ISABELLA SUELL, Grade 12. Murrah High School, Jackson, MS. Sarah Ballard, *Educator*; Eudora Welty Foundation, *Affiliate*; Silver Medal

Where I come from Mama's friends greet you with a "Hay Baby!" so loud your ears ring and you smile in response even though you're half grown and definitely no baby.

My home is sand filled craters in the ground; shopping centers with a wing stop, two hair and nail salons, and a laundry-mat. There's what used to be Fred's, with the obnoxious blue letters with the garish green outline but is now a profitless void.

Growing up was cursing the metal playground that blistered your skin upon contact, then praying for the rusted junk back when it's replaced with a singular red slide. One slide for a whole school to share between itself . . . that slide was the ugliest shade of red you ever remember seeing.

Living was walking to the store with your friends for cheap snacks. Feeling fifty types of grown when your ma lets you ride your bike down to the gas station with a dollar gripped in your sweaty hand. Ignoring the dogs barking day and night and at you. House and body and soul buzzing from a bass bumped so high in the car tearing down the street and you wonder if the whole block vibrated with you. It's trying to guess if that POP down the street was a firework or a bullet ripping out of a metal barrel.

It was "eat fast or not at all," your mouth smoking cause you popped a boiled peanut in fresh from the bubbling water on the stove. You never regret the burnt taste buds because you moan when the shell breaks apart and salty seasoned juice fills your mouth. Gumbo and crawfish etouffee always in need of more pepper or salt or Tony Chachere's Creole Seasoning.

I'm from broken desks chairs that pitch your thigh as you flip through the outdated, deteriorating textbook in front of you. Yearning for the dusted lockers that line the hall, with their complimentary art works of "Jasmine was here" and "Jasmine's a hoe." The smell of cocoa butter overwhelming your senses, burning your nostrils on each inhale. Teachers from Detroit and the deep country who tell you the truth cause no one gets anywhere in life being ignorant.

I'm from broken building that broken people are trying their damnedest to live in. Roads and sidewalks and parking lots that have cracked under the pressure of this life. Flinching at police sirens and watching through the blinds as screaming matches take place from the front door of the house across the street. Filling up the back of the toilet so you can flush cause the water had to be turned off for right now. Giving neighbors what you can because we're all the struggle and ain't no one got the business to struggle more then they have to.

I'm from "trying to find funding" and free lunches and metal detectors at every door. School clubs that have a GoFundMe cause the school is one strike away from being bulldozed. Home-cooked meals delivered to your door because the neighbor had a BBQ and doesn't believe in throwing good food away. Being friendly to everyone even when you don't like them because "My mama raised me right" and ready to knock out anyone who says a word against said mama.

I'm from the fixer-upper ghetto fabulous state of no head start, damn good comfort food, and a hospitality you can't get from anywhere outside of Jackson, Mississippi. ∎

Hate Is a Strong Word and I Know It

PERSONAL ESSAY & MEMOIR

JUSTIN HARTLEY, Grade 12. North Shore Country Day School, Winnetka, IL. David Grossman, *Educator*; Chicago Area Writing Project, *Affiliate*, Silver Medal

It was then I decided I *hated* them. They left mounds of wrappers, spoke at the top of their lungs,
they left their trash everywhere.

I hated them.

When they left, I looked into the tired eyes of the Latin woman as she approached the mess.

I hated them.

When she looked at me amongst their ilk—

"Sorry," I pleaded with her as I shoveled their refuse into my hands.
My feeble attempt to store away the privilege they left behind for another day.
She waved me off with quiet words.

I hated them.

It was if those quiet whispers broke. I had betrayed her.
I pretended to walk with them, as if the skin that bathed my body was their own.

I hated them.

Their pristine alabaster juxtaposing to the dark melanin that weaved into the fibers of my skin. It was the dark marrons mixed with the ferocity of jungle chocolates.

I was with them as if I had their money. I walked in secret with them—adorning their protection and removing it when convenient. What had I become?

I pleaded her for her subtle forgiveness, for her causal remorse.

I needed it.

It was my father who in the 90's worked the night shift at Denny's, cleaning up the leftover entitlements of those who demanded to be served by divine right and not in generous welcome.

Hate is a strong word, but I felt it in my bones, in my soul as she cleared the table, as I watched in utter intransigence as she washed its surfaces. It was the home she had made at $7.50 on the dollar.

When distant calls woke me, my anger only brewed.

"What was their excuse?"

It was then I started putting ice under my tongue when the anger appeared in fine institutions like that one. A new fear boiled within that perhaps one day I would "pop off" as they would like me to. That I would show them angst they would take as anger, discomfort they would take as wrath. I would become the caricature they feared, the one their grandmother talked about.

Steps to avoid fitting the stereotypes white people have set for you:

Develop a *thing*: cooling, painful, exhilarating ice under the tongue, pinching the skin, humming the powerful hymns your mother or your father taught you.

Take your space. You deserve. Perhaps, your ancestors didn't have it.

Transpose your anger and pain into power.

Think. Really *think* about what's happening.

If all else fails, *pop off* in whatever way controllable, educate through action.

In their wrappers, spit, and indifference all was created.

All was a gentrification.

The gentrification of a community. It's in the white families moving into the house on the corner, in and out for years. It's in the minivan full of faces taking pictures of an apartment across the street. It's the beginning of the end when BMWs and Porsches fill the streets, passing through in pallid glory—mocking the children who gawk, for if only they knew! There are quiet talks of North Chicago being sold to the little white village across the way because, the land there is sinking, falling into the waters of Lake Michigan, subsuming the mansions, consuming the privilege.

Make my community unsafe again. Make it so black mothers can raise their grandchildren when their fathers go to work over at the power plant in Waukegan. Make my community into the lambasted "ghetto" that marks your news cycle with every held breath. Make my community the uncultured place people, white people, look down upon. Make my community unsafe again for those who fear us but will never taste the lemonade of the little Latina girl who made a fortune last summer because *we* cared. Even though the lemons were bought from the not food-safe food market and the batch was made from salt and not sugar, *we drank the lemonade.* We told her it was fine when a child of not more than seven spat it out and bought another round. This is my community.

Give my black matriarchs the nice cars that years ago only those who sold could afford. Reopen the school system, give the lifeblood of this *home* back their elementary schools not, *private education centers*. Redefine us, fix our roads, and give us the affordable housing we deserve because not every family can buy a house, pay their mortgage and watch their child grow. For perhaps the greatest misnomer of them all is called my home, a place I love: North Chicago.

Fill my home's schools with names like Ayeshas, Imanis, Aaliyahs, Dejas, Demetriuses, and DeAndres, not with Mollys, Heathers, Jacks, Michaels, and Katies—or perhaps even Justins, like myself. I believe my mother regrets the name she gave me. She regrets giving me a colonizer's name. Something so easy to roll off their tongues. A name that their mouth formed with no pause and perhaps no mean. North Chicago is my community. She grows, she prospers, she curdles, she suffers. She is ornamented with her natural attributes like the gold and topaz of the street lights at night which to emphasize the shading of her flesh, greens, and browns and to offset her long, coiled black hair, her streets. With the depth and poise of deep purple calla lilies, my community can grow.

"When we moved here—before you were born—North Chicago used to be the place everyone wanted to be. The schools were good, all the sailors brought money, it was . . . was up and coming." Lacerating.

North Chicago is once more the place to be, however not for us. The schools have gone to the government, removing our control and yet, forcing them into further disorder. With every tax cut, negated budget we suffer as our tap runs dry.

We humble few withered. Our beautiful light amongst the world whisked away as its soul dispersed. The true treasure of home was fading with each recall and every inaction.

Our spirits broken.

Our spirits forever disappearing. ∎

The Schism

PERSONAL ESSAY & MEMOIR

JULIA MANSO, Grade 12. Saint Mary's Hall, San Antonio, TX. Amy Williams-Eddy, *Educator*; Region-at-Large, *Affiliate*; Gold Medal

"Jesus, it was taxing. It was not inter—"

"Don't take God's name in vain," my mother interjects. "Your great-grandparents would roll over in their graves, you know. I tell you this too often," she says, sighing, exasperated. Ah, yes, my great-grandparents, the fortieth generation Catholics, founded a church and currently lie there entombed, clasped in the darkness of its crypt, just under the choir. I wonder: Do they feel the organ and the churchgoers harmonizing; do the vibrations resonate with their bones? Do they feel my sacrilege; do their angelic forms writhe in torment? I murmur an apology, knowing I will probably slip up again tomorrow and repent, the perpetual sinner.

Pushing open the ancient wooden door of the cathedral, I looked up at the cavernous ceiling of Westminster Abbey, feeling my insignificance amidst the grandeur as I admired the tediously carved Gothic arches that reach together above the center of the room, intertwining and clasping. Arriving at the Abbey just in time for a guided tour, my mother and I sat down amongst the pews, securing the neon orange bands around our wrists as we prepared for the journey through the labyrinth-like chapel.

On my first day of Sunday school, the inklings of religious skepticism began: the rambunctious pupils who sought to joke, distract, and satirize the Bible did not learn about God's teachings but unabashedly disrespected his doctrines and way of life. Coloring a picture of Jesus while watching VeggieTales—*a television series documenting the Christian exploits of vegetables—and learning about the Ten Commandments should, I thought, be mutually exclusive tasks, never combined. Instead of giving me reverence and respect for Jesus and his plights, the class sowed the seeds of dissent, and I became tempted into disbelief, like Eve was enticed by the apple from the Tree of Knowledge.*

Beginning at the outside of the cathedral, the guided tour led slowly inward, past the monuments dedicated to military heroes and brilliant prime ministers, over the graves of great political minds, walked on both in life and death. How fickle man is, one day loyal like Noah, the next day like Judas. Strolling past the sanctuary, the coronation chair, and the choir pews, we ventured deeper and deeper into the Abbey, traipsing down a U-shaped hallway lined on each side by chapels—small rooms crammed with the graves of dukes, barons, patrons, and other nobles—pausing just behind the main altar. As a group, we slowly mounted a short flight of rickety steps, arriving in the "Heart of the Abbey," a circular enclave that is raised about nine feet higher than the rest of the chapel. On each side of the Heart are ancient wooden tombs, some of them dating back to 1000 C.E., which encompass the bodies of monarchs like Henry III and Richard II, but in the center of the Heart is a shrine to Edward the Confessor, sainted by the Catholic Church.

As I matured, the seeds had sprouted into a full-blown tree, growing symbiotically with the ivy of empiricism. "Interestingly, new research shows that Jesus was actually born in March," my science teacher informed me. A curious classmate, undoubtedly enticed by such an idea, posed the question, "Can you believe in God and subscribe to science at the same time?" Grinning, my teacher replied, "Certainly . . . you just have to pick and choose your miracles. You decide what you believe." While his answer was originally meant to soothe our prepubescent angst, I, if anything, felt more alarmed: what parts of the Bible—if any—are true? Since the truth means different things to different people, does each person bend her religion to her will or her reality? If science tells me to reject the improbable, like Daniel not being killed when tossed in a den of lions, I cannot reconcile such theories with acceptance of equally unlikely events, like Jesus' walking on water, for without proof, data, evidence, I cannot form a conclusion.

As I stepped off the staircase into the Heart, my eyes focused on the shrine, comprised of three layers: a large, rectangular stone box, plated in gold and accented by gems, with cutouts for pilgrims to kneel in so as to be closer to Edward; a second layer on top of his tomb, which looks almost like the facade of a Roman building due to its uniform arches; and a third layer mirroring the second one, only about half the size. To the monarchs who created it, the shrine clearly was a cornerstone of their personal faith, enticing them to donate their fortunes in order to entrench it in splendid wealth; likewise, the pilgrims who travel from near and far to visit the shrine share similar feelings, breaking off pieces of the gold and wrenching gems from the mosaics as "souvenirs." In hoping to never part from the comfort and salvation they felt praying to Edward the Confessor, these pilgrims, these *perfect* Christians, commit a sin; they break the Ten Commandments but feel no remorse, true humans clinging to their own desires. If Christianity doesn't prevent man from being a base animal, why does it exist at all?

Even as I silently questioned my beliefs, my mother and I would go to church like clockwork every Sunday evening, the five o'clock mass. Each week, we would go out for dinner afterwards, leaving my father to stay home with my infant brother, and to me, Sunday evenings were our special time. After communion at church, I would ask Jesus to watch over me, protect me from harm and evil, teach me the difference between right and wrong, good and bad. Kneeling on the cool tile floor, I would beseech God to help me, my fingers shaking, clasped in front of me, but he would never reply.

As the rest of the tour reached the top of the stairs, the guide began to speak about the shrine of Edward the Confessor, and while he explained the historical significance, I glanced at my fellow tourists, who were clearly enthralled by their magical reverence for God. Their admiration, intertwined with their humble awe, created a mist in their eyes and a fervor in their souls as each felt the divine. While the rest of the group wandered over to the wooden tombs of the monarchs, my mother approached me with glossy eyes, telling me, "You should pray and ask God to protect you, set you on a good path in life. This is the closest you will ever come to a saint. If you pray to him, they say your prayers will come true." Gawking with my jaw slightly agape, I stared at her with a feeling of earnest shock, bewildered by her request and her blind passion.

The questions only grew: Jonah survived in the stomach of a whale for three days—how could he breathe? Moses parted the Red Sea—what happened to physics? A star moved from its position in the night sky, leading shepherds to the newborn Jesus in a manger—impossible.

As she knelt in the alcove of the shrine, I stood by, cowering, watching, almost embarrassed. She performed the sign of the cross, and her face took on the impassioned look she assumes when begging for divine intervention. Upon completing her supplications, she whispered again, "Pray," and I bowed my head, clasping my hands before me. But I was not praying: I was acting. I was lying to myself, to God, to her, to everyone in the cathedral, for my mind would not allow me to suspend my disbelief, trapping me in the real world. I felt nothing.

I would love to believe in God, in heaven, in Jesus, in Biblical mysteries, in the idea that there is a universal plan. I would love to have blind faith, faith like my mother's, like my great-grandparents', like Joshua's in the Battle of Jericho, but I can never escape the nagging feeling in the back of my mind, a skeptical questioning that grows every day. It tells me: God isn't real.

As I looked up from my clasped hands, the group was beginning to proceed out of the Heart, and my mother asked me, "Did you pray?" I gazed at her, making no answer, and walked out of the Heart.

Even now, I cannot identify the root of my skepticism although I have attempted to discern a catalyst for my disenchantment. Had I never taken that Bible study class, had I never gained such a rigorous education, had I never subscribed to logic, had I never resisted slipping into the calmness of blind faith, I might be happier, healthier, heaven-bound. Am I going to hell? *I want to believe—I so want to believe, to surrender myself into the benign benevolence of God's plan— but I cannot. I remain in an indefinite grey area of skepticism, dark, ambiguous, and torturous.*

I climbed down the sloping steps, and instead of rejoining the group, I informed my mother that I was going to the restroom. I needed to escape: I was suffocated by the guilt, the lie I had perpetrated feet from a saint, directly in God's eyeline. Maybe he didn't notice? But God is supposedly omnipotent and omniscient, so he must have. Stepping over the graves of the men who had lived and died in greatness, I bolted towards a side exit of the Abbey, but as I pushed open the heavy, archaic door, my lungs filling with the chilling air of the London evening, I certainly did not feel cured. The poison of sacrilege had permeated my bloodstream, tainting my tranquility, growing and festering into a nearly lethal dose—will I ever be cured? Staring at the monk who stood across the courtyard from me, I slowly gained my composure, eventually becoming calm enough to return to the group.

From Monday to Saturday, I simply ignore the issue, preferring to live in oblivion rather than feel the crippling guilt, for I know that my great-grandparents, my ancestors, and every other soul who fought and died for religious freedom and the Catholic faith are undoubtedly disappointed, ashamed, and angry. Sitting in the stuffy pew of a dimly lit church on Sundays, the full force of their power ambushes me, and lost rationalizing in my mind, uncomfortable in my own skin, I vaguely listen, watch, and wait for divine indignation to befall me, seeking reparations.

After the tour reached an end in Poet's Corner, my mother and I were heading towards the nave of the Abbey when she caught sight of the rows of candles that pious believers light to honor loved ones. Stopping, she slipped a few dollars into the collection box, picked up a candle, and whispered a brief prayer in honor of her departed father. She truly believes: my mother sees her father in the natural world around her, as a butterfly that lands on her when she is upset, as a red cardinal who regularly perches on a tree in our backyard, as a rainbow that forms when there is hardly any rain. He is always there to protect her, even after life. And I want that.

In the meantime, however, I wait in quietude, smothering my doubts until I cannot, and they resurface in their monstrous glory, my very own Leviathan. Not knowing my silent qualms with religion, a friend once posed the question, "What is it like to live without God?" I don't know. ∎

Why I Say It Like That

PERSONAL ESSAY & MEMOIR

ELIZABETH TORRES-GRIEFER, Grade 11. South Brunswick High School, Monmouth Junction, NJ. Michael Dennehy, *Educator*; Newark Public Library, *Affiliate*; Gold Medal

The last time I saw someone who looked like me in my class was in eighth grade, when there were no arbitrary levels of difficulty plastered in front of course names that separated the student body into "dumb," "normal," and "smart." She had curly hair, like me; dark brown eyes, like me; and a skin color that, when looked at on its own, could be a mixture of all the shades of brown in the world, like me. In short, she was Latina.

It was an unspoken connection, between her and I. We were never friends, never even spoke to one another other than about class, but every time the teacher referred to the Chilean characters in the book we were studying as "Pedro? Maybe Pablo? I can't keep track of them all!", we were closer than any lifelong friends. When discussion began about affirmative action, and someone said, "I heard if you're Hispanic or black, they bump your SAT score by one hundred points," we were sisters.

I stopped seeing her after we "graduated" middle school. At the ceremony, I saw her with her mother, only her mother. Like me.

Then high school started, and the segregation began. My test scores shepherded me into a new class, one where college was a prize to be won, instead of a price tag, one where everyone had been in tutoring since the womb. It felt like I had been granted a mistaken accolade. Although I was certainly smart, as smart as any of my peers, I was not one of those kids. I wondered if my classmates knew that.

Academically, I could keep up. I found my new coursework challenging and exciting, and felt like, for the first time, I was really learning. But there was always the gnawing fact, the truth that underlined every day in advanced classes, that I was alone. No longer did I have anyone to look to when we learned about "the immigration problem."

So when I got up to present my project about a social movement in America, I said César Chávez's name as it looked to me. I explained about Dolores Huerta with no issues in pronouncing her name. To me, this was how you were supposed to speak.

The presentation came to a head when I said they, Chávez and Huerta, were champions of Latino rights.

And there the murmurs began, right after I said the L-word. When I quickly finished, and sat down, my friend asked me in a whisper, "Why did you have to say it like that?"

I knew what "it" was. As soon as the the *t* in *Latino* began its way out of my mouth, mingling with the *i*, and especially when the *-no* was left slightly open, the way my mother has always said it, I knew I had said something more than just the word.

In response to my friend, I shrugged. In my head, I wondered, "Was that too much? Will everyone think I'm obnoxious now? Do they think I'm dumb?" The obvious answer to fourteen-year-old me was a resounding yes to all of my questions. I thought about how best to recover from my fumble, to prove to everyone that I was intelligent again, to show the class that I wasn't *that* Hispanic, and if I were, that I certainly wasn't proud of it.

For the rest of the year, I cleaned up my mess. I stayed quiet during debates about racism and police brutality, I never picked an issue involving Puerto Rico or Latin America for my current events. I purposely butchered Sonia Sotomayor's name. Inside, I felt ashamed at my own disowning of my culture, especially in a space where it was so needed. But I was back in good standing with my peers; I wasn't the Latin social justice warrior or the trashy Hispanic. I was, to my own relief, just another student.

The political climate did not just make silence difficult: it made it a crime. While I played the part of tan white girl who was smarter than she looked, my people were being hunted by the government, my culture was being slandered by the most powerful man in the world, and my neighbors, ones I did not see in my honors and AP classes, lived in fear of deportation.

All of this, I did not speak of. I watched it in horror, but still, had relinquished my position as a Latina in the hopes that I could assimilate into academia without causing a stir.

As the national conversation on race and immigration escalated to new levels of disturbing, or at least, as I became aware of it, the torment of self-imposed censorship ate away at me. Entering my sophomore year, I came to school with resolve. If, and since, there was no one in my class to speak for my people, I would. Without mispronounced names, or a facade of indifference, I would be an advocate for a community being suffocated by a nation turned attacker.

So on the first day of tenth grade, I put my gold hoop earrings on. My mom looked at me before I left, quietly calling me a *boricua*. I smiled with soft pride.

During my debate conferences, I made sure to say the L-word, accent and all. Every chance I got in class, I'd bring up the financial turmoil in Venezuela, the inequality in Mexico, the political unrest in Guatemala.

Being a minority in an academic space puts you in the position of constantly having to prove yourself: that you're as smart as everyone else in the room, that you're not just being argumentative, that you deserve a spot in the conversation. It is lonely and it is exhausting. Often, it is embarrassing to consistently be the only one who cares. But if I have the privilege of speaking up for my community, I'm going to do it. If I have the platform, I'm going to use it. And if I have the accent, the one that sounds like the dancers in Colombia and the food in Puerto Rico and the perseverance in Honduras, I'm unmistakably going to speak with it. ■

All My Ink Is Brown

POETRY

RAJRISHI DAS, Grade 12. Philips Exeter Academy, Exeter, NH. Susan Repko, *Educator*; The National Writing Project in New Hampshire, *Affiliate*; Gold Medal

My English teachers never told me to write about race.
It was always more of an implication than an instruction,
the idea that if I had the nerve to write about myself in the English language
I had a responsibility to explain why, to provide a reason for my existence,
to provide an ethnic disclaimer for my inheritance of the
Anglican art form. My teachers meant well,
and gave me comments like,

"This is so powerful," and
"This writing is so crucial," and
"Thank you for sharing," and

whenever I wrote about racists I got good grades, so I continued
to write dramatic personal narratives of blatant micro-aggressions sprinkled
with italicized Bengali and *"red-hot tears falling*
down my brown cheeks like
the blood of my ancestors" and
my teachers and classmates drank it all like red
wine, with acquired pleasure in moderation,
because when you're reading your brown friend's narrative about
the people who call him "terrorist" it's so easy
to feel distanced,
to feel *woke,*
to feel as though by tolerating his English that you're not like the others.
White people love racism when they're not implicated. And so,

I began my career as a writer by mining
my life for explicit racial antagonism, for Racism with a capital R,
to provide my readers with free entertainment and a feel-good,
faux-political disclaimer for my literary existence.

This is why my ink is brown.

Blacks

POETRY

AAEISHA BAHARUN, Grade 11. Tomball Memorial High School, Tomball, TX. Canita Lee, *Educator*; Harris County Department of Education, *Affiliate*; Silver Medal

I have developed
this fear,
Of blacks,
Because blacks are
Loud,
Angry,
Thieves,
Abusive,
Robbers,
Rapists,
Guilty,
At least that's what I heard,
At least that's what
The police,
Movies,
Media,
And history claim.
But why
Am I
Afraid
Considering
The fact that
I'm
"Black"
Or,
As the cautious whisper,
"African American."
If I was labelled
As black
It would mean
That I was confined
To the same

Small box,
Limited,
Degraded,
Suppressed,
As the wrongdoers,
Offenders,
Villains,
Convicts.
The box that everyone expected me
to effortlessly fit into.
Because I'm supposed to fail.
I'm constantly working
To break
A mold,
A stereotype,
A label,
That does not define me.
For I am
Quiet,
Smart,
Loyal,
Peaceful,
Innocent, until proven guilty,
At least that's what I've been told,
At least they've said that, so far, I'm
"Not like other black people."

Why the Headline Doesn't Do It Justice

POETRY

ILANA HUTZLER, Grade 11. Pine Crest School, Fort Lauderdale, FL. Marisa Ortega, *Educator*; Young at Art Museum, *Affiliate*; Silver Medal

You lie in bed, staring into the light of your cell phone,
scrolling aimlessly, when you read the headline
17 Dead in High School Shooting
and you feel nothing.
After a day of hell, a day forever burned
into the backs of your eyelids,
17 Dead in High School Shooting
doesn't do it justice.

Close your eyes, you can hear
the fire alarm and the lockdown alarm
spinning together,
hear the jumbled footsteps of not knowing
whether to "File outside in an orderly fashion"
or to find a hiding spot in your geometry classroom,
not knowing until you hear the gunshots.
Old news articles churn in your stomach
and you know this moment will be on the front page
tomorrow. Pray your teacher locked the door
when you hear someone pounding on it,
and pray to God and hope
He can hear you from under your desk
but hope the man at the door
can't.

The shaking and crying and not knowing
whether the shooter was gone
because you couldn't look, couldn't move.
Not knowing who he shot
and were they okay? But mostly

who he shot.
17 Dead in High School Shooting
doesn't do this justice.

The police officer tells you to close your eyes
when you walk down this hallway.
There's nothing worth seeing here.
And you try to listen but for some reason
you open your eyes anyway.
And you finally see your parents
crying behind the caution tape. And they hold you,
and you haven't stopped crying yet,
and they don't let go.

You can't unsee the lifelessness,
can't un-hear the sound of falling bodies.
Flinch at the sound
of your mother knocking
on your half-open bedroom door.

Now your hands are shaking
and you can't read your cell phone
because you can't stop thinking
about going back to school.
Staring at the empty seat in the back row
of chemistry class as if nothing's wrong,
listening to the substitute call attendance
and she doesn't know which names she isn't supposed to read
and when she reads them everyone goes silent.
And a girl in the back row asks to be excused.
17 Dead in High School Shooting
will never do this justice.

Your phone clatters to the floor
because you've read this headline too many times
in your fourteen years,
and you don't know what to do
except pray and hope God hears you
because it feels like you're still underneath your desk.

Indirect Object

POETRY

OLIVIA LLOYD, Grade 12. American Heritage School, Plantation, FL. Ashley Hendricks, *Educator*; Young at Art Museum, *Affiliate*; Silver Medal

In my head I talk to myself about
   What happened
But some small part adds
   To me
As in "what happened to me"
As if I were prone
   Passive
A recipient of the action
Rather than a participant
No active voice

When he asked if I wanted to I said
   "Yes,"
Instead of
   "Yes."
I live and die by commas
A million things can happen between quotation marks

I think about the sentence structure of "he unzipped my jeans"
   How do I talk about this the right way?
   I did say yes after all
Subject, verb, indirect object
The subject is always him and the object is always me.

Dear Body

POETRY

CHLOE PHILPOT, Grade 12. Franklin County High School, Winchester, TN. Benjamin Smith, *Educator*; Region-at-Large, *Affiliate*; Silver Medal

Have you met my body?
She's usually the first thing people notice about me
It's like no matter what I try to suffocate her in, she always seems to make noise
my body is loud,
and she's not a passing loud-
she's a three step ahead of me,
too loud, in your face distraction,
that I can't seem to get rid of,
but I heard writing love poems helps you fall more in love with someone,
so Dear body,
when we were kids we used to dance-
at midnight
alone
in my bedroom
but I don't dance anymore
but you, you beg me to move,
force my bones against one another
but I don't dance anymore.
sometimes I forget I'm connected to you,
like I'm lying in bed beside you
and you won't let me sleep
but how could how could I ever sleep beside someone knowing they have the potential to hurt me
you are a suitcase of problems that I keep forgetting to leave at home,
baggage I am tired of answering questions about
and it's crazy,
crazy to think we used to be friends,
the last time I considered you a friend, was the last time I could look in a mirror and not have to remind myself that I am not you
because I am more than this body.
I am more than skin and bones and flaws I can't let go of

and despite what you might think,
I have become friends with parts of myself besides you, because you are not
the only part of me worth something
so dear body,
You may be me
but I will never just be you.

The Patina Effect

POETRY

SARAH SENESE, Grade 12. John Jay High School, Cross River, NY. Lena Roy, *Educator*; Writopia Lab, *Affiliate*; Silver Medal

It was fragmental thinking—
My father would close off the living
room,
An assembly line of dining room
chairs
—and spend hours rubbing the couch
With his large, rough hands
Tracing his fingers over the stitching
of the cushions
Not worth the oils of his weathered
soul.
It was fragmental thinking
To believe that the oils from his
fingers
Would create the patina he believed
Showed wealth, esteem.
We would watch from behind the
Chair barricade, as my father
Got down on his knees
Face parallel to the cushions of the
couch
Tracing his fingers over
The soft leather,
A slow, melodic push
The back and forth of a man
Who loved nothing more than
Wealth, esteem:
The state of his leather couch.

My siblings moved out,
Had kids, married well.
My brothers and my sisters

Acquired couches much like
My father's—
Couches that showed they had money
Had a life better than
Other around them.
The Patina Effect.
When my mother died,
My father spent the Shiva
Rubbing his hands over the couch,
Creating his dining room chair
Barricades
Inviting friends and family
To feel the soft leather
He'd created
With the Patina from his fingers.

When my father died
We sold the house.
I drove by it a short while after
To see my father's prized couch
Strewn on the side of the road.
The Patina Effect.

Two Ways of Looking at a Market in Chinatown

POETRY

JEFFREY LIAO, Grade 11. Livingston High School, Livingston, NJ. Susan Rothbard, *Educator*; Newark Public Library, *Affiliate*; Silver Medal

i. Portrait of a Corroded Nation
On Saturday afternoons, my mother and I visit
New York's Chinatown, where a confluence of spices and oils
stains the air. Old women with tongs prod at lobsters in wooden crates,
their calloused hands mirroring the topography of the Himalayas,
knuckles scabbed red from borders wrenched apart,
palms weathered with three generations of fractured bloodlines.
A wishbone beggar coughs black spittle onto a backdrop
of white brick facade, teeth yellow and decaying from the rotting syntax
of a muddled language. No one notices. An endless sea of bodies
pulses along with the hazy heat of summer, their eyes sloped downward like those
of old basset hounds, shoulders sunken inward as if to make themselves smaller.
My mother fights for the last batch of pigs' feet with another woman,
her lips pursed together like the pinched tips of folded *baozhi*.
The endless array of silver-scaled fish and bloodied shark carcasses
spills like wine across market stalls, the streets stinking of sweat and
heat and death. We pass by grandmothers with gleaming copper skin,
laughing over a deck of cards, their sun-spotted faces wrinkled like the
grooves of the Yangtze. Perhaps one of them is thinking of how
the little boy bicycling through a black puddle of rain—which splatters
across a crate of lychees and earns him the curses of the haggard vendor —
looks like the reincarnation of her late brother. Her brother, who, during the Japanese
invasion, was shot with his hands rope-tied and his eyes gouged out,
whose only eulogy were the words *please, please don't—*
I envy them now, these women, the way they carry on smiling,
the way my mother no longer flinches when the telephone rings static,
my mother who has not spoken to her own sister in decades.
Grouse soar upwards into the tangerine sun, along with tendrils of steam

from burning tea leaves, their paths diverging like the torn and missing words
between two sisters after the Revolution swallowed them whole.
My mother sighs, and it sounds like a lost threnody, like the rhythm of
chickens and ducks stowed away in barrels, clinging to the earth for some final
but hopeless salvation. Here, I observe the plight of an entire nation
numbed by hardship, of immigrant dreams whittled to smoke.

ii. Makeshift Homeland
Yet this market has never existed to please.
It reeks of a butcher's knife, of foul dragon fruit passed off as in-season.
Of English being a foreign language here. But it is a constellation of history
strung by our own hands. It is a roadmap of our resilience,
seen through Peking ducks and red lanterns and firecrackers at sunset.
This country has never been ours to call *home,* but Chinatown—where
century eggs rest in clay pots, where children race each other barefoot over dusty roads—
calls us hers. In the streets, girls in colored silk gowns dance along to ancient folk.
A village elder hugs his grandson, whose smooth face contrasts against the old man's
varicose veins and drooping chin. The soaring notes of a Huangmei opera song
drift in and out of open windows, and the footsteps of the crowd below
clap along like a refrain. I could never resent the toothless street vendor
trying to sell me a fake jade necklace, or the blue-veined straggler
cursing at my mother for not teaching me my native tongue,
his spine bent inward like the arc of a silver swan. For in this market,
the same place where I first discovered the disillusionment of an entire people,
I also hear solidarity in the din of Mandarin syllables, find comfort in the landscape of
raven-black hair and unfolded eyelids, this scene of reckless abandon.
Breathing in the scent of peanut oil beating itself into dough,
my mother and I walk onwards in this corner of the world
that exists just for us, this place which is neither peaceful nor harmonious,
as was expected of us, but rather engaged in utter yet
beautiful chaos.

A Green Line

POETRY

DAMAYANTI WALLACE, Grade 12. Chicago High School for the Arts, Chicago, IL. Tina Boyer Brown and Kenyatta Rogers, *Educators*; Chicago Area Writing Project, *Affiliate*; Gold Medal

When you board the green line
There is silence
You notice every race that sits on the train
It is almost America's perfect melting pot here
Until the 7 year old black boy yells nigga
Then all the white people dart their eyes at the few black folks on the train
The black people smile
As if they know nothing else to do
I laugh
The train is silent
And it breaks
"This a real nigga party—"
His words turn to gibberish
And everybody tenses
His mother begs him to shush
Somebody says something in Spanish
Darting their eyes at me
Apparently the only black girl on the train
That's in their eyes reach
I smile to myself
Wondering if I should take my phone out and tweet about this
About how they're already criminalizing this black boy cause he said nigga
Or
How they're dismissing the mother because she can't control her son
Or
How they're wondering what my thoughts are
Or
If they're just uncomfortable cause they can't join in
I smile and bask
This is the train ride I needed
To be completely comfortable

In the pit of everybody else's uncomfortability
Silence
"This a real nigga party—"
He continues

Ekphrastic

POETRY

MARY-KATE WILSON, Grade 11. Washington Latin Public Charter School, Washington, DC.
Rachel Breitman, *Educator*; Writopia Lab, *Affiliate*; Gold Medal

Joan Brown, *The Dancers in a City #2, 1972*

A song like a soft hand
     cradled on
        the small of my back,
something comforting and light,
      like dancing
    on an orange peel,
kicking off my shoes. If I close my eyes
  I can pretend my fingers rest
     in the palm of a girl,
       in a dress
like my grandmother used to wear,
pretend that instead of gloves I wear
    the hands of a dancer
        invisible in
        the city,
like the neon signs of a corner store
  or a lemon-colored taxi cab.
  I can walk New York at night
    like a hound or
     a ballroom champion,
       graceful and strong, on
       my toes,
leading with some foreign rhythm
    and not watching
      my hands or
       my feet
  as we glide down aisle 3
    and I hear a
   clique of heeled shoes
   following in suit.

I Don't Want Sorrow

POETRY

NATHANIEL HYLTON, Grade 12. Collegiate School, New York, NY. John Beall, *Educator*; NYC Scholastic Awards, *Affiliate*; Silver Medal

Momma, when I die
I don't want people to march.
I don't want the fires and explosions and those breaking news headlines
Cause if I die that way, chances are it was at the shriveled white-chalked
calloused hands of injustice.
Cause if I die that way, chances are I wasn't prepared.
Cause if I die that way, chances are you were sitting by the window waiting
for me to return home.
Cause if I die that way, chances are I was in the right.
Cause if I die that way, chances are I won't be remembered for my accom-
plishments
Oh Momma
If I die that way, your last photo of me will be the mugshot on the back page
of Sunday's paper
Hopefully you recognize me
But the strangers . . . they won't
They'll all say:
"Wrong place—wrong time."

All of the Pleasures I Will Not Allow Myself

POETRY

ELENA CASTRO, Grade 12. Fine Arts Center, Greenville, SC. Sarah Blackman, *Educator*; Region-at-Large, *Affiliate*; Silver Medal

Body I left abandoned
like a farmhouse
red and concave
in which moths
of all intentions
have decided
to make their home.
They are flapping
and frantic
in black corners,
trying to find the light
of a creamed moon
beaming in between
the rafters, the slow
rhythm of their search
echoes inside
stomach of a bull,
the vast beat
crickets mimic
in a symphony
of dying grass
repetition
like crop circles,
stalks of corn
leaning right
towards the sun—
signal the sheep
bloated, bellowing
breasts like poppies
tender and hanging,

expecting the mouth
of a lamb, expecting
the hands of a farmer.
Let it be known
I did not betray
my pastoral
there is so much
I wish to say
about wanting this back—
because the body
is not the body
until it is given what it wants.

Spring Has Passed, Winter Is Coming Again

POETRY

GINA KILLINGBECK, Grade 9. Saginaw Arts & Sciences Academy, Saginaw, MI. Jared Morningstar, *Educator*; Kendall College of Art and Design, Ferris State University, *Affiliate*; Silver Medal

You were the winter,
freezing me to the core,
sticking pins into me
like an old doll,
repurposed and reused,
but never able to find a home.
You cut into me with your sharp tongue,
leaving me like a warm day,
passing me by.
You caught me from a 4-foot drop
and threw me off a tower,
making me fall lower than I have ever before.
You are too sharp for my gentle petals,
and you'll continue to cut into me.
I used to wait for the day,
when the warmth would come,
consuming me and letting me bloom.
Yet that day isn't here,
and I'll wait in the cold,
for the flower I was
can't bloom with the snow surrounding me,
but you're not here.

Last Breath

FLASH FICTION

MAYA ALI, Grade 8. Gray Middle School, Union, KY. Kara Nixon, *Educator*; Art Academy of Cincinnati, *Affiliate*; Silver Medal

I've been underwater for twenty-three seconds. I always go up after twenty-four. To go up, I plant my feet on the soft sand, and with a powerful push my arms stretch out, forcing my body upward. With my feet, I begin to make small, rapid kicks. Now, it's been twenty-seven seconds. I am inches away from the surface. At twenty-nine seconds, I start to lift my head over the water to catch another breath. Just as my forehead touches the hot air above me, a forceful wave shoves me back down before I can refill my air.

I try to fight the water all around me, but in this battle, I am losing. Thirty-one seconds have passed, and I am still sinking rather than rising. Thirty-three seconds. I cannot stay in the darkness any longer. As I open my eyes, salt rushes onto their surface. They burn like the sting of a large bee. My vision is weak and blurred. Thirty-six seconds. Just as the water begins to release me, the ocean calls another wave to visit me. This one is more powerful than the first. I am pushed into a neverending front flip. Forty seconds. The air I have left in my lungs has now converted into carbon dioxide. My lungs hurt. They deflate hopelessly. I watch the air escape from inside me. Bubbles float up to the surface. I wish I could join them. Now, not just my eyes sting; my everything stings.

Forty-three seconds. Every limb attached to my body is fighting to break loose from this death machine. The ocean is giving me a bear hug. I feel its weight pressing on my skin. I feel its arms wrapped around my neck. Forty-five seconds. I wonder if this is it. I think of the headlines, "Local Girl Drowns on a Day at the Beach." I think of my family and home. I think of girls gossiping at my school about my death. This is my last breath.

Forty-eight seconds. I feel empty inside. Fifty-one seconds. Fifty-two seconds. Fifty-three seconds. My body sends in adrenaline to save me. I kick harder than I've ever kicked before. My arms flap like wings. Everything hurts now. Fifty-seven seconds. The ocean finally releases me from its murderous waters. With one powerful, forceful kick, I use all the energy left in me to push myself to the surface. Stella one, ocean zero.

My head jolts up. I open my mouth larger than it's ever been stretched before. Oxygen pours inside of me. My lungs have been empty for so long, the air feels heavy. I swallow in more and more air. I cannot keep my head above the surface any longer, so I let my body sink back downward. I kick off the ocean floor and begin swimming to the shore. I swim quickly, afraid if I slow down the ocean will drown me. Once my feet touch the bottom, I start to walk more than swim. My waist is above water now, and I run frantically with my entire body. My arms swing out far and hard, helping me run out. As I touch the sand I drop to the ground. The dry, harmless ground. Thousands of sand grains crawl onto my skin. I breathe deep and with great speed. I am living again. This is my first breath. ■

A Procession

FLASH FICTION

ADAM KRASNOFF, Grade 12. Charleston County School of the Arts, North Charleston, SC. Danielle DeTiberus, Francis Hammes, and Elizabeth Hart, *Educators*; Region-at-Large, *Affiliate*, Gold Medal

His mother died on a Tuesday.

It had been coming. He'd be lying if he said he didn't know that. But, he reasoned to his then girlfriend, a curly-haired girl with roundish glasses, you could know for sure that a snowstorm was going to hit a particular Tuesday and still slip on a patch of ice. *That's a stupid analogy*, she said. *I know*, he replied noncommittally. *I'm sorry*, she said. *Is that what I'm supposed to tell you?* It was leukemia. It was three months' work. It was his mother gritting her teeth and refusing medication. She didn't want to live in pain. She wanted everything to happen naturally. She wanted to be buried under an oak tree. She wanted Cat Stevens played at her funeral.

His father wanted none of this. Mostly he wanted his wife to live. Certainly, if she was to die, he didn't want to have to moan and cry at her funeral while some good-for-nothing hippie crooned along. A Tuesday, anyway. He flew in early that morning, three-ish, held her cold, wet hand for as long as he could stand to while she lay dying, not being able to say much of anything at all. His father waited outside the bedroom door. *Call me in when it's done*, he said, and he went to go make himself some coffee. It was done by seven. He left the bedside and went out into the hallway and gave his father a long hug. *Oh*, his father murmured. *Oh, oh. Not all of that.* He went into the bedroom and looked at his wife of thirty-five years and nodded a couple of times.

Later that night, his father insisted on cooking dinner, and he had chicken breasts on the stove when he started to sob. He took the pan from the burner and flung the meat at the small kitchen window. He took the pan over his head and banged it on the formica countertop, then brought it back up, a second time, a third time, a fourth. Hearing the noise from the other room, he ran in. *Dad*, he shouted. *Dad, Dad, Dad,* until the pan was rattling against the tiled floor. His father shuffled over to him and wheezed into his shoulder.

The cemetery was a point of contention. There were three or four other relatives buried where his father wanted, so they decided she should be too. No oaks. And it was forty minute's drive from the funeral home. So the service finished, and his father was in disarray, and there was this huge procession across the whole city, twenty or thirty cars, and somewhere along the way it started to really pour down rain, and he was in the car with his father and his father's cousin Steve, and Steve began to tell an elaborate story about when he had had a heart attack and stayed at this rehab facility for a few months, and it just went on and on, and the cars on the road trailed thick tails of mist down the interstate, and his father burst out *shut up, goddamn it, did you have to ride in this car with us,* and that shut Steve up for the most part, and eventually the procession reached the cemetery, and the road going down the center of it was dirt, and the dirt was mud, and the rain had slowed but now hung in the air as a cold, still mist, and when he got out of the car he slipped and the knees of his suitpants became covered in mud, and he winced, and his father was complaining about the cold so someone forked over their jacket and eventually everyone had come so they made their way over to the site, where they had pitched a white tent for people to stand under, and everybody took their turn shoveling dirt onto the casket, and the rabbi said something, but he wasn't really listening, and someone muttered something about just how cold it was, and someone else muttered for them to be quiet, and everybody went back to their cars after a time, and drove to a nearby synagogue, where there were hundreds of bagels and plates of lox and rugelach and pitchers of water and Diet Cherry Coke, and his father looked at the spread and said *I need some wine.*

He stayed for four days after that while his father sat shiva. He just couldn't bear it after that. He went back to school. He went back to his mousy girlfriend. She consoled him a little. He wasn't inconsolable. He was disconsolate, though. She never liked that. She liked to be made to laugh and smile. *Fuck off,* he shouted at her when it was over, *fuck the fucking fuck off,* and he couldn't help but to think as she walked out of his dirty little dorm room, that though he thought he hated her, he wanted more than anything to grow old and bored with her, to know the kind of comfort that allowed a person to nod at their lover's dead body. For weeks after he found himself in tears, not over his mother, but over the tight little coils of hair on the girl's head. He broke down in his car on the New Jersey Turnpike, in the line at the Trader Joe's, eating by himself at Ruby Tuesday's one night. She was mist and rain and he was Cousin Steve, that fuckhead, who had a heart attack at forty-five, who quacked and quacked, clinging onto other people's lives. ∎

A Heart in Two Cupped Hands

FLASH FICTION

MIKAELA PRESTOWITZ, Grade 12. Davidson Academy, Reno, NV. Rebecca Coleman and AnnElise Hatjakes, *Educators*; Region-at-Large, *Affiliate*; Gold Medal

The summer with the guavas taught me what it was to be low hanging fruit. We were throwing guavas in the garden because our grandmother said we could. That's a lie. We were throwing guavas in the garden because we could and because daybreak in the tropics hadn't yet resorted to heat and because grandmother hadn't yet awoken to tell us not to. The itch of a midsummer morning drove us out of the house and into the garden; the guavas called down from their roosts and told us we could reach. My sister mounted the tree, her feet like snakes, the coils of her painted toes curling around the branches and drawing her upwards. Fruits of the bottom boughs, where the tree gave up its young fruit easily and often, were still tinted with the green of fresh growth. As my sister ascended, she dropped the guavas to my waiting hands, cupped and open. We were used to things being simple. We were used to things that were round and easy to catch.

We had been used to the firmness of the bottom fruits; we were unprepared for the ease with which the uppermost rind gave way.

The fruits of the apex branches were bright against the sky, where they were too high for grandmother to reach. They were so easy to see, to grab. No green tint in sight. Only yellow. When my sister dropped the guava for me to catch, I did not expect its softness. I had not known that things grew soft in old age, when left in the sun for too long. I did not predict the whorls of my fingers collapsing into the overripe flesh. The pulpy heart of guava shivering in the cool morning air. The humidity not quite risen, the sun only just. Our grandmother, inside sleeping, dreaming about her heart in my child hands. Two girls in the garden in the morning mist, wide-eyed, the juice running a river between us. The bruise of waning fruit against the blue morning sky; grandmother in her bed, ripening away. ∎

The Waiter

FLASH FICTION

OLIVIA SNYDER, Grade 11. Seacrest Country Day School, Naples, FL. Adison Lax, *Educator*; Region-at-Large, *Affiliate*; Silver Medal

The restaurant was nothing special, but the night was unusually cold. It was closer than Wendy's and so Mom had made the executive decision to go there instead. So there we were, my brothers and I rubbing our hands together to get some warmth back in them while Mom asked for a table for four.

Soon enough, one of the hostesses showed us to our table and we were seated. Our waiter was taking our drink orders when It happened.

"And what can I get for you, young man?" the waiter asked me, pen and paper in hand. Too shocked to actually think of anything, I asked for a water. He didn't seem to notice his mistake, and my mom and my brothers didn't either. Good. I wanted this warm feeling in my chest to stay as long as it could.

As dinner progressed, I made my voice a little bit lower than normal when I was talking to the waiter, and I didn't really look him in the eye. I was afraid he would notice the softer, more feminine features of my face instead of my short, boyish haircut and my baggy sweatshirt that hid the curve of my waist and the lumps on my chest. I didn't want him to notice his mistake, and I prayed to whatever deity exists to not let my mom or brothers call the waiter out on it.

It reminded me of the time I had used the family restroom instead of the gendered ones on a school trip. The bathroom itself wasn't anything special, but it was the way I thought of it that made it so. Instead of "just a family bathroom" I saw it as a "non-gendered bathroom." That's where the difference was. It wasn't gendered. It wasn't a place where I had to fit in and make sure I had to dress more femininely or put on makeup to "look presentable" every-day. It was just there, no expectations, and no preconceptions. It was scary, how much more comfortable it felt, because of a little sign.

And that little sign, it was like something had just clicked or slotted into place. The next four hours on the bus I spent researching and worrying if any-one had seen me coming from the family bathroom. But if they did, I at least had the excuse of the girl's bathrooms being too crowded.

The use of male pronouns used to refer to me sent a warmth fluttering through my chest, like using the right bathroom did. It felt right, comfortable. Meanwhile the anxiety of the waiter possibly stopping and using female pronouns curled up in my gut. Hot and cold. Or rather, hot and double cold, since I worried that maybe I was showing that I liked the male pronouns too much, which might make my brothers or worse, my mom, question me.

When getting our food, Mom remarked on how I'm such a potato girl. My stomach dropped and I smiled, praying the waiter doesn't notice the "girl" bit. He didn't (thank you deity), and the rest of dinner went without another incident.

"Isn't it funny how the waiter thinks you're a guy?" My mom asked after she paid the bill. I smiled, trying not to show that my stomach was leading a revolt and the warmth of the "young man" was fading fast.

"Yeah, but I guess it's too late to do anything about it now," I said lightly, as we exited the restaurant. Mom hummed in agreement and I jumped in on my brother's conversation about video games.

Late that night as I'm falling asleep, I think back on the waiter and feel right again. ■

Down in the Bayou

FLASH FICTION

JOSHUA SOGADE, Grade 11. Stratford Academy, Macon, GA. Susan Lolis, *Educator*; Savannah College of Art and Design, *Affiliate*; Gold Medal

Down here in the bayou, cypress trees tower over you, judging your worth. The trees can judge, they live longer. Bayou water doesn't flow like the Missis sippi River does: a continuous flow of urgency and responsibility. Bayou water takes its time. It goes nowhere. It is everywhere. It is resigned in its journey, as with the drowned souls in its mucked limbo. It does have purpose, however. The barbues and 'gators need the water and they make a fine fillet. Humans make fine fillets, too; bayou water is the best place to marinate them.

Down here in the bayou, all meetings are business meetings. Selling land is business, selling guns is business, selling drugs is business, selling men is business. It started with the land business. Metal balls did business by bur- rowing into their backs, bursting out their chests, and spraying out rotten Ta- basco. The alternate proposition came later. First the myalgia, then the fever. You prostrate on the earth, and you bury your face in the remoulade that you vomit and soil your pants with excrement because you cannot lift yourself out of your own filth. Either your skin breaks out with cysts littered on your body like sugar on a beignet, or your it begins to look like crème brûlée as blood seeps from within your veins. Sometimes you start shaking violently, and the now-red remoulade splashes everywhere, all as the light fades from your eyes. If you lived, you were embraced by powdery shackles and chains. If you looked like trouble, you might have been taken to the center of stage. An audi- ence stands before you as the braided leather fwèt repeatedly tears bright red stripes across your back. A pretty face upon ravenous eyes meant you might have been taken backstage, as mèt bent you over and emptied himself into you.

Down here in the bayou, you are a witness or you are a statistic. The pat- terns are crystalline. The slave quarters still look relatively dilapidated. They call it the Lower Ninth Ward now. The slave trade's still booming in business, more than just niggers now. Metal arrows still erupt from chests. The bows are usually black. People are decorated with multiple holes. Men in hoods use them, men in uniform use them. They all kill. Folks die. Often those who die are the people that followed the rules.

Down here in the bayou, it's ill-advised to drink from the water. Streams keep moving, sometimes carrying remnant pathogens. Better that it be the pathogens. One taste from the depths and it's easy to understand why. Bayou water does not move much. You only taste the prejudice, the racism, the crime. Reach down deep enough and you'll taste the diluted bodies of eight women, floating down the bayou. It's all just gumbo. ∎

Flickering Lights

FLASH FICTION

DEDEEPYA GUTHIKONDA, Grade 9. Edina Senior High School, Edina, MN. Theresa Bademan, *Educator*; Minnesota Writing Project, *Affiliate*; Gold Medal

Their words echoed in their actions. They stayed away from me.

During partner projects, they hurried to the other side of the room, getting as far away as possible. I was the sole loner sitting on the bench at recess, eating in the teacher's room during lunch.

They pretended not to notice me but they knew I was there.

Sometimes I stood in front of the mirror, I wondered what they would think if I was as white as them. My skin blending into the cold and bitter walls of the room, unnoticeable . . . but still there. I never failed to imagine the impossible.

"How is it?" My friends back home would ask excitedly, their voices scratchily blasting through the tiny microphone. They peered into the camera excitedly, unaware of all that was happening behind me.

"It's good," I would say painfully, cautiously protecting my voice from breaking, aware that Ma and Papa were listening behind me. They would ask me to say more, but the words I wanted to say would not come out. I would end the call, becoming more distant from them each time. The time difference was too much, our own differences were becoming too much.

We all suffered silently. Evenings that had once been cheerful, full of talking and eating, had now become a silent routine. Disappearing into rooms, hearts aching and faint whispers to ourselves caught and trapped by the solid cement walls. What had once been a whole complete family, with *dada* and *dadi* and aunts and uncles and cousins had simmered down to . . . just us. Only the four of us.

Morning would come and Ma would cook some of our own food, the only time we could eat it, safe in our own homes away from the eyes of the people. For lunch she would distastefully pack those sandwiches on plain white bread, as white as their skin, filled with nothing but the fake sweetness of the peanut and jam. It was a silly thing, to think the soggy bread would make others want to come closer in the lunchroom.

One evening Papa came home with a box, a brown cardboard box wrapped aggressively with thick layers of tape.

"What is in it Papa?" Anjali asked, with her new English words coated in a thick Indian accent.

"You'll see," Papa said, setting the box down after heaving it up the endless flight of stairs it took to get to our little apartment. We peered over his shoulder and watched him as he cut through the box with the sharp blade of the knife.

Green prickly bristles were revealed as the flaps of the boxes opened. We stared in amusement. I thought of the trees that had stood tall and strong in front of the apartment building since we got here. I mouthed what they were called, *pine trees,* stretching my jaw far wide open to pronounce it. Papa lifted it out of the box and set it up so it was standing straight and tall. It was a short, green little thing.

"What is this Papa?" Anjali asked curiously, gazing at this tree that was sitting indoors.

"It's a Christmas tree." He said dubiously, stumbling over his words, spitting out "Christmas" in what I knew was the wrong way. He couldn't help his accent, none of us could.

"But we don't celebrate Christmas," I chimed in for the first time. Papa pondered for a bit, and Ma watched him. A new realization had arisen in both of them.

"Well, now we do," Mama said, filling in for Papa. She smiled and looked at us. Anjali jumped up in excitement.

"We celebrate Christmas! Christmas!" She said, running around the tree. I didn't think she knew what it was.

The tree brought something new into our lives, a new hope. Perhaps, things would become different. It was a far-fetched dream, but it rested in our hearts nonetheless. That night I gazed out and peered into our neighbor's window, the fuzzy lights of their own tree appeared vaguely.

"Look Anjali," I said, pointing to them. "Our tree is just like theirs." She giggled with excitement.

Only, our hopes were crushed long before we could even finish dreaming. When we were sharing what we did over the weekend, I, along with everyone else, said "we set up the Christmas tree," careful not to let a wrong word or sound slip out from my thin lips. I had recited this very phrase in my mind countless times as I listened to the others.

They all looked at me peculiarly, even my teacher. "Now, did you really?" She asked, slightly mockingly. I flustered, my face burning with embarrassment. My penny-colored skin covered it all up and I appeared unflinching to them.

"Yes," I answered, and she told me to sit down.

That was when I realized that we would never be the same. As long as our skin remained the color it was, even our distinct features, we were in two completely different worlds, and it would be that way forever.

The tree sat short and stout in our mostly empty living room, serving as a reminder. We strung some lights around it, lights that Papa had gotten from the dollar store. There was no use.

It must have been past midnight when I went out there, the apartment indulged in complete darkness. I sat next to the tree, the lights reflecting dancing shadows onto the carpet. "Why?" I whispered to it, tears at the brim of my eyes. The lights blinked, and I watched, mesmerized by my own torn feelings. I ripped the lights from the tree and leaned against the raw wall, the heaping pile of lights glowing in my hands, flashing a grim shadow of my face onto the empty wall. They blinked on and off, hesitating nervously. Finally, their cheap bulbs gave in and they fluttered until finally disappearing, blending in with the silent darkness.

Come back, I whispered.

I am still here. ∎

Break

SHORT STORY

HALEY RENEE BORN, Grade 11. Olathe North High School, Olathe, KS. Molly Runde and Deirdre Zongker, *Educators*, Greater Kansas City Writing Project, *Affiliate*; Silver Medal

You can't take it another minute, the shift of tight packed bodies, tobacco fog thick in your nose. Bottles in customers' hands clink like chains tying you here with their emptiness.

"I'm taking my fifteen," you call to the shapes at the bar, knowing one of them is likely your manager.

"The hell you are, we're too busy!" he shouts back but you've already grabbed your jacket, swinging it up and over your shoulder.

"You'll manage." Replying through gritted teeth.

"Get your ass back here!" You ignore, blowing through the heavy double doors. Your pupils dilate in reverse, shrinking from the bar's dull light to the flare of setting sun sparked on low-hanging clouds.

Pulling a pack from your jacket, you read the boldface warning but slip a cigarette past your lips anyway. You quit a few years ago, at your girlfriend's request, but it's all just too much. Working wears down your nerves until your self-control is in shreds.

Maybe that's why, when you hear the barker call *Carnival, free entry!* you wander from beyond the awning and approach the pop-up fair. Music plays from a few staticky speakers and flashing florescent lights battle the sun for dominance over the sky. You take an acrid drag of smoke and imagine tar clinging to your lungs like the black crust where asphalt gives way to dirt. On a whim you begin down the path, looking at the ticket booth and Ferris wheel, the hall of mirrors you want nothing to do with. Something catches your eye and in a moment your ear.

"Step right up and take your shot! One dollar a blow, this old car has got to go! Who doesn't want to let loose for such a low price?!"

A middle-aged woman stands in front of a piece of junk car. Her eyes have light sketched wrinkles and her hair is graying. No, not graying, silvering. She wears a red striped blazer to match the chipped paint job of the Chevy Malibu. Four once-ruby doors.

"Let off a week's worth of steam cheap?" She beckons you forward. You fish around in your back pocket for the dollar bill you tucked there half an hour ago. You look at the car, imagining it belongs to the man who gave you the one.

He had shoved it down the front of your shirt when you leaned forward to grab his plate, which now you suspect he purposefully left out of your reach. It took all your self-control not to let the dish clatter back down in front of him. Seeking refuge, you leaned your back against the kitchen wall and removed the bill from the lip of your bra. That was when you noticed his phone number scribbled in the upper right-hand corner. It was the only tip he left.

You hand the woman the dollar and she hands you the bat.

"You've got one swing, use it wisely," she says jovially and winks. You heft the bat experimentally, heavier than the ones you used for softball in high school. You like the solid weight in your hands.

In your head, you're still trying to pick where to hit but your hands have already decided. The side-view mirror is the weakest.

The connection of bat to mirror is unexpectedly satisfying, like a hit of nicotine. You almost feel your heart tighten, but it's not even broken. It hangs at an odd angle and the reflection of the draining sky is splintered, but it's not enough. Not yet. Again, before you know what you'll do next you hand the silvered woman a five, trying to buy yourself peace in pieces.

This time you shift your feet and tighten your grip. The mirror comes clean off with a plasticky snap, spinning out of sight, out of mind. The fluorescents catch on the perfect, unburdened curve of the car's hood. You're reminded of the way men talk about their machines, about how long you have to listen to a conversation before you can tell if it's about a woman or a car. Usually what gives it away is how much they care about breaking it.

You bring the bat down over your head and into the hood once, twice, three times before it's misshapen enough for you. You've got one swing left. Somewhere you know it's been fifteen minutes, but nothing matters except the blinding moment, the song of this second.

A cloud of breath and a crack as the bat hits the windshield. The glass is thick, you knew that, but you were unprepared for the new claws in your lungs. You barely consider letting go, going back to work and suffocating, before the bat is resting on your shoulder and you're leafing through your wallet. Not something you can afford but you fork over the twenty.

"Whose is it?" She asks.

"What?" You're distracted by the continued wholeness of the windshield.

"Whose car do you wish you were beating on?"

"No one in particular. Some guys from work I guess." You almost don't notice her knowing nod. You can't leave until there's a hole in the glass. If you tried you don't know what you'd do. As the cracks grow and meet to make fault lines in the windshield, you're reminded of the not infrequent urge to grab a grimy piece of cutlery or shatter a bottle and bury it in one of the customers' roaming hands. Just to make them feel it, how far they push you, how much it hurts, but it'd never work. That knowledge, the only thing that stops you.

Right now nothing does. Finally, the glass collapses, sending shards into the soft cushions of the seat. You flinch from memories of being pinched. Gritting your teeth against the flare of helplessness you do to the brake light what you wish you had done to the man who cornered your girlfriend when she came to visit you at work. This time she's not here to talk you down.

Your arms are tired but your blood is fire, rancid as gasoline and sparked. You can't stop until every piece is as twisted and broken and useless as you. You can't see anything but the dent you left in the hood, a dent like bruised hips and breasts. You hit their hands away, marring, scrapping red paint. Your nails dig into the grain of the wood.

Thoughts race, eating up the memory of your manager talking to a table, saying *She's nothing special but she's all we've got.* Your hands, with the help of the bat, begin to dismantle the driver's side window. Like you were a dish served lukewarm. Now it's his car and you slam down the bat until the window's nothing but a web of cuts.

What had he said? That time some drunk shoved you up against the wall and knocked a glass out of your hand? It scattered into pieces that you spent ages picking up, a thousand tiny cuts. Then you were naïve enough to ask him why he was taking it out of your paycheck. What had he said to you?

Twenty hits and the window's more cracks than glass, but still not broken. One more, just one more swing, and you know it would buckle.

Nothing breaks for free. That's what he had told you.

You break the fucking window.

"Don't think I wasn't counting, young lady."

The bat drifts, top landing between your feet in the dirt, handle loose in your hands. You expect you've got blisters. Your hands aren't the only things that feel stripped raw. You let rage flicker and fade, returning to the slow simmer.

You retrieve another dollar, leaving only a five and some checks that would bounce in the wake of your breakdown.

"Nothing breaks for free," you mutter bitterly, holding it out. She eyes it for a moment but doesn't move to take it.

"How about this," she says. Her skin has lines like smiles, but she's serious now. "I'll give you that last one pro-bono and you'll make me a promise."

Remembering a halfhearted warning about selling away your soul you raise an eyebrow.

"You keep the one if you promise to quit your damn job."

You take a breath. A breath and a moment to look past everything at the freshly turned night sky. Put away your money. Walk home. ■

Broken Pieces

SHORT STORY

JENNY HU, Grade 9. Seven Hills School, Cincinnati, OH. Mark Beyreis and Chris Caldemeyer, *Educators*; Art Academy of Cincinnati, *Affiliate*; Gold Medal

She used to play the instrument because Baba made her practice for hours on end every day, his face drawn as he watched her fingers tangle in the strings and stumble over the notes. Sweat dripping down the back of her neck, sometimes intermingling with the tears that dotted her cheeks when the strings dug into her fingers so hard that her skin broke and bruised and bled. Sometimes when she finished he would smile, or clap; he'd place his rough hands on her shoulders and say that she played the most beautiful music in the world and it would all be worth it, all the silent sobs and the pierced hands and the hurt. Other times he would frown and scowl and glare. Say that the sound didn't flow through her fingers and the strings like creek water, say that she broke the music. That he didn't know why he was wasting his hard-earned money on lessons for her if she was just going to slack off, that if they were still in China then she wouldn't have grown up to be so lazy, that if they were still in China life would be good.

Those days had passed. For years now, she'd played the instrument simply because she loved it.

Funny, how the *guzheng* had once been the target of all of her anger, all of her hatred. The stringed instrument with the sound like bells and wind whistling through the tall grasses, the instrument that sang a song of glass and chimes and streams of silver moonlight woven into the snow. She'd forgotten how to love the music, her fingers brittle and stiff as she plucked the strings, her callused fingertips still bruised. Each note sounded like a tear.

Why did she still listen to Baba? Why did she let him force her to play?

She had long since stopped trying to answer the questions, locking them away instead and letting the music fill the hollow void that they left in their wake.

* * *

A strange thought—it had not been Baba who had picked the instrument for her.

She could hardly remember it, could hardly remember when she was still shorter than her aunts and wide-eyed with innocence, before she knew of the rice wine that Baba snuck back to America in his suitcase and her fingers began to bleed. They'd gone to China that year, Baba taking her everywhere he went. She looked just like him, the same dark, lilted eyes that could speak a thousand words and the same strong nose that looked better on a man than a girl. Baba had bragged to all his friends how his daughter was like his little mirror.

One of those friends had taken them to his home, had made his own daughter come and play on a long instrument, a horizontal harp of sorts resting on two stands, her fingertips covered in picks secured to her skin by a sticky bandage. The girl had played, and it had been so beautiful that she'd asked Baba immediately to learn the *guzheng*, too. Baba had been so delighted he'd picked her up by the waist and spun her in a circle. *Finally,* he said, *you want to learn about your motherland.*

As soon as they returned to America, Baba bought a *guzheng* for her, paying for it to be shipped all the way from Shanghai. He proudly told her so, saying that she ought to practice hard to make up for all the money he'd spent.

And she did. "Fisherman's Evening Song," "High Mountains Flowing Water," "Three Variations on a Plum Blossom Melody," she played them all. Baba's favorite was a passage from "Harvest Nights," a slow tremolo melody with arpeggios as the harmony, dancing up and down the strings. He insisted that the tune was a bittersweet one, nostalgic, a song that sounded like home. *If you listen carefully,* he always said, *you can hear the street vendors selling suan-mei candy and the sound of your great-uncle's voice calling for everyone to come to dinner.*

Back then, it was a rare occurrence for him to talk about his childhood in China, only when he was in a good mood, swept up by her music. His stories were a rare treat, a gift given in return for her hours of practice and the dried blood that stained the strings. He spoke of his great-uncle, who'd raised him in Nanjing when his father was in the military, of how he and his cousins had played war games in the mountains and ruled the streets of the city that was always so bursting with life. Of how things were good until he'd left China to come to America and marry her mother.

If I were still in Nanjing I would be a rich man, Baba liked to say. She always hated those words, even though she loved to hear his stories. Baba was a master of a storyteller, his voice warm and rich and golden like honey in the sun. When he spoke, she wished he would always weave that beautiful world of his childhood in Nanjing, rather than shout at her to go practice.

Yet soon enough she would learn that his stories preceded the rice wine. And the rice wine was when the nightmares began.

* * *

Mao-tai, it was called. Baba often snuck the liquor in his suitcase across customs when he came back from his trips to China. He said he went back to visit her ailing grandmother, but they both knew the real reason was to get drunk with his old high school friends on *mao-tai* and memories that no amount of alcohol could water down.

When he drank he became that man who hated her music, that stranger of a man with the accent so heavy she couldn't distinguish his words, that man she could hardly recognize at all. She couldn't reconcile him with the Baba who'd kissed her fingers the first time they bled, the Baba who'd bought her a *guzheng* and taken her to concerts in China and taught her to listen to the undertones in the music rather than just the melody—*what is beneath the music is what pulls at the heart*, he'd said.

She'd done as he said. The arpeggios that climbed across the tremolo tune were in a minor key while the tremolo was in major, giving the song that bittersweet touch that Baba loved so much. The smooth crescendo of a melodic scale building up underneath a strong chordal melody made it lilt and waltz instead of falling flat. Likewise, the desperation and frustration that bubbled beneath Baba's shouts and fits of anger gave her hope that maybe he was the same man, just . . . broken, and trying to break others with his own misery.

The notes were her escape now, when his face turned the crimson red color of the *qipao* dress he bought for her in Nanjing so many years ago, when his voice raised and rumbled and shattered the air. The soft, stirring melodies that sounded like a fine filigree of starlight wrapped themselves around her heart in the place where Baba should've been, filled the gaping void that remained beneath her ribcage, the space that felt so very empty now that *mao-tai* had stolen Baba away.

She often thought that this rice wine must be magic, like the magic that danced in her music but darker. Midnight instead of starlight, depths of the ocean instead of crashing waves. A magic that could change a man from one person to another, in the blink of an eye.

* * *

The notes glide and dance on her fingertips. She feels like the most powerful girl in the world, to have the ability to manipulate sound and weave it into beautiful things, songs made of snow and fractured light.

The Baba she remembered had woven stories rather than music, painting a different world for her to step into, built of imagination and days long past. It was her turn now, to create a land just beyond memory, a land without *mao-tai*, a land where Baba didn't regret, a land where they could be a family once more. A land held together by her fingertips.

Baba taught her to love music and she did. Baba taught her to hear the songs beneath the surface and she did. And Baba taught her to create an escape, a place in her mind to hide from the world when everything came crashing down.

Sometimes she wonders if music is her *mao-tai*, intoxicating notes and drunken glissandos that pull her under dark waters. But whereas Baba is an empty man searching for the light, she cradles brightness in her hands and refuses to let go. Only when her heart is teeming with song does she dare to let herself remember memories so poignant that her tears splash onto the sound box, mingling with the crimson from her bleeding fingers, diamonds and rubies and melodies that sing of days long past. But she smiles as she plays, for she knows there is not a thing in the world more beautiful than the music she spins, the stars she holds in her fingertips. ■

Holodomor: Death by Hunger

SHORT STORY

NATHAN PHUONG, Grade 11. Homestead High School, Fort Wayne, IN. David Price, *Educator*; Fort Wayne Museum of Art, *Affiliate*; Gold Medal

In memory of the victims and survivors of the Holodomor, the Soviet-Ukrainian Famine and Genocide of 1932-1933 under Stalin.

Bat'ko's forehead is runneled with time. It is creased and cavitied like the soil-flecked skins of potatoes that were our dinner. Every night, he stays up late guarding our last loaves of bread, rifle angled wearily at the front door. His breathing has been run ragged with paranoia, and he coughs and paces during his twilight vigil. He can't face silence anymore—it makes him feel hunted. But from the lust in his eyes when he talks about our long-dead pigs and from the greedy way Mama watches my younger siblings lick grimed kitchen pans for months-old grease, I am sure that our family wouldn't mind an overbearing thief. It was only a year ago that I had never truly understood how many people a corpse can feed. And it's been so long since we've had meat . . .

Two years ago, the Red Train rumbled through the main road of our village, thick dust churning beneath the horses' hooves. The Train, a procession of a dozen muddied carts, cut through the scattered huts of the village toward the central gathering area. Bat'ko and my older brother, Marko, had run to the stained storage shed at the rear of our house and dragged a weighty burlap sack of sugar beets to the front porch in preparation for the collector's house-to-house inspection.

Under Ukraine's new Soviet Socialist government, swaths of private farmland had been merged into massive, publicly owned "collective farms." Rural families were now assigned harvest quotas of crops cultivated on these farms. The season's harvest from each Ukrainian village would be amassed, transported to the nearest distribution center, and subsequently allocated to families. When the Red Train was away, I would hear the elder villagers mourn the "old days," when Ukraine still maintained its sovereignty. They would discuss Stalin, oppression, and the murmurings of a rising Ukrainian national group. I helped Bat'ko in the public fields, tending to his assigned equipment while he guided the workhorses toward his all-important quota. A month passed uneventfully.

A drowsy summer had now simmered into autumn. But in the dusk-toned evening, the fields of wheat had fallen into flames. The village's men stood around the public farming plot, stirring and muttering bitterly as a balding Soviet official made bland attempts to explain the burn. He had come from the nearby Soviet administration center as the overseer of this month's Red Train collection cycle. "Рутина," he repeated to the shifting mass of farmers— "routine, a standard procedure." The growers wouldn't be appeased. Finger-nails caked in crusted dirt, one man hurled a rock at the officer. His attendant guards instantly stepped forward, rifles leveled at the crowd. The farmers quieted and began a slow, backwards shuffle away from the blazing field and the soldiers' gleaming guns. In the dark hours, the Red Train wound out of the village with embers and ashes on its tail. The village went without bread that week.

Four days later, the Red Train returned. Confused villagers stood in the front doorways of their houses, caught between trodding back to their storage sheds for more produce and demanding an explanation for the Train's early arrival. As the Train rolled past our shack, clouding the front porch with fine dust, I noticed that the wagons held many more soldiers than usual. Soviet troopers sat under the carts' ribbed canopies, heads swaying in time to the road's bumpy tempo. They were arrayed in full military outfit with cutlasses buckled onto their chafed leather belts. They kept their muskets beside them, barrels propped against their legs. "That cotton must be in high demand," Bat'ko quipped. "An armed escort for this week's Train? General Secretary Stalin must love his shirts." The Train stalled near the village commons, its soldiers piling out of the sagging wagons. And then, the slaughter.

The Soviets stormed the village, flowing past the villagers before challenge could be made. At our house, a contingent of three rifle-brandishing officers kicked down the crude network of fences in our yard, moving swiftly to gut the cow and the three pigs within. They drew greasy bayonets from their sides and hacked at our livestock. The village's thin Ukrainian soil sponged up the rivulets of animal blood.

By now, Bat'ko had retrieved his battered rifle. He blasted above the heads of the soldiers conducting the slaughter. "СТОП!" my father called. "Stop!" But despite his plea, the soldiers scarcely glanced away from their butchery. They knew as well as Bat'ko did that he would not dare to harm them. As long as they were operating under State orders, Bat'ko might as well be another of the snuffling swine, three lazy slashes away from death. Bat'ko let his rifle clatter to the ground. He had only loaded one round, knowing that it would be suicide to threaten the Soviet soldiers with any more than a single shot. He joined me in anxious observance by our house's splintering front door. We exchanged grimaces as shearing metal shafts disemboweled our animals; intestines and livers alike crumpled wetly against the ground, their surfaces still ragged with connective tissues. If entrails could ever be read, these would fester with ill omens.

The next evening, our family visited the decimated grain fields surrounding the village. Bat'ko and Marko strode together through the powdery remains of one plot of barley, the smooth soles of their boots scuffing over a leveled, ashen plain. Intermittently, the gray sky's gusts shifted direction and I became downwind of their conversation. With newly airborne flecks of soot flaking through my close-cropped hair, I listened in on their sporadic, bitter commentary. "By all accounts, the Red Train's work was a sight to behold," my brother remarked with disgust. "Picture for a moment the planning, the organization, the effort, the *discipline* that must have been required for the Soviets to massacre our livestock *while simultaneously* burning the remaining grain fields!" "Indeed! Truly, an astounding feat!" Bat'ko replied, a wry-vicious smile wavering on his lips. He and Marko, like all of the other villagers, had begun to make the pointed distinction between "those Soviets" and us, ethnic Ukrainians. Before the Red Train's pillaging, I hadn't even entertained a difference. But in the lantern-lit walk back to our home, I couldn't help but grasp Mama's hand even tighter. "The State will return our food, right? Mama? Please?" She didn't comment on my last, rattled question, only resting a calloused hand on the back of my neck to guide me forward, always in the warm-wicked womb of my father's lantern light.

Within the next two months, *holod*—hunger—had ground our family down to emaciation. Because our home was far inland, creased into a remote Ukrainian valley, we could neither confirm what little news we received nor access smuggled foods. Potatoes were our main nutrients. Two weeks into the *holod*, we cursed ourselves into finishing the limp potato peels at the bottom of the dead pig's trough. Then, stale bread. The two last loaves of grainy bread were doled out in the thinnest of slices, a luxury beyond measure.

Next, we gnawed through the tanned leather outers of our shoes. The treated material was acrid and sour with each stiff swallow, but it was undoubtedly more palatable than the mossy, wooden roof shingles that were soon to follow. I had long since lost hope in aid from the State. The villagers only ever glimpsed Soviet officers at a distance now. But even those few spotted were likely only taking estimates of the village's death toll. We even heard rumors that the Soviets had sealed off Ukraine's borders, barring crucial food stores from reaching the starving masses.

Yet after another three weeks, we began to eat the soles of our shoes. These had occupied a small, dusty haven by our living room's far wall, becoming that last, tacitly approved reserve. At hunger's call, even the oblong flaps of rubber were welcome.

Then, the rough floorboards. These made for a fleeting alternative, long splinters of oak gouged out by crusted fingernails as a stale snack. My younger siblings' luck didn't last for long. Two promptly slit their fingers to the bone, and the gray-green pus slicking their palms reeked of gangrene.

At eight years old, my younger brother, Vasyl, was the first to die. Once-mirthful eyes bleary with thirst, he had crawled to a nearby pond to take a drink. Over the span of two days, cholera had coiled his intestines into a death-bound spiral. Bat'ko and Mama were too exhausted to shed tears; each held Vasyl's hands in silent prayer. As night drew on, they left him there on the bedroom floor, legs stiffly together and arms outspread. They chose to leave him inside the house, not willing to wreath his body in the yard's blasphemous, crimson soil.

The next morning, Vasyl's corpse was gone. My parents turned their eyes upward—toward Heaven—at this act of Godly grace. But when they had retired to their bedroom, noise from a neighboring house drew me to the living room window. I hadn't heard the clangor of kitchen pots and pans in over a year. And when I worked the window open, I smelled frying flesh, heard the thick sizzle of congealed blood. I smiled at the thought of someone having a good meal today. Abruptly, an unexplained sense of calm overcame me for I could feel Vasyl's aura and touch his presence on the morning's biting squall. ■

This Negro Speaks of Rivers!

SHORT STORY

DANTE KIRKMAN, Grade 11. Palo Alto High School, Palo Alto, CA. Lucy Filppu, *Educator*; Writopia Lab, *Affiliate*; Gold Medal

My white grandfather was in the Navy, so on the Monday after I turned eighteen I took his officer's cutlass out of the display case in the study and headed out. It was a pure silver ceremonial replica sword, with a twenty-six-inch blade, a bone grip, and a black leather scabbard. Totally badass. Why did I take that knife? Well it stood for something, for his honor and strength I guess, and I wanted to bring it to the Navy recruiters to show them I was for real. His name was Alistair Lycurgus Holden, and he was a naval commander who died for our country. Drowned in battle actually. His life meant something.

There was no recruiting office near my house up on Sunset Boulevard in Beverly Hills, or anywhere in West L.A. for that matter, but I Googled a location over on Slauson and Crenshaw, down in South Central. I told Mom that I was off to school, but instead of heading up the canyon road to good old Harvard-Westlake prep, I hit the 405 and sat in the morning commute. They had given me their old Mercedes CLK for my birthday, Stanford red with white interior, so I didn't mind the traffic. It gave me time to think about what to say to the military recruiter:

Name: Peter Moses Holden Compson
Age: 18
Race: African-American
Highest Education Level: 12th grade
Medical Conditions: None
Hospitalizations: Only one
Requested Duty Posts: Sniper (is that a thing in the Navy?), Submarine, Sailor

But should I tell them why I want to serve? Is it fair to say that I just need to get out?

That I've been sheltered my whole life and stuck with my parents' rules even though they broke my only wish. Stay a family. And still they went and got divorced over their whack shit. So I need to leave. I need to explore and break the rules. Besides, with my miserable grades there's no way I'll be getting out of here by going to college.

For some reason the interview didn't go well. Do they usually turn people away? I don't think they should have disarmed me when I pulled out the sword. Screaming "knife, knife!" was really too much wannabe Navy Seal bullshit by those whack Gomer pencil pushers. Submission holds are not comfortable! And I was just trying to tell them about my grandfather, how he was an actual decorated naval hero. To show them that I'm authentic, the real deal! That's all I was trying to do.

To be fair though, "brandishing a weapon," as they put it, does make it sound like some kind of a crime. Maybe that's why they called the police, who warned me and let me go, probably because of the address on my driver's license. Before the cop left, I asked him where the Los Angeles River was. He asked me if I was being a wiseass, and I had to say no. I told him I was serious—that I had heard there was a river running through Los Angeles and I needed to get to it. He told me, "Shut up Billy Budd before I put a 5150 hold on you," and I complied.

Still, despite all that, I don't know why I slashed the leather interior on the passenger seat so many times as I sat in my car in that whack strip mall parking lot next to a wig store. Or carved up the airbag compartments with X's. It was my own car I was destroying. But honestly I felt rejected, like when Dad left, and like having Stanford come to your house and personally tell you that your application was a hilarious joke and how they all stood around their prestigious office and laughed their whack asses off. So self-annihilation didn't seem out of the question. But I did want to know about that river since I figured the day was a bust and I might as well make something out of it.

I was already down in South Central, so I decided to ping my uncle and head over to his house. My Dad grew up down here before he made it big and married my Mom. I was sure Ant would understand how I felt, because he was basically a loser like me, but to be fair, in a good way. He was the right guy to go to when you're feeling self-pity. He wouldn't intervene or coddle or call therapists. He'd just let you do your thing and maybe commentate about it

He would understand that I'm having doubts about what I should do next. He knows they disapprove of my girlfriend Phelicia, who is in fact my future wife, and very mature (not ditching school), a real Miss Perfect. But she doesn't pass the paper bag test. It's such a hassle dealing with everything, and hearing what my parents don't like, which honestly makes me want those things even more. To be fair, Phelicia and I did have a fight last night; for some reason she took their side again over the whole whackness thing.

Anyway, the time I got to Uncle Ant's house I decided enough of the Juuling; I wanted to get high. Just to take a step back and plan my day. I was eighteen, a man of the world. He was home, since his weed house was his home office, so

I pulled up in front of his little magenta-colored, cracker-box house. It looked like it was held up by match sticks and duct tape. Ant looked straight African in his white overalls, as he and my Dad are pretty dark-skin'ded, though I turned out high-yella.

"What took you so long? I've got things to do and I've been waiting on you!"

"Sorry Unc, the day's already a bust. If you can believe it, I just got rejected by some whack assholes at the Navy recruiting office.

"So I decided to just cruise Crenshaw and take Rosecrans all the way over here because I hate the 110 and the 705. Really you know I hate most of the freeways here in L.A. because they've been built along the river, but they're really a concrete tomb for it, an ugly movie set for stupid chase scenes."

He interrupted me. "Ok well I see you're feeling 'tragic' again," he said, using air quotes, "but son I'm not gonna talk about god damn rivers while you're out here skipping school. What you need to realize is you're Blessed and all you have to do in life is stay Black and Die."

"Fine then, just give my my birthday present and I'll be on my way."

"I thought about it actually and sorry you came down here, but you can just be on your way. I ain't finna be part of your drama no more. So just head on home. I already texted your parents, so they know you're down here playing hooky. They said they already knew because a cop gave them a courtesy call."

"You did what? You know what pretentious whack fools they are."

"Boy, your parents ain't phony; green is the new Black. You're the one who's ruinous and disrespectful, riding a wave atop a sea of trouble and pretty soon you finna sink for good. And Boy, you better check yourself—I'm not one of these little Niggas out there, I'm your Uncle. Say something like that again against your family and you're going to start a fracas you can't finish little Nigga, now get outta here and don't come back until you get it together!"

"Well fine then, if it's going to be like that. But I want to go see the river first, so just tell me the way to the L.A. River then. I'm eighteen and I'm captain of my own motherfuckin' ship whether you like it or not."

"Why be like that Pete? Why this insanity? Go and find the damn river by yourself—I'm done with your curly, squirrely bullshit. Simple fact—you think way too much and there is no god damn white whale to find. But truth—you look wrecked, you should really head on homeward, son."

"So now I can't score off'a you? I'm out!"

I had had enough of that. What is the use of a moralizing, drug-dealing, equivocating, hypocrite felon of a relative? So I drove off. On the next corner I saw some slick young brothers leaning on a cherry Impala, chromed-out with candy-paint, and pulled up to score. Their apparent leader greeted me. He was a real Wesley Snipes brother, straight out of New Jack City.

"What's up fancy Nigga? You flamed up for real today son, what set you claim up there in Beverly Hills, or wherever you come from!

"You ain't no MOB Piru Blood, you think you cool with your baboon colors?"

"No I'm just Pete, my Uncle Ant Compson stays over here. I'm not affiliated, I'm only looking to score some dope."

"You hear this Nigga?" exclaimed Lorenzo, turning to his crew sarcastically. "Lorenzo not believin' his ears! Nigga talks so white, out here saying i'M jUSt lOoKInG to SCORE SuM DoPE, Nigga sounds so white and square as his name. I don't care who your narc-Oreo-whack-ass-self uncle be!"

His crew started laughing and calling me a punk and a trick and worse. So I said, "Ok fine then, would you please then just tell me if you know where the L.A. River is from here, and I'll be out."

But Lorenzo started in on me again with some theater and loud talking. "This Negro speaks of rivers! Who are you Old Man River? River Phoenix?" His crew took the cue and started singing "Dat ol' man river," kind of Vaudeville Mammy style, and doing some mock Irish dancing. To be fair, they really deserved originality points for all that. "Rivers, rivers, rivers! River-dancing Nigga!"

Still, it pissed me off, so I grabbed the cutlass and brandished it for real at their whack asses. They just laughed even harder and yelled "Bitch," "Carlton," "Crash Test Dummy!" Then they showed their weapons, so I burned rubber before they changed their minds because their guns did beat my sword.

Around the corner on Guildenstern I spotted an old crack bag doing business and pulled up to her. She had a messed up weave and twitched like a real clucker. To be fair, her ebony skin did still have a royal shine to it against her scarlet velour sweatsuit.

"Looking to score from Little Skittle my young, gifted and Black man?"

"Yeah I could use a couple blunts I'm outta paper."

"Sure I can hook you up for a Benjamin and take good care of you Mac Daddy!"

"Fine, whatever—do you know the way to the Los Angeles River? My phone says it's not far from here."

"Sure I do hon'! There's a park right across the 710 up here, Burnam Park it is, we call it Burn-Out Woods—just a few blocks up ahead. Let Little Skittle come party with you and them hazel eyes, and she'll show you some delights to charm this filthy air! The Blacker the berry, the sweeter the juice—the deeper the magic from this old sailor's wife!"

"That's all right, I ain't looking to get robbed today any more than this," I joked as I handed her a $100 bill and outta the side of my neck added, "Or catchin' nothing off of you no-how. You are one Weird Sister."

She heard me though. Ok, to be fair, I was disrespectful to my elder, but that particular skank was way past disrespecting herself before I was born.

"You talkin' daggers at Little Skittle? Don't want none'a my milkshake, none'a my chestnuts then? Try these then, they're a special 'Power-Courage-Pride' blend of reefer. Just what you be needing down by the river. Watch out when you party with trees though boy, they'll be coming for you!"

I split and continued on Rosecrans, passing under the 710, which by the way, like I've been saying, was built along the river system. From there I got to the park, to be fair right where her mythical self said it was. I sat in my car and smoked a bit, but you couldn't even catch a glimpse of the river from down there. You had to climb the service ladder of the concrete mountain at the edge of the park to see down into the river and its Thunderdome, its Terminator motorcycle raceway.

Anyway, this weed was not chilling me out. That mother fucking Little Skittle, whack-ass weed-grocer, and her voodoo-witch's brew! I was getting agitated and feeling kind of paranoid, but I felt a great strength in me, almost manic, triumphant. I grabbed my cutlass for protection. I raised my silver sword like that whitey Commander Alistair Lysurgus Holden and charged towards the river! Everything was kind of spinning and there was a loud clicking noise in my head, but I was noble, a Mandingo warrior, a Zulu. Not white or whack. So I made up an African ceremony where I cut an X in each of the palms of my hands. It was pretty bloody but I wasn't feeling anything but exalted.

I ran along the top of the concrete levee, but then I slipped on some broken glass and fell hard down the sloped concrete wall about one story into the river bed. I think I was unconscious for a while; I'm not sure. When I got up I could see that the riverbed was almost dry, so I couldn't go down with the ship like the Commander. So I sat in the mud and put war paint on. I had found the ancient river. It was the Euphrates, the Congo, the Mississippi, the River of Grace and Wisdom, all in one. The river I always knew existed! Turkey gravy smell! Thanksgiving! Hallelujah! Then I saw flashing pictures in the sky of blue and red chirping sounds, and then the metal dinosaur birds attacked. I had the strength of ten warriors until the lightning bolts went through me and it got dark.

They told me it was PCP, so that's how I got this ESP. Phelicia doesn't live with me, but she does visit the house when she's home on break from Stanford. She says she's not my wife, but I know she is so I let it go. Mom and Dad converted the pool house for home care so I could leave the hospital place again. They took my sword but I still have my warrior scars. I'm Peter Moses Holden Compson. A rock, a prophet, a phony with a Mississippi slave name. Between you and me, when no one's looking I'm going to find a way to part the water in this swimming pool just like Moses, and if I am whack or if I am worthy, sink like the rock that I am and drown myself just like that damn-cracker part of me Alistair Lysurgus Holden. And go home, once and for all, for real. To the ancient river. ■

Follow Me to the Edge of the Desert

SHORT STORY

KELLY MARTINEZ, Grade 12. Northside College Prep, Chicago, IL. Kyra Doherty, *Educator*; Chicago Area Writing Project, *Affiliate*; Gold Medal, American Voices Medal

BEFORE

I.

WAKING, I WAS MET with an unwelcome ring in my ear. Metallic hum. Discordant rhythms: a single mother hushing her children, the steady tap of sleets on glass, gusts of laughter as college students drifted in. Staring out, it was as though I'd landed in a dull landscape of one of the Dutch masters my father taught—Vermeer or Frans Hals maybe, the colors outside, mixing and mingling into muted tones. I could picture the university students, fixated by the quick, muscle twitch movements of my father as he spoke breathlessly on the Golden Age, in a room populated by glossy replicas; then as they fell into the warm embrace of the train car, their gaze catching the same strokes of color layered on the dull haze, the careful droplets of white rain on glass. Tearing your eyes away from art to drinking more art. Was it coincidental? Or subliminal? Small bits of beauty that we instinctively yet subconsciously dug for, telling ourselves it was readily available when it wasn't.

Before his death, my father and I'd taken the train to the university nearly every afternoon, his head tilted against the metallic frame of the car, lids pried shut, expression transmuted to a distant, preoccupied dreaminess. It was as though somewhere in the darkness, he'd followed the soft lantern glow of memory into my mother's embrace, the lonely comfort of past beauty. She'd died in car accident on one especially particularly grim winter's storm. Her pallid figure had been nearly imperceptible against the snow when they'd finally spotted her. And I hadn't stopped dreaming about her since, trying to make out her voice, straining for not words, but the bend of her mouth and the shine of her eyes, until I was sick, almost convulsing with agony. I'd waken up every night, nearly certain she'd be there. Kiss on my cheek. *Good morning, cupcake.* Soft hands. Avon makeup.

I guess that's all my father had ever wanted, to take these un-savable fragments—her face, emanating a jarring otherness, dark skin and eyes glinting as though they possessed some truth we knew not of—and force them into something that breathed as she had, full of delicate but luminous energy. He'd spend the entire day at a canvas, silent. It upset him to be interrupted. We'd stop eating dinner together a week after my mother passed and seldom spoke unless he'd sent me out for more paints or books he'd left behind in his office at the university.

On one of these evenings, returning from the rich, flowing halls of the art department, I'd walked into pools of light spilled at my feet from lamps torn to their sides, untidy stacks of clothes and perfumes, my mother's favorite gloss-covered art books sitting in boxes, the ivory sheet of canvas cut down the middle, her eyes now half-moons. And then, I'd caught sight of my father, silent and puffy-eyed, listening to the bright blue record player my mother had spotted in a tiny antique shop before giddily bringing it home. For a moment, it was only me and the crooning voice of my mother's favorite singer drifting about as I stood there, blinking in the dim corridor.

Follow Me.
Follow Me.
To the Edge
Of the Desert

The ground beneath me felt oceanic, washing and working through my ears, my eyes, my heart. My father turned his eyes to me, then back to the mess, before falling into a rack of sobs. I pressed the small of my back to the wall, halos of light spilling around me, listening the run of the record, his raw gasps for air, wishing again for silence.

II.

SINCE THE ACCIDENT, my father produced any reason to take the subway. Gas stations owners too haughty with their prices. Car keys left in his office. Burnt exhaust valve. I'd come along dutifully, rewarded with a weary, ghost of a smile. And secretly, I adored it. The feeling of going somewhere and being nowhere, a glorious in-between, as the city faded into a faraway thought. Now I'd began riding the train by myself, stopping at the sort of end of the road places, landing in deserted ends of the city. *Outlandish* was the word. For hours, I'd walk down uninhabited bends, scrutinizing the muted storefront signs, old fast food restaurants with chairs upturned; quiet marks of the past, a reminder that they truly had *been* and still *were,* even if it was only the outline or skeleton; that time could only steal them partly, that there was some shout of hope in the void.

Now, this routine gleaned a happiness I failed to possess in ordinary life. I could shut my eyes and imagine before—nights at Chinese restaurants, harsh lights down on us as I studied and he worked on lectures. Sitting at bookstores in Chinatown. Watching *Le Mystère Picasso* for the tenth time.

But even as they re-opened, his death colored every end of my vision, exploited every crevice, wavered at the surface of every hanging mirror as my mouth curved to form his name. Every now and then, the veil would lift and I'd catch sight of him—an apparition against the subway tunnel's blackness; lingering on the platform, as if awaiting someone; on the edge of his seat, heavy with laughter; next to me, our eyes converging for a moment, a visitation from two contradictory planes: life to death, highest peaks to ocean depths, suburban realms to provincial lull, reality to rabbit holes. And then some noise—the stalling of the doors or the shifting of footsteps—would send me rushing back to consciousness.

I knew it was unhealthy. Still, the status quo seemed so hideously unbearable that I resolved live on the edge of consciousness, never submitting to full awareness. I'd scroll past but never read articles about students at the local university, reminiscing on their beloved professor. I'd only *just* register my name as I slipped into the market, the sounds slipping down the street, slick from a downpour. Slowly and all at once, my life unfolded into a series of last-minute runs over metal thresholds, biting glares of platform lights, and half-conscious wanderings until someone took pity on me and bought me a ticket back to Essex.

He'd died at the start of fifth period (I later found out), sophomore English, taught by a skittish, young woman in round-framed glasses. I could remember the morning, the touch of summertime that dragged my classmate's faces into vacancy. Heavy with perspiration, they gleaned like caramel candies, dripping into their seats. I was engrossed in the metal window latches that'd embittered us all as we'd made effort to open, ultimately with no avail. The next hour passed in a warm daze.

And it was drifting past the stream of students, that I realized for the first time in years, my father was late to pick me up. I'd decided to wait in the library, encapsulated in its dusty, towering rows, for a long time, keeping my trepidations hidden, focusing on the Whitman readings, making small talk, asking for the book locations I already knew.

I'd returned home on the 6:00 o'clock train. I'd torn up four flights of stairs, a monochromatic green and white rush past my eyes, and with agitated impatience, rattled open the door to our apartment. Stepping in, its vacancy was immediately clear. Lamps shut off. Books still in the tidied manner I'd left them, that was so unlike my father's usual disarray. Still, I passed painfully at each room, checking for signs of him. I'd even found the old home line—hidden beneath piles of *National Geographic* and leaky pens—to check for messages on the answering machine.

I tried to imagine he hadn't made it home. Meetings. Students neurotic over final exams. Congestion in the subway. Maybe he'd stopped in at a bookstore or market and hadn't seen the time. My mind bent, tortuously composing could-have scenarios until exhausted, I found the number for the front desk at the university stuck onto the refrigerator. Pulling my thoughts together, I phoned, quickly greeted by a voice I recognized as Horace Conway's. The name for many, conjured up thin, gilt-framed spectacles, silvery hair piled in tight screws, and a warm, unassuming manner. He was, really a receptionist. (Though no one of sound mind would say such a thing within earshot.)

"Horace," I said, my voice almost tearful with relief, "my father hasn't made it home yet. Have you heard anything from him?"

"Carmen," he paused, "Oh my dear, you must come. Come here. There's been a terrible accident . . . " his voice shuttering off.

I don't remember much about the rest of what he'd said. Time felt imaginary. I pulled on my sickly green coat, swept my hair, dark and coarse, into my father's black baseball cap. I bore out into the nighttime, lightning carpeting the sky. Within an hour, I'd made it to the ivory colored steps of the university, water-sodden and uneasy, wavering as though I'd cross the threshold and step into some new, chaotic world.

III.

STEALING THROUGH THE entryway, the warm, bookish of the university came over me. For a while, I drifted between the lines of commemorative plaques (one for each graduating class), large vases, and freshly waxed lecture halls. I found Horace in what I expected to be in his place of permanence: peering over the edge of his great oak desk (strewn with files and ballpoint pens) in deep conversation with a student.

I drifted to him not pausing to excuse myself before I say, "Horace."

He turned to me, absent his usual cheeriness.

"Oh . . . Carmen, yes. I'd been meaning to call you dear—but you see it's all been so much and it must've slipped my mind. Yes, yes, why don't we get somewhere a bit more *private*?"

Just behind his desk was a stuffy office, much like a broom closet but stacked endlessly with photos of his children, old Russian novels, fashion magazines (his sister worked at *Elle*), and notes that read things like *"and the sun still rises"* and *"ask if New Wok delivers."*

He hands me a small mug, filled with tea gone cold, but I take a sip anyway. He lets out a half-audible sign, then turned to me.

"Carmen, your father, I'm afraid they found him . . . they found him here, at the university, his car, well . . . oh—they say the damage is irreparable. Your father, oh well, he's *dead*, Carmen."

I'd already made it to an exit from the university when the office door shut. I worked my coat on, not bothering to check if I'd fastened it correctly as Horace came after me.

"Carmen, you must let me explain!" he shouted, his voice slipping away as I made out into the nighttime, rain catching over my eyes, before stealing away into a quiet, shadowed street I seldom took but was all too necessary now.

And I remember the walk back, how the ground shifted as I trudged past the acidic glow of business signs. The night seemed to shout his absence. I fell deeper into Essex's sprawling backways and shadowed corners, spotting empty restaurants we'd frequented when neither of us felt like cooking—my father's favorite a tiny, pastel-toned diner tucked in a corner between a jewelry shop and fish market.

Intermittently, shock spilled through me. I missed the street to our apartment building a second, then a third time. I tried to think of the last conversation we'd had. What had it been about? I strained for exact words and inflections, trying to retrieve any saveable fragment. Leaning my weight against a bare bicycle rack, I felt an unwelcome swell of emotion. I stood there for a long time, under the phantom streetlights, half-tranced. I was almost certain it was all a dream. My hands pinched at the muted green fabric of my coat, its sodden, worn material shifting between my fingers. I can't explain what it felt to not start then, not to find my head raising over piles of books on a desk as I blinked away sleep.

I felt myself collapse against the blacktop in an almost drunken stupor. On my back, I fixated on a set of grand, wavering eyes, honey-colored, as the clamor of sobs racked through me. The sky seemed to deepen, spilling out before me in an oceanic void. Cars hum by. A young couple passes, laughter rising clear and hopeful in the air.

And in the vast, depthless space before me, I find him, his memory, the glimmer against the black; It was the convergence of light and laughter, the thin, shining point of exactness where stained glass fractures; The swallowing sounds of silence before the next note, the thin patches on the asphalt where flowers are to bloom. Beauty, only sustained by absence.

And what an absence it was.

NOW

IV.

I LEFT IN a hurry, though I could still remember the shock of the nighttime air, eyes wavering over beaming celestial disorder. I was seventeen but still wearing the green overcoat I'd arrived in, hair tangled, eyes strewn with something heavier than I was, something I'd tried to forget but never would. Outside, it felt the way midnight at the ocean would: black and gusty and eternal. Soft signs of life: two-toned diners, emptied gas station lots, the faint glimmer of lights at the window, of the person who'd yet to sleep. Just like Abue, my grandmother, who soon, the sigh of the bedsprings, the pad of her slippers, would go calling *Carmen* to bed, the "*r*" always as though she'd draped it over a metal edge—too harsh.

But even then, I couldn't help but think of Essex. In fact, I could only think of Essex. The pulsing throb of the subway; the quiet line of apartment complexes; the roar of tourists through Chinatown, clad with freshly bought rain gear to fend off the looming downpour; the tiny flat my father and I'd lived in, warm and illumined against the stark New England haze. Echoes of memory, disjointed and fleeting, but with a quality of tangible permanence that left me fitfully chasing fictive realities that would bleed into fictive futures.

The seasons had bled into one another, days drifting soundlessly. I'd wake up at the house of Abue, the bathroom of the library, the subway, anywhere. But never *here*. As the end of summer began to close its mouth over me, I'd found myself on a train back to Essex. I stood in the stuffy, carpeted hallways of our apartment building, eyes drinking in the details around me, shocked with unaltered state of it all. It'd been over a year since I'd left. But here I was, met with the same forest green paint, shaded windows, mundane heaviness.

The evening sounds had all but settled as I ease the door open, greeted with the quiet exhale of particulates. I didn't know what to expect, really, as I entered the empty flat. I pressed the lights on. They wavered over the striped wallpaper, shadows erecting themselves into haunting forms. The beep of the answering machine, then his voice, a low apology for missing their call. About the corner, *sorry, I'm not home.*

His absence hummed at every detail, the quiet contradiction of what had been and what would never be. The lantern glow at his study. The bowl of takeout he'd left untouched. The peculiar slew of patterned rugs that populated the living room. Books at every available space. Department store china left on armchairs and side tables. The thread-and-bare black cap he'd worn *that* day. *Yan-*

kees, the sort of contradiction one could only avoid in Central Boston. Hand in mine, we'd endured the steady, light-hearted remarks from passersby, as we'd peered into the caverns of a Chinese antique shop, candied red and gold, his bookish smell that only a decade as a professor could produce.

I drifted through every end of the apartment until I found myself at the doorway of his room, lingering at the threshold, as though my entrance would disrupt the highest orders of ignorance, the almost certain emptiness inside a disastrous stroke on my portrait of oblivion. He needed to be there. Working my hand over the gilt doorknob, I slipped into the small, honey-lit space.

Emptiness stared back.

I fell to the floor, listening to the hum of the evening tunes; The ceiling sheen swelled about me until reality fades into the bareness, and all I could think about was the hard-wrought beauty of life: My father's distant, swarming eyes that centered intermittently. Restrained laugh, that only unwound when he'd been alone with my mother. A warm embrace, a habit of not combing his hair.

There's something about the small, un-saveable grains of his life that brings an unwelcome surge of emotions, something akin to an electric shock or a dousing in ice water. It was the figure at the study; it was the guiding hand after skinned knees; it was the voicemail that he'd be late, but he'd be home soon. It was . . . it was . . . it was. Because everything now could only be *was,* an inexhaustible series of *what-ifs* and hypotheticals; a perpetual ring that burned resonant against the nighttime, unfolding slowly, as though a strain of musical notes in lullaby, lulling and distant, before delivering me to the dark thrall of subconscious thought and finally, the blackness of sleep. ■

Where Flowers Grow

SHORT STORY

VANESSA VASQUEZ, Grade 12. Fort Hamilton High School, Brooklyn, NY. Niki Maratos, *Educator*; NYC Scholastic Awards, *Affiliate*; Gold Medal

"Go kill yourself while you're at it,"

and with that, Mama took a puff and imprinted the butt of her cigarette on my arm—marking the 25th scar to what I had begun to regard as birthmarks for the sake of keeping the truth at bay. Grinding the pink off my lips till the pain subsided, I quietly picked up the stubs that had begun to form a ring around her toes—dumping her ashtray to the part of "home" where my fingers grew raw. There, against the nestled corner of the yellow-lit kitchen where mold peaked through the crevices of the walls, I scrubbed the filth off Mama's belongings until the sun sought its bed—never ceasing until I felt the shove of her knuckles against my bones.

"Get the fuck out," she would say.
And, like any child would, I set the chores down, and got out before she had a chance to mark me with the 26th.

My father left before I was born—met a light-skinned woman along the sky-scrapers of the Detroit River and left before Mama could even muster a sound. *Our baby,* I imagine a pregnant Mama saying after finding my father rushing to stuff her little jewels inside his luggage—the same jewels she had kept wrapped in silk cloth for the sake of feeling like a rich woman. Feeling like she had worth in spite of living in a broken home tucked in the heart of what people had begun to call "Murder City." But Mama knew she'd never be a rich woman, so she settled for love. And when love slipped through her hands and rotted the flowers she had begun to grow, it crippled her. So Mama substituted love for hatred until that too became too strong—too potent for her severed soul to exert on her five-year-old daughter. So Mama turned to alcohol—shifting the calendar of when to beat and bury my remnants from weekly to daily. If there is any truth in this world, it is that I was never a part of "our" baby for that would mean that, at one point, Mama wanted me. I like to imagine that she did. I like to imagine myself as the little, pig-tailed girls pictured on the covers of children's books. The ones adorned with tiny tiaras and clean, round-toe shoes because their Mamas wanted them to look their very best. Because their Mamas *cared* and *loved* and *nurtured* them. Because their Mamas let them know that they were *wanted*—an idea that my Mama has come to let me know, time and time again, I was not. Where these Mamas taught their daughters the alphabet through songs and silly little faces, my Mama was ahead of the game— teaching me words like: bitch, baggage, burden, and even the sentence: "I wish you'd never been born." But Mama doesn't only remind me of this. She makes sure that when I stare at my reflection, I see that engraved across my skin.

I remember when Mama said her first "I hate you." We had sat along the rim of a beaten, oil-greased dining table—separated by piles of Tupperware and week old take-out boxes that had begun to form a barrier between us. I sat silently and picked at the pieces of skin that fashioned themselves across my cuticles. You see, for an eight-year-old, I was intuitive. I knew that if I smelled the musk of Mama's breath, the heavy tang so familiar to bottles of cheap rum, I needed to crawl into myself because, that way, I could survive. With this in mind, I decided to make a cautionary list that warned me of all the moments when not to make Mama angry because angry Mama hurt me, and I was tired of being hurt—of having to hold onto the fray of my sleeves when I lifted my hands because no one wanted to be friends with the girl who had burns and blisters across her arms. And so, I picked up a pen and wrote against the bleeding marks.

*1) When Mama pulls the glass bottles
from under the sofa, don't speak or
look at Mama because Mama will
hurt you.
2) When Mama takes a puff of her
cigarette, don't stand too close, or
else Mama will burn you, and you
don't wanna be burned.
3) When Mama takes a puff of the
stinky-feet smelling cigarette, you can
go out and play in the garden because
Mama is calm and calm Mama doesn't
hurt you.
4) But don't spend too long in the garden
because you will get dirty and Mama
doesn't like you bringing dirt in her
house.*

5) Mama loves you.
6) Even when you think she doesn't—
Even when you believe the tirades
against your existence—
Mama loves you in her own special way.
Mama has to love you.
She has to.

Sitting there, in the place where Mama blocked the kitchen exit—her breath forming a cloud of Bacardi in the air—I knew I had to brace myself, and as I did, she followed the first "I hate you" with the second, the third, the fourth, and so on until she beat down that childlike intuition. I never looked at 5 and 6 again.

Mama used to tell me that flowers would never grow for as long as I was alive. That's why when I stepped out into the garden to lose myself among the flowers—to forget and to be alive—I lost myself all together. And so, when Mama sucked the burning green leaves from their paper blankets, I broke through the smoke and into freedom—sinking my hands into soil until they rose with seeds from the garden of weeds and wilted stems. One by one, I lifted their shells from the ground until I could hear their song rustle in the pockets of my pants, and when Mama rose her hand to brand the outline of her fingers across my cheek, soil-stained hands rupturing the fourth rule to my simple list, I'd reach for those seeds and press them against my body—hoping they would make me feel as I did among the unkempt field where I was repotted and reborn.

And so, with every venture into Eden, I watch as the marks turn from 25 to 27, 27 to 35, and 35 to 1 as the scars begin to fuse themselves together. And as they do, as the blacks and blues decorate my body like roots buried beneath, I take those seeds and plant them inside me.

So guess what, Mama?
Flowers do grow here
And I carry them with me.

A Modern Fable

HUMOR

VANDER ENGLAND, Grade 8. Wheaton Christian Grammar School, Winfield, IL. Daniel Huttenlock, *Educator*; Region-at-Large, *Affiliate*; Silver Medal

Once upon a time there lived a young princess, who was growing up in the castle with the queen and the king. Soon, however, along came the socialist revolution that kicked the "royal" family and what they would call "their" knight-in-training out of the castle (although kicking out the knight was largely unnecessary, as he was largely incompetent and unknowledgeable, which wasn't helped by the fact that he hit his head on the way out). The people involved in the revolution, being people of above average levels of compassion, decided to kick the family out of the castle and make them live how they did for a change.

Not long after, the ex-queen passed on due to the culture shock of living like the normal populace. Her husband was so brokenhearted that, neglecting the well-being of his own daughter, married another woman almost immediately. Not very soon after that, the ex-king died of a broken heart, because his decision to marry this new woman was just a wee bit rash and he missed his old wife (this is not to say she was age enhanced, just his original wife).

As the young princess grew older, she viewed her stepmother in a worse and worse light. Now, her stepmother wasn't mean or evil or even cruel, simply misunderstood. Soon, the young princess, who some uneducated people might call foolish, decided to run away to the forest, thinking she could fend for herself. She stumbled onto a small cottage that used the native soil as walls and, being unskilled in the ways of the world, decided to just barge on into the house.

In it, she found seven little bowls of extra fibrous, boosted vitamins, non-GMO oatmeal with prunes, however she believed that three were too hot, and three were too cold. One she found to be "just right," temperature-wise, although others might not agree with this statement. She did find the nutritious food to be less than delicious, however.

After she ate the oatmeal, she felt full, so she went into the next room and came upon seven small chairs. Again, three were too hard, three were too soft, but one was "just right." She promptly sat down, although the chair soon broke under her above average but beautifully normal weight. Not wanting to be caught at the scene of the crime, she decided to go on to the next room.

In this room there were seven completely equal piles of straw on the floor, which she presumed served as these primitive creatures' bedding. Her assumption that these beings were primitive was a rash one, and if she was better schooled in the ways of the world she wouldn't make such presumptuous and arrogant statements. She found that all seven of these natural beds paled in comparison to the perceived "comfort" of the castle beds, although she was able to fall into a restless sleep in the last one.

When the owners of this house came back, they first noticed the missing oatmeal.

"Someone's been eating my extra fibrous, boosted vitamins, non-GMO oatmeal with prunes!" one said.

"Someone's been eating MY extra fibrous, boosted vitamins, non-GMO oatmeal with prunes!" another interjected.

"Mine too!" one replied.

"Me too!" another suggested.

"Same with me!" one of the men exclaimed

"My bowl hath been eaten out of!" one of them uttered.

"Someone ate out of mine, and now it's all gone!" the littlest of stature nearly whispered, followed by a loud gasp of all of the others. Disrupting their equality was the highest crime in their micro, but still fully functioning, society.

While some of the men readied themselves to take revenge, gathering all the pens and paper necessary to write a sufficiently long strongly worded letter, the rest went into the next room and saw their chairs. They could only prove that someone sat in one of their chairs—the broken one- but each secretly thought that their own chair was sat in as well, although none would say it out loud, for fear of becoming a pariah due to a false accusation.

After the letter was readied, both groups converged in the last room, and all parties checked in their bed, each saying that their sheets looked ruffled. When they turned to the littlest-but-still-beautiful man, he said "Someone's been sleeping in my bed, and they're still here!"

When the princess came to, she found seven small men looking down at her. Her immediate reaction was disgust at their untamed hair and short stature, which was an extremely mess-ist and height-ist thought. She recoiled, and so did the men. They apologized for their appalling behavior and invasion of her personal space, than told their story.

They explained their lifestyle, then expounded on what happened upon finding it was interrupted. After finding the princess in one of their beds, they waited, wanting to give her sufficient time to rest, under the possibility of her not getting enough at home. Being good, upstanding citizens of their self-governed commune, they offered to incorporate her into their micro-society. She was originally naïvely opposed to the idea, until the little men showed her their presentation on socialist micro-societies. She promptly fell asleep, which the little men took as a "yes."

When she awoke, the princess found that the little men had built her a room of her own. She had warmed up to this lifestyle, and soon enough she grew to like it. The little men skilled her in what you should and shouldn't say, who to vote for, and the other ways of the world.

The princess soon grew up to be a beautiful, but mostly strong and independent, woman, but the men of the kingdom focused on the first adjective. Many men came to try to take away her freedom, including the original royal family's idiotic knight, but she always remained free, and even managed to talk them into taking her money to buy themselves healthcare.

One day, when the princess was out on a leisurely stroll to become one with the universe, she noticed what looked like an innocent creature in trouble. After trying to help it, she realized that it was in fact a large dragon. This dragon caught her up in one of its claws, and whisked her away to a tower, where she was promptly dropped. This dragon was not wrong in doing this, because the reason it did this was largely because of its upbringing.

The dragon was catching small creatures for her to eat in the beginning, but this was a horrendous thing to do, because the princess was a devout vegan. After much humble asking, the dragon eventually started growing a garden and gave it to the princess. Again, she wasn't happy, because the dragon used pesticides, but she did have to eat.

Back in the commune, the little men were getting worried when the princess wasn't coming home. Believe me, they trusted in her ability to provide for herself as a strong independent woman, but after two weeks they began to wonder. They got out their pens and paper to write a strongly worded letter, but then wondered, "Who can we possibly write to?"

They discovered that they had to leave their commune to investigate.

Shortly after, the knight was skulking at the edge of the city, mad at everyone for rightfully shunning him. When he heard that the north tower was being occupied by a dragon, he decided that this was his time to shine He was about to investigate.

At roughly the same time, seven small men and a very large, but rather incompetent and uncouth knight showed up at the north tower, for entirely different reasons. The little men had heard the princess singing, and were just getting ready to write a strongly worded letter to the "owner" of the tower, when the knight came up and was putting on his leather climbing gloves, just like a true predator. The little men, righteously enraged, lectured the knight on the evils of the cattle industry, then tried to burn his gloves. The knight shook them off and, like a true predator, threatened them with his sword.

After the little men begrudgingly backed up, the knight started to climb the tower. When he got to the top he promptly killed the dragon, then was ready for the fair maiden to—stereotypically—fall into his arms, however, much to his surprise, she slapped him.

"You are a true predator! What has this dragon ever done to you?" she cried.

"I was rescuing you!" the knight retorted.

"Well I say! I am a strong independent woman, and I do NOT need your help! That dragon was completely innocent, as him victimizing me was largely a result of his upbringing!"

"But . . . he kidnapped you!" the knight retorted.

"That's it! I'm taking you to court!" the princess sobbed, which is perfectly okay, as she had a good reason.

"For what?" inquired the stupid knight angrily.

"Oh, I don't know, MURDER?" answered the princess with perverse relish. She wasn't wrong in doing this, as the knight's idiocy and the grief of the dragon—an innocent creature—dying naturally clouded her judgment.

BANG BANG BANG

"Order in the court," came a wheezing old voice. "Now, will the prosecutor bring the charges to the table?"

"This man should be locked up for killing the dragon!" answered the princess.

"I trust you wholeheartedly," stated the wheezing old judge.

"What about my side of the story? What about bringing witnesses to the stand?" exclaimed the knight very rudely.

"ORDER IN THE COURT!" bellowed the wheezing judge. "For that, I'm making your cellmate a bed-wetter."

"But that's a cruel and unusual punishment! And what about due process?" exclaimed the wrongfully angry knight.

"You're a cruel and unusual person," wheezed the judge. "As for due process, it's unnecessary for someone as obviously guilty as you. Now, without further objection . . . "

"Yes, there is an objection, your honor!" came a voice from one of the little men from the jury.

The other little men chorused their agreement.

"Shouldn't our society be based on equal representation, no matter what, despite the atrocious acts of the defendant?"

The moronic knight grumbled quietly, but was ignored.

"Furthermore, shouldn't we welcome anyone, even if they're a threat or a hindrance, with open arms and giving them as much or more than the already wealthy?"

Six hours passed, then . . .

"Which is why we should welcome the knight, feebleminded as he may be, back into our society. Everyone is a winner!"

Everyone clapped except the dim-witted knight, who had fallen asleep.

"I wholeheartedly agree," said the princess, "and I'm sorry, knight, that I ever got so angry at you, even though I had cause for it, and you are so very dense."

"Yes. I think we can all agree that we should now present the knight a choice: give up his predatorial lifestyle and join us in perfect harmony in nature, or face multiple lifetimes in prison. What do you say, knight?"

What do you think the knight would have said?

We'll always be wondering, as the knight was struck down by lightning before he had a chance to answer—evidently because of his idiocy.

Everyone rejoiced, because they guessed what the knight would have said, and they didn't want to give him out his punishment.

In this, everyone lived equally happily ever after.

Moral: Don't be the stupid knight, and you will always succeed, no matter what. ∎

Trendy Restaurant Menu

HUMOR

LYDIA WEI, Grade 11. Richard Montgomery High School, Rockville, MD. Molly Clarkson, *Educator*; Writopia Lab, *Affiliate*; Gold Medal

FRITTATA WITH CHORIZO AND FRESH SPRING GREENS
Our creamy, custardy frittata is filled with smoky chorizo bits and tender spring greens to power you throughout your day. As a socially conscious restaurant, we pledge to use free-range eggs, which allow chickens to go outdoors for brief periods while still living in otherwise enclosed factory farms because the USDA's definition for the label is so loose!

BUTTERMILK BLUEBERRY PANCAKES
WITH LEMON-RICOTTA WHIPPED CREAM
Start your morning off right with a stack of our buttermilk pancakes, studded with blueberries harvested by vulnerable and impoverished immigrant workers! These light, fluffy pancakes are garnished with a bright lemon-ricotta whipped cream that perfectly disguises the bitter taste of wage theft, poverty, hostile working conditions, and intimidation from large corporations controlling immigrant work visas!

AVOCADO TOAST WITH SMOKED CHILE FLAKES AND LIME
A signature brunch dish! Our farm-to-table partners (or, large corporations) harvest avocados in water-deficient valleys in Chile, drilling deep wells to provide nutrients for the plant and lowering the regional water table so that impoverished locals lack safe drinking water. These exquisite green malnutrition bombs are then smeared onto toasted sourdough bread and confetti-covered with chili and lime for an extra zing!

SESAME-SOY AHI TUNA POKE BOWL
A bright and colorful bowl with a delightful sesame crunch and savory soy sauce, our poke is made with yellowfin tuna, a near-threatened species with a strong mercury content from industrial emissions! Our seafood is always fresh because we only use quality-sourced ingredients (and because our distributor only uses carbon monoxide to preserve tuna's pink color)!

NEW ORLEANS-STYLE SHRIMP JAMBALAYA

Authentic New Orleans-style jambalaya gets a kick of heat with jalapeños and a generous dose of hot sauce. This dish is also bursting with tender Asian factory farm shrimp most likely uninspected by the FDA, which inspects only 2% of seafood imports. And if your shrimp from Thailand contains klebsiella, a bacteria resistant to numerous antibiotics, consider it a real taste of the Big Easy!

BURGERS WITH CARAMELIZED ONIONS AND CHIPOTLE KETCHUP

Soft, toasted potato buns, caramelized onions, tangy chipotle ketchup, ruffles of lettuce, and succulent patties all come together to form our perfect burgers. With a sizzling griddle and the perfect fat ratios, our patties are crunchy and compact, oozing out rivers of juice much like the cattle manure that accumulates on factory farms and flows into waterways and drinking water. Careful—you'll need a paper towel for that!

PORK MEATBALL BANH MI WITH PICKLED VEGETABLES
AND SECRET HOT SAUCE

A modern twist on the traditional Vietnamese sandwich, this banh mi is fully loaded with crisp, pickled vegetables and pork meatballs, all tucked into a crackly baguette. Our pork comes from farms whose operations are as secret as our hot sauce due to Ag-Gag bills making it illegal to take farm jobs undercover or as a journalist. The meatballs add the perfect hearty bite to this towering sandwich full of underhanded policies and contrasting flavors!

FOUR-LAYER CHOCOLATE CAKE
WITH DARK CHOCOLATE GANACHE

Treat yourself to a decadent slice of silky-smooth chocolate cake, prepared in-house by our expert pastry chef. It's the perfect guilty pleasure: moist, indulgent, and the force behind deforestation in the Ivory Coast as farmers clear tropical forests to plant cacao trees and meet the global demand for chocolate. But shh—your hips and African deforestation will be our little secret! ∎

Woodbury High School Newspaper

HUMOR

BRIDGET PEGG, Grade 12. Incarnate Word Academy, Saint Louis, MO. Claire LaMarche, *Educator*; Greater Kansas City Writing Project, *Affiliate*; Gold Medal

Government Teacher Tries Really Hard to Be Impartial

Stewing behind her desk while watching a presentation on the constitution devolve into a rant about the current governor, government teacher Ms. Smith wondered if she was allowed to inform the student that the U.S. tax plan was, in fact, *not* a product of communist Russia.

"It's so difficult in these divisive times to be informational, and not let my biases show through," she told us. "Especially since the class is primarily based on discussions of some hot-button issues."

In her first year of teaching the subject, Ms. Smith seems disappointed that her fourteen- and fifteen-year-old students appear to be incapable of nuanced political arguments and debates on the nature of governance.

"Just last week, a student said, 'I don't think there should *be* a government at all. Like, can't we just pay somebody a little bit of money every once in awhile to build the roads and schools and keep us from getting killed?'

To which I replied, 'That's what the government *does*.'"

Following that comment, the school received a barrage of angry phone calls and emails from parents upset.

"Why can't these teachers *one*, reinforce my family's personal beliefs," said angry parent Nancy Wilcox,

"While *two*, teaching the basics of civics. It should be simple!"

In response to the criticism, Ms. Smith has adopted the policy of only replying to students' opinions with,

"Well, that's one way to think about things."

Despite the controversy surrounding her class, Ms. Smith says that she can at least take comfort that her students are doing better than the current U.S. government: "Sometimes they even finish their work on time!"

Meanwhile, Woodbury's English department head, Mr. Jefferson, was debating between affixing a Greenpeace or Socialists of America sticker on his classroom door.

Drama Teacher Regrets Teaching Theater Warm-Up

Woodbury's resident drama teacher, Ms. Laird, reportedly immediately regretted teaching theater warm-ups to her Introductory Theater students.

"At first, they were shy, mumbling," she said. "But then . . . they started to roar, louder and louder . . . like the crowd at my regional production of Chekhov's *Three Sisters*. Then, within minutes, there were people trying to split into four different octaves, students unnecessarily stretching, quotes from *Hamilton*."

At press time, a disconcerting chorus of twenty hyper theater kids sang as one, "When I *took* my *tea* I *took* my *tutu* out."

"I will admit this doesn't look great," Ms. Laird mumbled, "But they didn't want to read *Waiting for Godot*."

Following another round of noise exercises, Ms. Laird took another swig of coffee and put earplugs in.

"What?" she asked. "They're sanity measures."

Investigation: Accumulating Ball of Hair Tumbles Through Hallway

Many students have claimed to have witnessed a mysterious ball of hair slowly drifting through the halls, growing in size as it traveled. Also known as "the Blob," "the Hairy Horror," and "Tumbleweave," none have successfully captured or destroyed the Ball, though many have tried. The administration claims that there is no evidence for the Ball, and denies its very existence. They blame increased sighting of the Ball on stress-induced hallucinations.

However, maintenance worker Tommy Willis believes that this is merely a cover-up: "I've seen it! I don't care what those paper-shufflers in the office think or say. They don't want this to get out, that's all. I've been hunting the Ball since the eighties. I came close last year, *so* close . . . But the leftover perm glues everything together, and the flattening from the early two thousands makes it hard to grip. It just kept rolling through the hallway, and no one did anything . . . rolling, rolling, rolling . . . "

Geometry Teacher Replaces Chemistry Teacher as "the Cool One"

Ever since she started attaching "fresh memes" and "spicy tweets" to the last page of her tests, geometry teacher Angela Wilson has been on the rise, replacing Alex Johnson as "the Cool One."

"Yeah, Mr. Johnson blows up things all the time," said one sophomore, "but I *feel* those memes. Sometimes, she even puts emojis in the equations. Stuff like, 'Solve for Dancing Lady' instead of x."

Wilson is reportedly ecstatic, telling her husband, "I know teachers aren't supposed to have favorites, but it's nice to know that I'm the *students'* favorite."

Mr. Johnson, inconsolable, said that he would try to throw in an extra day of slime making to win back the teenagers' fickle favor.

"Do you know how hard it is to make chemistry *interesting?*" he lamented. "I set everything flammable on fire, I doused half my classroom in acid, and they *still* move on to other teachers. I can't lie—I feel betrayed. I guess I'm going to have to start throwing out candy to stay relevant."

Teachers Still Baffled by Technology, Study Shows

For the fiftieth year in a row, a recent study conducted by every exasperated IT worker has concluded that teachers continue to be perplexed by all manner of classroom technology. Teachers particularly struggled with difficult tasks like shutting off the overhead projectors, sending emails, and turning their computers on and off.

Despite recent difficulties, the Conglomeration of Technology Experts in Schools remains hopeful for the future, putting out the following statement: "We're working to give them new tablets, new SmartBoards, and all new programming next year. That'll definitely clear things up."

The teacher's union has requested books instead.

School President Congratulates Himself on
Proposed Plan to Raise School President's Salary

Saying that it was his best decision in years, School President Wilson has decided to raise his own salary. The proposal was unveiled at the most recent school board meeting, where it was met with unanimous, if reluctant, applause.

"I need to do what's best for the school," He said at the meeting, "And what's best for the school is me having more money!"

The president reports that his 5 percent raise will be funded largely from teacher's salary cuts, as well as the destruction of the music department.

"Look," Wilson said, "these teachers . . . they've got twenty students in a class, and I've got, well, if you carry the two . . . I've got more than that! The entire school!"

Updated College and Career Prep Curriculum Instituted

In the midst of a rapidly changing economy, Woodbury High School has introduced a revolutionary new College and Career Prep class. Developed from Millennial Guru Toni Klasing's confessional *How I Learned to Stop Worrying and Love my Pensionless, Dead-End Job*, juniors in the class focus on embracing the death of the American dream and enduring comments from baby boomers complaining about their generation's laziness.

"The first week, we work on basic techniques, like the inevitable break-down call home for money during college," said Mrs. Brachman. "Then we move onto more advanced steps, like the 'attempting to network my way into an entry-level position' maneuver, or even the 'splitting a two-person studio with fifteen other people and their cousins.' That one can be especially tricky when there's a health department employee downstairs." Students additionally learn meditation techniques to deal with the overwhelming stress from student loans. To help prepare them, Mrs. Brachman plays audio of loan collectors leaving urgent messages over the speakers. "My favorite is the one with thirty minutes of some guy shouting 'Debt! Debt!'" She told us, "That one gets me every time."

Woodbury's College and Career Prep differs from other high schools, School President Wilson believes, in that it's realistic.

"No one needs all that 'pursue your dreams' shtick," he says. "My bet is that there'll be all of five jobs *not* taken by robots by the time these kids have graduated. We want to acclimate them to that near constant level of economic anxiety surrounding the economy. You've got stagnation, housing crises, gentrification, debt, a shrinking job market. Best thing they can do is learn to just suck it up and live with it. Unless they don't have insurance. Then they won't be able to live with it . . . "

When we visited the class, two students were sobbing in the corner, each clutching their scholarship letter. Mrs. Brachman screamed that, "This is a *sharing* economy now! But do you know what we *don't* share? Our feelings!"

She then turned to us and whispered, "Proudest moment a teacher can have. Look at that. They're crying. And *that's* how you know they understand the material." ∎

Love with Romeo and Juliet: A Parody

HUMOR

JULIANNA REIDELL, Grade 10. Jenkintown High School, Jenkintown, PA. Tamara Craven and Shannon Hackett, *Educators*; Philadelphia Writing Project, *Affiliate*; Gold Medal

Little Will's Junior Classics: Love with Romeo and Juliet
Adapted from William Shakespeare
Retold in the style of "Fun with Dick and Jane"

See Fair Verona.
See us lay our scene in Fair Verona . . .

See the families.
The families are rich.
The families are noble.
The families are powerful.
The families love tax loopholes.

See the Montagues.
The Montagues do not like the Capulets.
See the Capulets.
The Capulets do not like the Montagues.
Why do the Capulets and the Montagues despise each other?
Who knows?

See the Capulet servants.
See the Capulet servants meet the Montague servants.
See the Capulet servants bite their thumbs at the Montague servants.
See the street erupt into a brawl.

See Benvolio.
Benvolio wants to stop the fighting.
See Tybalt.
Tybalt is a Capulet.
Tybalt does not want to stop the fighting.
Why does Tybalt not want to stop the fighting?

Tybalt is a dolt.
See Benvolio and Tybalt fight.

See the Prince.
The Prince is angry.
Why is the Prince angry?
The Capulets and Montagues have disturbed the peace.
See the Prince say that the next Montague or Capulet to fight will be punished with death.
The Prince is having a bad day.

Meanwhile . . .

See Romeo.
Romeo is a Montague.
Romeo is sad.
Why is Romeo sad?
The girl he loves, Rosaline, does not love him.
Romeo is certain the world is a black place.
Romeo is very much an overemotional teenager.

See Benvolio.
See Benvolio try to cheer up his cousin Romeo.
See Benvolio take Romeo to a party.
See Romeo mope all the way there.

See Mercutio.
Mercutio is Romeo's and Benvolio's friend.
See Mercutio go to the party with Benvolio and Romeo.
See Mercutio endlessly talk about fairies and dreams.
Why does Mercutio talk about fairies and dreams?
Mercutio is a drama queen.

See the party.
See the Capulets at the party.
The party is a Capulet party.
Oh no, Romeo!
See Juliet.
Juliet is a Capulet.

Juliet's parents want her to marry Paris.
Why do Juliet's parents want her to marry Paris?
Juliet's parents get lots of money and power out of the deal.
See Juliet hold no opinion of her own and agree to check out Paris.
See Juliet's Nurse talk for 33 lines straight.

See Romeo.
See Romeo see Juliet.
See Romeo fall head-over-heels in loooooove.
So long, Rosaline!

See Romeo and Juliet dance.
See Romeo and Juliet make comparisons to saints and pilgrims.
See Romeo and Juliet kiss.
Romeo is a Montague.
Juliet is a Capulet.
This does not bode well for their long-term relationship.

See Tybalt.
See Tybalt see Romeo.
See Tybalt get mad at Romeo for coming to the Capulet party.
See Tybalt vow revenge.
See Lord Capulet call Tybalt a saucy boy.

See Mercutio.
Mercutio is angry.
Why is Mercutio angry?
Romeo has run back towards the Capulet house.
Romeo is running to see Juliet.
Run, Romeo, Run!

See Romeo.
See Romeo sneak into the Capulet garden.
See Romeo hide under Juliet's balcony.
See Romeo talk to himself about Juliet.

See Juliet stand on the balcony.
See Juliet talk to herself about Romeo.
See Romeo watch her under the balcony THE WHOLE TIME.

See Romeo come out from under the balcony.
See Romeo and Juliet make promises of love.
See Romeo and Juliet agree to get married the next day.
See Romeo and Juliet make several disastrous choices.

See the Friar.
The Friar likes plants.
See the Friar talk about his plants.
See the Friar talk to Romeo.
If only Romeo were as smart as his plants.
See the Friar reluctantly agree to marry two emotionally questionable
teenagers in the hope of keeping Verona's peace.

See the Nurse.
See the Nurse take an entire day to find Romeo and make certain he wants
to marry Juliet.
See the Nurse's attempt to slow down the fastest relationship ever, in hope of
more sensitive heads prevailing, ultimately fail.

See Romeo.
See Juliet.
See Romeo and Juliet get married.
Congratulations, Romeo and Juliet!

See Mercutio and Benvolio.
See Mercutio and Benvolio hang out like cool dudes in the town square.
See Mercutio and Benvolio trash talk Tybalt.
This is justifiable.

See Tybalt.
Tybalt is angry.
Why is Tybalt angry?
Tybalt wants to duel Romeo for coming to the Capulet party.
Romeo is nowhere to be found.
But will Tybalt give up?
No, Tybalt will not give up.
Tybalt, the cretin, will keep looking until he has somebody to fight.

See Mercutio.

See Mercutio see Tybalt.
Mercutio is angry.
Why is Mercutio angry?
Mercutio is looking for a fight.
Mercutio has it coming.

See Romeo.
See Romeo see Tybalt.
See Tybalt call Romeo names.
See Romeo attempt to diffuse the situation in the least effective way possible.
See Mercutio lose control.
See Mercutio duel Tybalt.

See Romeo.
See Romeo attempt to stop the fight.
See Tybalt.
See Tybalt fatally stab Mercutio under Romeo's arm.

See Mercutio.
See Mercutio wish plagues on Romeo and Juliet's houses.
See Mercutio die.
Die, Mercutio, Die!

Romeo is enraged.
Why is Romeo enraged?
His own actions have led to the death of his friend.
See Romeo snap and kill Tybalt.
See Romeo call himself "fortune's fool."
See Romeo high-tail it off the Verona streets.

See the Prince.
The Prince is angry. The peace of Verona's streets has been broken.
See the Prince banish Romeo from the city.
See Benvolio get the heck out of dodge and vanish from the play, never to be seen again.
Vanish, Benvolio, Vanish!

See Juliet.

See Juliet talk about Romeo.
See Juliet talk about wanting to cut Romeo into little pieces to illuminate the sky.
See Juliet, for a brief moment, sound even more terrifying than Lady Macbeth.

See the Nurse.
See the Nurse arrive in a panic and not specify who is now dead.
See Juliet in emotional crisis.

See the Nurse.
See the Nurse find Romeo at the Friar's.
See Romeo overreact about his banishment.
Romeo's life is a stream of overreactions, but this one especially takes the cake.

See Romeo.
See Romeo sneak to Juliet's house.
See Romeo and Juliet-

THIS PORTION OF THE TEXT HAS BEEN CENSORED DUE TO ITS INAPPROPRIATE CONTENT.

See Romeo and Juliet, the epic two-day couple.
See Romeo and Juliet say a tearful goodbye.
See Romeo escape to Mantua.
Escape, Romeo, escape!

See Lord Capulet.
Lord Capulet is happy.
Why is Lord Capulet happy?
Lord Capulet has just agreed to let Paris marry Juliet.
Lord Capulet will get money and power from this agreement!
Congratulations, Lord Capulet!

See Juliet refuse to marry Paris.
See Lord and Lady Capulet threaten to disown their daughter if she does not marry Paris.
Oh no, Juliet!

See the Friar.
See the Friar help Juliet.
See the Friar offer to come up with a plan.
See the Friar give Juliet a magical potion that will mimic death in its effects, upon which time she will be carried to her family tomb, only to be rescued by Romeo, whom the Friar will have notified of the ruse.
The Friar is a man with a plan!

See Juliet.
Juliet is afraid.
Why is Juliet afraid?
It's a long story . . .
See this author skip over her tirade.
The play must go on!

See Juliet drink the potion.
Drink, Juliet, drink!
Chug chug chug chug chug!

See the Capulets.
See the Capulets find Juliet.
See the Capulets think Juliet is dead.
The Capulets are sad.
Now, they will get no money or power from marrying off their teenage daughter to a man more than twice her age.
Poor Capulets.

See the Friar.
The Friar is worried.
Why is the Friar worried?
The Friar has discovered that his message never reached Romeo.
His plan is falling apart.

See Romeo.
See Romeo see his servant Balthazar.
See Balthazar mistakenly tell Romeo that his wife is dead.
See Balthazar do NOTHING to prevent Romeo's clearly intentioned suicide.

See Romeo instantly buy poison and race back to Verona!

Race, Romeo, Race!

See Paris.
See Paris grieving at Juliet's tomb.
See Romeo.
See Romeo see Paris grieving at Juliet's tomb.
See Romeo and Paris get in a fight.
See Romeo kill Paris.
See Romeo lay Paris's body beside Juliet's tomb.
See Paris's body lie there for the rest of the play, unnoticed by all.

See Romeo.
Romeo is sad.
Why is Romeo sad?
Romeo thinks that Juliet is dead.

See Romeo.
See Romeo drink poison.
See Romeo die with a kiss.
Die, Romeo, Die!

See Juliet.
See Juliet wake up.
See Juliet wonder about Romeo's whereabouts.
See Juliet see Romeo.
See Juliet instantly attempt to suck poison off Romeo's lips.
See Juliet's attempt ultimately fail.

See Juliet.
Juliet is sad.
Why is Juliet sad?
Romeo is dead.
See Juliet decide that her life is nothing without Romeo.
See Juliet notice Romeo's dagger.
See Juliet stab herself.
Stab, Juliet, stab!

See the Capulets and the Montagues find Romeo and Juliet (and Paris).
See the Friar find Romeo and Juliet (and Paris).

See the Friar confess the plan.

See Romeo and Juliet.
Romeo is dead.
Juliet is dead.
(Paris is also dead, but really, who cares?)
The pair of star-cross'd lovers have taken their lives (and Paris').
See their grieving families make peace.

See mushy, starry-eyed, idealistic teens and adults form this story of raging, unchecked hormonal emotions into a timeless love story for centuries to come.

. . . And see Rosaline live Happily Ever After!

The End

Applying to College, Correctly

HUMOR

MISHA REKHTER, Grade 12. Carmel High School, Carmel, IN. Eugenie Baum, *Educator*; Clowes Memorial Hall, Butler University and Hoosier Writing Project at IUPUI, *Affiliate*; Gold Medal

Dear respected college,

I have poured my heart and soul into providing honest answers to your poignant questions. I recognize my standardized testing and GPA are clearly insufficient in conveying my abilities so I appreciate that you have gifted me with seven versatile prompts through which I can prove my worth. I hope you find my answers, which are listed below, satisfactory and enjoyable. It has been my parents dream that I gain admittance to your selective community for the entirety of my life. I look forward to your thoughtful response to my application.

How did you spend your last two summers? (50 word limit)

I co-parented twelve obnoxious fifth graders and taught roughly fifteen words of English to Taiwanese children. In the sweltering heat of a Jewish sleep-away camp in rustic Wisconsin and a makeshift classroom in rural Taiwan, I had strikingly similar realizations: most of life occurs outside the classroom.

What historical moment or event do you wish you could have witnessed? (50 word limit)

I wish I could have witnessed the 1618 version of the Defenestration of Prague. I appreciate the way the situation was handled. It would have brought me great joy to see grown men fly out of windows. A satisfactory resolution, indeed. Additionally, Prague is simply gorgeous during the spring.

What five words best describe you?

Are you serious? I'm Batman.

Imagine you had an extra hour in the day—how would you spend that time? (50 word limit).

I would attempt to scale Mount Everest in a metaphorical effort to overcome my physical shortcomings. However, I suspect this undertaking would prove to be detrimental to my dream of eating hot chicken on a regular basis. Thus,

I would learn how to grill so I could achieve that goal.

Reflect on an idea or experience that makes you genuinely excited about learning. (100 to 250 words)

My co-worker was robbing the store as I was washing dishes in the back.

It was at my esteemed place of employment, Jersey Mike's, where I first became intimately familiar with fiscal irresponsibility.

You see, the person, let's call them Hank, had stolen roughly $700 in the past month. Interestingly, their paycheck, in the same month, was easily over $2500. Eventually, I realized, Hank was not an idiot as I had presumed, he was just unlucky. Mismanagement of money permeates the air we breathe, unfortunately for Hank, theft is illegal.

After the incident, I increasingly began to notice poor financial choices. People were dumping money into high ranking, out-of-state colleges instead of attending solid, cheaper universities. I was buying delicious spicy chicken at outrageous prices. Homeowners, completely blinded by square feet and high ceilings, were signing contracts with ludicrous interest rates. It was pure madness.

Correspondingly, I read *The Undoing Project*, a nonfiction novel about behavioral economics, at the suggestion of my dad following this mild case of burglary.

As I turned the final pages, it became clear: rationality and being human were mutually exclusive ideas.
That foolish robbery broke me. I was now constantly probing for irrationality.

Why would I watch *Fight Club* instead of learn derivatives for my impending test? Why would Hank steal such an insignificant amount? Why is debt rampant in the capitalist utopia of America?

I have no explanation for my actions. I just want to know why Hank stole that money. I really liked Hank, he was my favorite co-worker.

Tell us about something that is meaningful to you and why. (100 to 250 words)

I belong in the exclusive guild of outrageously spicy food enthusiasts, more commonly known as the OSFL. Our numbers are few, but our reach is infinite.

Residing in jalapenos jars and habanero sauce canisters, relegated to hidden corners of households and restaurants, plagued by doubt from servers at our requests for "extra extra spicy," and worst of all, having to tolerate the bland nothingness of communal mild dishes, it's tough being addicted to hot foods. But I have no other choice: this organization is my world.

When your older brother chooses to feed you Tabasco infused pelmeni (Russian dumplings) as a four-year-old, your taste buds adjust accordingly. You become accustomed to a certain fire. You develop a need for heat. You keep buffalo sauce on you at all times. Sriracha packets line the inside of your lunchbox. You do not enjoy medium or mild or tweener. You eat hot.

The OSFL has instructions for new members:
If there is a promise of spice, you try it.
If a member succumbs to a spice overload, they will be banished.
You do not ridicule the mild taste buds of others.

The OSFL has had a profound impact on my life. In the search for spice, I've traversed the globe. I've met Bedouins in Jordan and Vikings in Iceland. I've baked in deserts and shivered in caves. And in the end, I learned that people are only willing to disregard race, religion, and ethnicity for one thing: good food (preferably spicy).

Virtually all undergraduates live on campus. Write a note to your future roommate that reveals something about you or that will help your roommate—and us—know you better. (100 to 250 words)
I have a tendency to practice nude tai chi during the wee hours of the morning. This schedule is malleable though and can be adjusted per request. On the weekends, I usually focus on practicing the dark arts; however, consultation with registered voters in the community could easily sway me to use my powers for good. Currently, I'm an advocate of dogs. I love Joella's hot chicken and a variety of ethnic foods. I watch a lot of football which is usually accompanied by a plate of buffalo wings. I do not believe that exercise is worth it; however, exceptions are made for meditation and recreational sports.

It has been said by certain people of unmeasured importance that messiness is the culmination of creativity spilling out the skull and pouring over bland patches of reality. I agree with this sentiment.

My mother has mastered the fashionably late arrival. My father has mastered the unreasonably early arrival. I agree with my father's method.

Ernest Hemingway once said something valuable. It read: "I love sleep. My life has the tendency to fall apart when I'm awake, you know?" I like this thought. I find great usefulness in sleep. It makes reality sticky and less likely to crumble into dangerous shards.

Religion just doesn't do it for me. Not a fan of the commitment, not afraid of a mythical man, but very tolerant of other cultures. I respect devotion.

Ultimately, I don't take life too seriously: my odds of survival aren't high enough.

Thank you,
Humble Student

Eight Essential Things to Do as a Loving Parental Unit During the Formative Years of a Human Child

HUMOR

NAME WITHHELD, Naperville, IL. Region-at-Large, *Affiliate*; Gold Medal

One. USE PROLIFIC CORPORAL PUNISHMENT. Strike your child whenever you can with whatever you can. With a cane—with a belt—with a shoelace, a lamb shank from the local Mom & Pop shop, an April 15th tax deadline, a queen-sized mattress, a fast-moving gasoline-powered motor vehicle. Know hitting your child like the back of your hand. Every "homework" excuse to get out of unimportant household duties should have scarring repercussions. You had children for selfish reasons: the continuation of your genetic line, self-validation, the satisfaction of your wealthy great-aunt, the guarantee of a caretaker during old age. Hitting your child ensures the fulfillment of those desires.

Two. CLEARLY DELINEATE PHYSICAL BOUNDARIES. Contact is dangerous. Ask Carl Sagan. Avoid touching your child in most all cases except to beat them. Don't touch your child during diaper changing; use a wooden back-scratcher or a plastic claw. Don't touch your child to put on their seatbelt; take advantage of your child's high body fat percentage. Don't touch your child when they fall off their bike on the pavement; Band-Aids do not contain child-safety locks for a reason. Touching your child will teach them that physical intimacy at a young age is acceptable and in fact coveted. This type of mentality foments adolescent pregnancy, sex trafficking, gigolo work, pornography, and, in especially rare cases, pediatric dermatitis.

Three. NEGLECT TO VACCINATE YOUR CHILD. There are no good kinds of shots in this world. Gun or vodka, basketball foul or hot, or even scientifically backed but ultimately futile attempts to improve public health—no shots do anything positive for this world. Hospitals are too clean to be trustworthy. Nurses are too prissy to be reliable. Vaccines often contain mercury and formaldehyde; getting immunized is essentially equivalent to swallowing a thermometer and eating a car engine. Your child may develop congenital defects after receiving vaccines. You do not want to have to pay that high of an insurance premium.

Four. SPEND MINIMAL TIME WITH YOUR CHILD. Choose a fundamentalist private childcare center, and enroll your child. Make up the medical documents, or just smile and clutch your rosaries when the secretary calls yet again. Perhaps you will be lucky and they will not ask for such a thing at all. Fully maximize their operational hours, and always wear powdered makeup and pearls when you pick your child up to communicate that you are wealthy, and most importantly, in charge. The loving embrace of a daycare cot and the affectionate disinterest of a near-catatonic preschool teacher will nurture your child to be beyond apt at emotional disconnection with all other humans they meet.

Five. KEEP THE HOUSE DEVOID OF MELODIC NOISE. Most all music is rebellious. Pop music is explosive. Dance music is not spiritual but rather silly, full of average people rolling on psilocybin. Music is freeing and therefore dangerous. Allow anything more than "O Holy Night" in your house and your child will start smoking cannabis at the dinner table while saying grace and thanking God "for the great ganja."

Six. CLOSELY MONITOR MEDIA CONSUMPTION. Handheld mobile devices depress the sleep schedule; your child should never go to bed later than 7:15 p.m. Do not allow garbage like CBS, NBC, CNN, BBC, or any other member of the media alphabet soup; they are full of scary, true things about the rest of the world. QVC, however, is acceptable: it will condition your child to be more receptive to your accelerating lower back problems. *SpongeBob Square Pants* is also a permitted program, as it will teach your child about stealing, condiments, and self-deprecation. *Duck Dynasty* may also teach your child some core values about casual racism and—bonus!—sometimes even misogyny.

Seven. FLUCTUATE SELF-ESTEEM IN YOUR CHILD. Make the ego sinusoidal. Glorify your child with plaques and framed photos. Emasculate them in front of the neighbors at the block party. Humiliation is key. Follow up the next day with photocopied pages of your child's exemplary resume—world's loudest crier, preschool book club group leader, superior roly-poly torturer—hammered to each neighborhood door, a manifesto about your parental success. Never enter or leave a family dinner without deploying a litany of compliments and a deluge of insults. The surefire effect is a child so unsure of themselves they *need* you to be able to live with themselves, but so confident that they can bully other people into realizing your excellence as a parent.

Eight. LOSE YOUR CHILD AT A BUSY SUPERMARKET, OR SOME PUBLIC AREA OF COMPARABLE SIZE. During this time, you will have time to visit the Swedish spa and the confession box, although in the latter you will find men that have violated Rule TWO with other children. Abandoning your child is a magnificent way to teach your child what an illusion of autonomy feels like, for certainly they will marry it to paranoia and deem it undesirable. It is vital that your child remains dependent on you. Who else will sit stupidly in your house for a few hours a day, mouth-breathing loudly and wasting away their life while your husband is doing some extra hours at a "coworker's place?" Besides, purposefully losing your child in a public area will impact neither your wallet nor you. If nosy strangers are miffed and call child "protective" services, there is little to worry about. Perhaps they will peer into your windows—perhaps they will come to the door and knock, thick peacoat and wire-rimmed glasses and all. You will open it, crinkle your eyes when you see the handprint badge on their chest, and smile with your faux white teeth. They will look over your shoulder and see the neatly laid silverware and wax candles and laughing humans and dandelion wine, and walk away, head shaking, apologetic for disturbing such idyllic suburban peace. *Never mind, ma'am. Wrong house. Sorry.* As they should be. Nothing's wrong. ■

An Educator's Guide to
The Best Teen Writing of 2019

Prepared by the National Writing Project

Use the works of these National Medalist teen writers to inspire discussion and guide writing exercises with students.

1. Short Story

The relationship between setting and mood— *35 minutes*

Goal: Students explain how authors establish mood through details of setting (time and place).

Activity: Choose a story for review that contains many evocative details of setting (time, place, weather, etc.). Ask students to read with a highlighter, making note of the plot elements.

List on the board.

Discuss: What would it feel like to be here? Why do you think so? Choose a "favorite element." How did that particular detail add to your feeling about the place?

Revising for mood: Students choose a story they are working on, or a story from *The Best Teen Writing*. Add details of setting to enhance the mood being conveyed. Share with a partner for response.

2. Short Story

Writing with focus on characterizing the narrative—*35 minutes*

Goal: Students restructure a narrative with another narrator, creating the same story with a different perspective.

Activity: Ask students to take on the voice of one of the other characters and tell the story from that point of view, filling in blanks that the original narrator left. Challenge students to use important characterizing details in the reading to give color to their entries.

3. Poetry

Writing with focus on form—*30 minutes*

Goal: Students write using different structural techniques.

Activity: Have students write two poems on one topic of their choosing. Begin with a prose poem, in which they write freely on that topic; then have them write another poem on the same topic with a focus on line breaks to emphasize changes in rhythm or highlight specific phrases. Discuss the differences after sharing the results.

4. Personal Essay & Memoir

Writing with a focus on structure and pacing—*45 minutes*

Goal: Students will write an organized and coherent memoir imitating the format of a *Best Teen Writing* piece.

Activity: Select a Personal Essay & Memoir from the anthology to read out loud with your students. Talk about the format in which the memoir is written. Discuss the choices made and how those choices are inherently personal, therefore inherently suited to convey a personal essay.

Ask your students to write their own memoirs modeled after the memoir you have selected. Have the students share their work and discuss choices that each student makes, including how those choices convey something personal to the reader.

5. Genre-Shifting Exercise

Blackout Poetry—*40 minutes*

Goal: Students will explore form's relationship to function by distilling the language in a single piece of prose, into a piece of poetry.

Activity: Have the students choose a page of prose in *The Best Teen Writing*. Students then scan the page for words that are interesting and lightly circle or underline those words with a pen. Next students read the page from top to bottom, looking for more interesting words, or words that might relate to the circled words. They should circle these, too. Finally, students begin to black out all the words on the page that they aren't using, in a sense "whittling away" the words that aren't part of the poem they've found within the text.

6. Blog Exercise

40 minutes and homework time

Goal: Students will use critical-thinking skills to offer critiques and analysis of specific works or the anthology as a whole.

Activity: Ask students to write a blog post expressing thoughts about a specific piece of their choosing. Posts will be sent to the Alliance for consideration to be included on the Alliance blog.

• Students should express their opinions, offering positive feedback or constructive criticism, on a specific work in *The Best Teen Writing*. Alternatively, they may discuss the anthology as a whole.

• Posts may be emailed to info@artandwriting.org, with subject line "*The Best Teen Writing of 2019* Student Blog Post."

Educators: Continue the discussion! Explore with your peers even more ways in which *The Best Teen Writing of 2019* can inspire students in your classroom! Feel free to share new ideas about how to use *The Best Teen Writing* by sending your ideas to **programs@nwp.org**.

Major Supporters

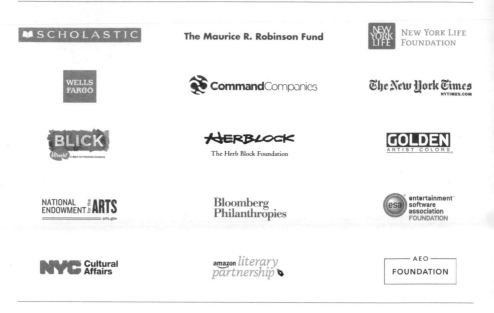

The Alliance for Young Artists & Writers, a 501(c)(3) nonprofit organization, relies on the generous support of its donors and supporters to carry out programs that recognize and empower creative young artists and writers, primarily through the Scholastic Art & Writing Awards. Their generosity is key to the success of our programs, and we are most grateful to them. Join us in fulfilling our important mission of supporting creative teens through scholarships, exhibitions, workshops, and more.

To make a tax-deductible contribution, visit **artandwriting.org/donate**.